AWAKEN, CHILDREN!

*Dialogues with
Sri Mata Amritanandamayi*

VOLUME 2

Adaptation & Translation

SWAMI AMRITASWARUPANANDA

Mata Amritanandamayi Center, San Ramon
California, United States

AWAKEN, CHILDREN!
Volume 2

Published by:
Mata Amritanandamayi Center
P.O. Box 613
San Ramon, CA 94583
United States

In India:
www.amritapuri.org
inform@amritapuri.org

In Europe:
www.amma-europe.org

In US:
www.amma.org

This Book is Humbly Offered at the
LOTUS FEET OF HER HOLINESS
SRI MATA AMRITANANDAMAYI
The Resplendent Luminary Immanent
In the Hearts of All Beings

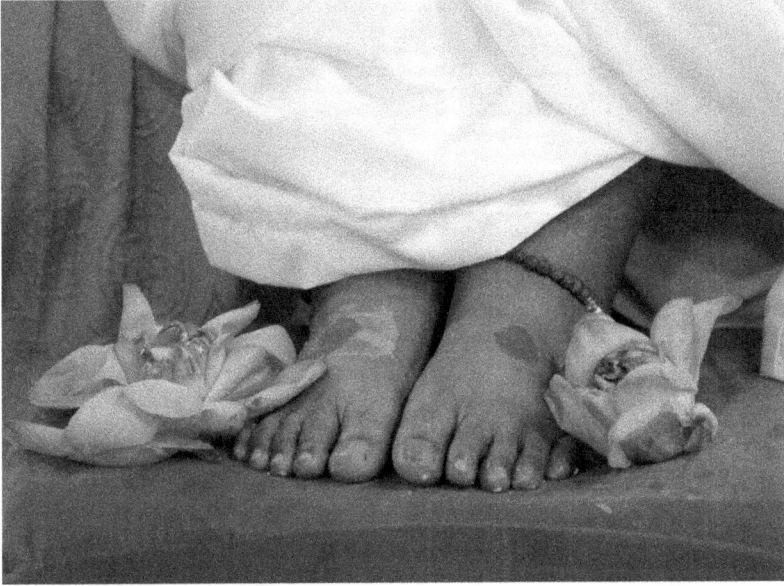

Vandeham saccidānandam bhāvātītam jagatgurum |
Nityam pūrnam nirākāram nirgunam svātmasamsthitam | |
I prostrate to the Universal Teacher, Who is Satchidananda (Pure
Being-Knowledge-Absolute Bliss), Who is beyond all differences,
Who is eternal, all-full, attributeless, formless and ever-centered
in the Self.

Saptasāgaraparyantam tīrthasnānaphalam tu yat |
Gurupādapayōvindōh sahasrāmsena tatphalam | |
Whatever merit is acquired by one, through pilgrimmages and
from bathing in the Sacred Waters extending to the seven seas,
cannot be equal to even one thousandth part of the merit derived
from partaking the water with which the Guru's Feet are washed.

Guru Gita, verses 157, 87

Contents

Preface

Dear brothers and sisters, herein is contained a direct translation of Holy Mother's *divya upadesha* (divine advice) into the English language. The tremendous blessing that is bestowed by presenting the Mother's teachings to the English-speaking world is not yet fully realized. Now it is left to the reader of the material and a whole-hearted practice of it in daily life.

Several points should be remembered in order that this translation is approached with the right understanding. First of all, these conversations have occurred between the Mother and Indian house-holders and renunciates in the cultural context of India. Also, the Mother's teachings are given according to the level of understanding of each person to whom She is speaking. Often a word-for-word English translation falls short of conveying the totality of what the Mother has expressed through Her mother tongue, Malayalam. One must consider these factors when contemplating Her words to achieve deeper insight.

Secondly, the Mother's use of language is direct and earthy. Her words convey an immediacy and intensity of purpose to transmit the Essential, particularly when speaking to sadhaks (spiritual aspirants). For instance, when it comes time to bring a point across to a renunciate, the Mother does not mince words. Thus we can understand Her expression, "Worldly pleasure is equal to dog excreta" to be sound advice to one whose sole aim is God-Realization.

In a separate conversation with a householder, the Mother's advice takes on an entirely different tone. "Mother does not say that you must give up all desires. You can enjoy them, but do not think that this life is for that only." Keep in mind that in the Mother's language, the word 'world' literally means 'that which is seen' as opposed to the invisible Reality or God. Knowing this will be of great help in interpreting Her use of the word 'worldly.' When the

Mother contrasts that which is spiritual to that which is worldly, She refers to the attitude with which actions are done. Spiritual actions are those actions which lead one to God through selflessness and purity. Worldly actions are those actions which lead one away from God, performed as they are in a spirit of selfishness.

Finally, the Mother speaks to us from the exalted state of sahaja samadhi, the natural state of abidance of a Self-Realized Master in the Absolute Reality. The challenge in translating is to render the Mother's transcendental vision into English for the layman. The vital ingredient in this process is the contemplative mind of the reader. Abandoning all superficiality, may our mind and intellect become subtle and assimilate the Eternal Wisdom of the Mother's words. Firmly established in our practice, may we all revel in the direct experience of the Supreme Absolute without delay.

My heartfelt gratitude is due to Professor M. Ramakrishnan Nair, the compiler of Mata Amritanandamayi Sambhashanangal, the Holy Mother's conversations in Malayalam. The present book, Awaken, Children! 2 is a faithful translation of the same, interspersed with some additional materials which were recorded by me. I would like to thank my spiritual sisters, Sabari, Meera and Astrid who edited and typed the text, Brahmacharin Nealu who did the typesetting, and all of the Holy Mother's children who took part in producing the book.

Introduction

With joy we present this second volume of "Awaken, Children!" to the readers and devotees of the Holy Mother Amritanandamayi. As in the first volume, I have interspersed the conversations with material which has been personally recorded by me over the years.

Words of Mahatmas are not merely meant for superficial reading. Mother does not want us to read and forget. She wishes that we should apply at least a little of Her teachings in our daily life, born out of our conviction of their practical utility. As She says,

> *"Faith gained through telling, hearing and reading will not last long, but faith gained through experience will last forever. You will not get sweetness if you write 'honey' on a piece of paper and lick it. Neither can you milk the picture of a cow nor live in the blueprint of a house. Practical experience is needed."*

The Mother is Herself an embodiment of all that She says, a living witness to all the eternal values mentioned in the texts of all religions of the world. Both Her teachings and Her life stand as a tremendous source of inspiration for people from all walks of life. How many scientists gained new insights into their particular field of research through Her words! How many scholars have felt thrilled to hear Her simple and lucid explanations of subtle and complex scriptural statements! How many doctors have been wonderstruck on seeing the miraculous cures effected by Her! How many engineers have been amazed at Her efficiency in planning! How many political leaders have gained courage and self-confidence through Her words of advice! How many householders have found solace in Her loving protection! How many spiritual aspirants have been uplifted by Her presence and loving guidance! And how many countless lives have been set right and put on the path of integrity by Her gracious blessings!

Loving obedience to the words of the Guru is the meaning of "self-surrender" as told by Mother. Therefore, let us strive and try as best as we can to live by Her instructions so that we, Her children, may awaken to God-consciousness and thereby fulfill Her wish.

Swami Amritaswarupananda

In the beginning, many people who visited the Holy Mother were interested only in gaining material ends. They had very little knowledge about spirituality. Many of them thought that the Mother was like an astrologer or a fortune-teller who predicts the future. There were many who believed that the Holy Mother was visited by Devi and Krishna three times a week. Almost all the people who came in those days had no real spiritual background at all. Once their desires were fulfilled, they would never return until another problem or wish arose. They could not understand anything about the Mother's Supreme Realization. Soon things changed; the visits of people who were only interested in worldly things decreased, and people who were primarily interested in spiritual practices started coming to see the Mother. Eminent scholars and serious sadhaks, scientists and people from different walks of life greatly interested in doing spiritual practice started flowing to Mother. They realized that the Holy Mother was a unique soul and a storehouse of Supreme Knowledge. Then they, out of their longing to know, asked the Holy Mother various questions about their own spiritual practices. At this time She started manifesting more and more of Her Guru Bhava (Masterhood).

All those who asked the Mother questions found great joy, peace and inner contentment in Her answers. Even eminent scholars and learned people gained new ideas and insights into many subjects which they discussed with the Holy Mother. Once they met Mother, they became very drawn towards Her and came to see Her time after time.

Tuesday, 1 November 1983

The brahmacharins were meditating at ten o'clock this morning since there was no scriptural class. The Holy Mother was sitting in the hut deeply absorbed in Herself.

The young men who had come on the previous day returned today. Seeing the Mother in an abstracted mood, they waited outside the hut. After some time, cheerful and smiling, the Holy Mother invited the young men inside.

Amma: Children, were you standing outside for a long time?
One among them: No, Mother, we were simply gazing at you.

The Holy Mother lovingly asked them to sit down. They sat down after prostrating to Her and one of them said,
Young man: We are here with more questions today. Who else can we turn to except you, Mother?
Amma: Questions and doubts should end; acceptance should come.
One young man: We agree, Mother.
Amma: (Smilingly) Good, at least you have accepted that (the young men laugh).
Question: Mother, is devotion a spiritual practice (*sadhana*)?
Amma: Son, devotion which is based on real spiritual principles (*tattwattile bhakti*) is a *sadhana*. But devotion prompted by desire (*kamya bhakti*) cannot be considered a *sadhana*.
Young man: Mother, what is *tattwattile bhakti*?
Amma: *Tattwattile bhakti* is selflessly loving and taking refuge in God who has become everything, without thinking that there are many gods. One should understand that the Supreme Lord is omniscient, omnipresent and omnipotent. One should proceed with the sole aim of realizing God. It is useless to move towards the west when you want to go east. What meaning is there in simply wandering about with no direction in life? There should not be any delusion concerning the goal of life. For that, a *Satguru's* assistance is

absolutely necessary. If *sadhana* is performed under a Guru conflict and confusion will not arise. Attempting *sadhana* without a Guru will lead to trouble.

Question: Who is a real *karma yogin*?

Amma: A real *karma yogin* is one who always remembers God throughout every action in which he is engaged. A real *sadhak* works seeing God in everything. This means he offers the action and its fruit at His Feet. Such a person's mind is not in the work but in God. It all depends on practice. In other words, one who thinks of the fruit of action while doing work will not be able to perform the action fully applying his ability or talent. He should forget the fruit in order to get the full benefit of the work that he is doing. Sincerity in the work one is performing is very important. If actions are performed sincerely and wholeheartedly, they must bear good fruit. Instead, if you worry about the fruit, not only will you fail to put forth the necessary effort, but you will not get the expected result either. A certain amount of dedication is needed for any and every action.

Haven't you seen the folk dancers who dance while keeping a pot decorated with flowers on their heads? They will do all kinds of acrobatics with the pots remaining on their heads. They will dance according to the beat (tala) and sometimes even roll on the ground. The dancer's mind will be on the pot even while displaying all these tricks. If for only one moment he withdraws his mind, the pot will fall down. This is how you have to act. Whatever action you do, the mind should be on God.

Question: Can the Vision of God be had through this path?

Amma: Yes, children, but who can do so? Such people are rare, are they not? Who is able to see God in their actions? It is possible if you try. The path of action is good, but the actions should be performed selflessly. Most people are after name, fame and position. If they don't get it, they will fight for it.

Question: Mother, in order to walk in the path of *karma yoga*, is a Guru necessary?

Amma: Certainly, a Guru is necessary. Even though the wind blows everywhere, when we stand under a tree, a special coolness can be felt from the breeze which filters through the leaves. Likewise, even though God exists everywhere, being in the presence of a Guru is something very special. Though air is everywhere, one gets a special feeling when sitting near a fan. A fan is beneficial when it is hot. In the same manner, when we are living in the midst of worldly pleasures, a Guru is necessary to control the mind. After reaching a particular state, these problems will no longer arise.

Isn't there a difference between studying in school and staying at home to study? When we sit at home, desires like wishing to go near our mother and to be held by her, will arise. If any guests happen to come, then the mind will be with them. The child will not study attentively. That is why children should be taught at school. The child will sit there and learn attentively when he realizes that he cannot go home till the afternoon. Likewise, in the beginning it is difficult to do sadhana sitting at home. Different kinds of worldly thoughts will enter the mind. Therefore, the best way is to do one's sadhana in a pure atmosphere. For proper and specific instructions and guidance, a Satguru is necessary. Guru and God are one, but we have not grown sufficiently mature to realize that.

Some people say that an external Guru is not necessary and that the Guru within will guide us. Some others might say that they are themselves the Guru. It cannot be said that a child studying in the kindergarten and a student who is studying for a Master's degree are the same. We need to learn in order to reach the latter's stage. If we think both students are equal, it is utter ignorance. It is like saying that an apple tree full of ripe apples and an apple seed are one. The former can give fruit and shade to the people and quench their hunger, but the latter cannot. A seed can become a tree and give fruit; but to become a tree, it has to pass through several stages. In that process of becoming, if it is not properly taken care of, it may even get destroyed. It has to overcome and withstand adverse climatic conditions and also be protected from stray animals. Similarly, in a sadhak's life many impediments will arise both from within and without. For that, the presence of a living Satguru is needed. Satsang, also, is beneficial to remove ignorance.

Question: Mother, will one go mad through devotion to God?

Amma: Yes, son, but that is the madness for God. Worldly people are mad for the world. By realizing God, one becomes the King of the world; others are only beggars and slaves of the world. If one really goes mad as a result of one's devotion, it is due to pursuing the path without knowing the essential principles behind it. Anything can happen then. One will not go mad if one travels along the path of devotion, rooted in its principles.

Question: Mother, it is said that some devotees are deranged.

Amma: Son, are you asking about the craziness of the devotees? Do you know what kind of madness they suffer from? It is madness for God. From our point of view, they are crazy. That is not ordinary craziness but God-intoxicated craziness. If one has that, one has succeeded.

In reality, who is mad, devotees or worldly people? A devotee, through his craziness for God, saves thousands and thousands of people from going madly after worldly pleasures, and getting drowned in them and dissipating their energy. Whereas worldly people get completely caught up in worldly affairs and become un-balanced, thereby destroying their own lives and the lives of others as well. Some commit suicide or fight with each other even over silly things. They dissipate their energy in smoking, drinking and other indulgences. Now tell Mother who is really crazy and which craziness is better?

Question: Mother, what if one doesn't approach a Master?

Amma: Child, never do spiritual practices on your own. This is a serious matter. There is a difference between doing without study-ing and having studied and then doing. One needs a teacher in order to practice. Practice is not like reading books; there must be supervision. Even to gain worldly knowledge, a teacher is needed. Since this is the case, think how much more imperative it is to follow the advice of a Master while practicing the spiritual science, the king of all knowledge!

Question: Mother, why is it said that a *sadhak* should not move closely with the opposite sex?

Amma: In the same way that our mouth waters when we see a delicious mango pickle, our mind will unknowingly vacillate when we see the opposite sex. It is just like the ground getting muddy when it rains. Even if the holy Ganges water falls on the earth, it will become turbid. In the beginning, a *sadhak* should always keep a distance when around them. Always consider a woman as mother or sister and a man as father or brother. Remember that, no matter how alert we are, there are possibilities for falling into trouble. If that fear and strong discrimination are there, we will not look at the external appearances, but only at the subtle aspect of each person. Then every woman's breasts will appear to be the breasts of the Divine Mother. Otherwise, looking at a woman as a mere woman, you may end up walking in the wrong path.

A male sadhak's greatest enemy is a woman, and a woman sadhak's is a man. Not only that, women are weak-minded by nature, but they can become more steady than a man if they develop some manly qualities. However, most of them do not do so. There are some women who have transcended sexual feelings, but they are only one or two in a million. There may be only one woman in a million who could instruct a man in spiritual principles even when he approaches her with a lustful mind.

For a sadhak, a woman is like a whirlwind. In the beginning a sadhak should not go near women. No harm will happen once the mind has been controlled. He will not vacillate even if a woman happens to come near him stark naked.

My daughters might think, "Why is Mother putting the blame on us by calling us weak-minded? Are not men equally to blame for their faults?" Children, women have a natural softness and compassion with them. However much they may try to conceal that, it is very difficult for them to do so. Their mind will easily melt if a man shows a little love for them. It is enough if a man looks lovingly at a woman. Her inborn nature of surrendering her all to a man is awakened and she forgets everything else. Seeing that soft and surrendering nature of hers, a man feels an attraction for her and forgets himself as well. This compassionate and soft nature of women always leads them into danger. Both men and women have their weaknesses and strengths. Why should anyone be blamed? Mother will try to awaken true knowledge in both through Her instructions.

Those who are overly attached to sports, games and movies should not keep the television in their room. The temptation will be too much for them to resist. During the period of sadhana it is best to keep away from circumstances which will arouse one's passions.

Do you know why the opposite sex becomes an enemy, spiritually speaking? When our parents had sexual intercourse, they never had a desire to have a virtuous and brilliant child. It is the same samskara that is lying in us. Weren't we born from the same blood? The thought that lies in one's mind is that the opposite sex is only for one's pleasure. In order to remove this vasana, one should keep one's distance, while perceiving them in a brotherly or sisterly way.

Question: Is that easy?

Amma: It is not easy, but it is also not impossible if you have the determination. Son, we do not feel anything when we see a child's nakedness, do we? We are supposed to be like that. The mind is the cause of everything, isn't it? Our mind does not become impure when we perceive someone as a small child, but it becomes lustful when we think that person is a grown-up. Everything depends on the mind.

Even the world appears because of the existence of the mind. In the waking state the mind functions; therefore, the world of plurality exists. Whereas, in the deep sleep state the mind stops functioning;

therefore, the world and the objects do not exist. In the morning when we wake up, the mind comes back and the world arises as well. A Self-Realized soul, through constant spiritual practice, restrains all thoughts by focusing the mind on the Supreme. Thus when the thoughts stop, the mind also subsides because it is nothing but thought waves. Then there is no world of plurality as we now see it.

Question: If one tries, can God-Realization be gained after crossing all these obstacles?

Amma: It is possible if you try, but who has the determination? Even to try requires a certain degree of spiritual disposition inherited from the previous birth and the desire to reach the goal.

Most people in the beginning show a lot of enthusiasm. They think that they can experience or gain that state in a few days, and when it doesn't happen, their enthusiasm slowly disappears. Constant and sincere practice is needed. But in some people you can see spiritual experience dawning at an early stage. This is due to their spiritual samskara inherited from the previous birth.

At this time a family from the eastern side of Kerala came to see Mother. The entire family prostrated to the Mother. The eldest lady of the family expressed a wish that the Mother be the first to give her grandson some solid food. This child had been born due to the blessings of the Mother.

One and a half years ago this woman's daughter and son-in-law had come to the Mother praying for a child. It was seven years into their marriage and still there was no child. The Mother had taken a banana and, after blessing it, had given it to the couple asking them to share it. She had told them that the woman would soon conceive and give birth to a son on a particular day in a particular month. She had also told them that since the child would be a Godly one, they should be very patient with him and cautious in their actions towards him.

As foretold by the Mother, the woman did indeed give birth to a male child on the exact day that the Mother had indicated. It was to this child that the family wanted Mother to give the first solid food.

The Mother lovingly told them, "Children, Mother will give the food tonight during Devi Bhava. She usually gives it at that time." However, the grandmother objected saying,

Grandmother: This child is very adamant and will not sleep without a cradle. Also, he may become sick from the sea breeze here. Therefore, we must reach home before dark. So, Mother, please do the ceremony now.

Amma: Is that so? Suppose the child were sick and you had to take him to the hospital. Would you tell the doctor that you must take the child home before dark because he won't sleep without a cradle? Children, patience is very important, especially in regards to this child. He is not an ordinary child but a Godly one.

In spite of the Mother's words, the elderly lady insisted that the child must be taken home before dark. Hearing that, the Mother kept silent and closed Her eyes. After a short while She opened Her eyes and was asked by one of the young men, "Mother, may we ask a few more questions?"

Amma: Yes, children, go ahead and ask.

Question: Mother, will God appear to us in the form in which we think of Him?

Amma: Son, definitely God will give us His *darshan* in the form in which we think of Him.

The Holy Mother stopped abruptly. She seemed to be immersed in deep contemplation. With tears flowing from Her eyes, She sat there motionless like a statue. After a few minutes, opening Her eyes, She sang,

Creation and Creator art Thou,
Thou art Energy and Truth,

21

Creator of the Cosmos art Thou,
And Thou art the beginning
And the end, the Essence of
The individual soul art Thou
And Thou art the five elements as well,
O Divine Mother!

As She called "Devi...Devi," the Mother shed tears of bliss and once again entered into spiritual ecstasy. After a long pause, upon regaining Her normal consciousness, the Holy Mother continued.

Amma: Son, certainly God will come in the form in which we think of Him but we must have the longing to see Him before He will manifest. The omniscient, omnipotent and all-pervading God, the *Nirguna Brahman* (Attributeless Reality), can definitely assume any form according to the wish of His devotees. *Nirguna Brahman* becoming *Saguna* (with attributes) is like ice becoming water or butter becoming ghee. The form which He assumes as God or Guru should not be considered as made up of the five elements, but rather as the embodiment of Pure Existence, Awareness and Bliss Absolute (*Akhanda Satchidananda Brahman*). He will also come in different forms in order to test the devotee's renunciation and devotion.

There was one devotee who did severe penance to realize God. One day a stranger came to his house and said, "It seems that you are a great renunciate. If so, let me see the depth of your renunciation; give your wife to me." Without any hesitation, the devotee gave his wife to the stranger. Having received the devotee's wife, the stranger came out of the house. As he was leaving the compound, some friends of the devotee happened to see the stranger accompanied by the devotee's sobbing wife. They mistook the stranger for a miscreant who was forcibly taking away their friend's wife. They caught him and beat him till he was black and blue. Hearing the uproar, the devotee came out of his house and was shocked to see the pitiful condition of the stranger who was breathing his last.

With unbearable pain in his heart, he said, "What is this? What have you done to this poor man? I willingly gave my wife to him." He continued, "O Lord, please forgive my friends. Please save this man by giving my life to him. O Lord, take my life instead." As soon as he uttered these prayers, the stranger disappeared and the Lord Himself stood before him. Everything which happened was His trick to test His devotee's devotion and dedication. The Lord was testing whether the devotee had any selfishness. The Lord did not appear when he gave up his wife, but only when he had the willingness and mental attitude to sacrifice his own life in order to save someone else's life.

Children, it is our duty towards God to be compassionate and loving towards the poor and needy. When somebody is suffering, we should sympathize and take pity on him. But that alone is not enough; we should be ready to help him because God is everywhere, in everything. When we develop compassion and love for ailing people, His grace will spontaneously flow into us.

Sin means ignorance

Young man: Mother, the Christians call everyone sinners. Why is this?

Amma: Son, in fact, sin means ignorance or *vasanas*, i.e., the tendencies inherited from the previous birth. It is meaningless to hate someone, labelling him as a sinner. No one is without faults. Otherwise, everyone should be hated because all have some blemish or other. What is called "ignorant" in India is called "sinner" in the West. That is all. *Papa* (sin) is a synonym for *ajnana* (ignorance). Those actions which take one closer to God are meritorious, while those which take one away from God are sinful.

Question: Mother, many saints say that he who goes on saying "I am a sinner, I am a sinner," will become a sinner. What does that mean?

Amma: That is correct. When he goes on thinking and saying that he is a sinner or is weak, he will become unable to undertake any kind of useful work. Ups and downs are the nature of life and are unavoidable. An individual who thinks that he is weak or is a sinner will collapse before them. A sinner is one who does not have the mental strength to confront the problems of life. No doubt he will become weaker and weaker if he continues thinking "I am weak, I am a sinner. I cannot do anything, I cannot accomplish anything in life." Whereas, he will gain more mental strength to face the challenges of life if he thinks, "I am not a sinner, nor am I ignorant or weak. I am strong, I am the Supreme Self or I am protected by God, I am His child."

Fruits of action can be overcome

Question: Let it be so. Shouldn't the fruit of actions be experienced?
Amma: Not quite, son. They can all be gotten rid of if we are really determined. The fruit of some actions can be cancelled through other godly actions. Mother can narrate a number of incidents to prove this point.

Suppose we are fated to be stabbed to death due to certain evil acts which we committed in our past birth. If somehow in this birth, we are instructed by a great saint or spiritual person to start doing spiritual practices, such as observing vows, chanting mantras and the like, then when the predestined time would come, someone might stab us, but instead of it putting an end to our life, we might sustain only a minor injury. Pre-destined fate will follow its course, but its effect will be weakened. Son, fate, of course, is powerful, but the strength of good actions is even more so.
Question: Mother, is there an actual incident to demonstrate the point?

Amma: There are a number of such incidents. (Turning to Brahmacharin Balu) Balu, my son, tell these children one incident to demonstrate the point.

Balu: A couple used to visit Mother every now and then. One day the wife seemed to be very worried and mentally depressed. When Mother asked what was wrong, she told Her that she had visited a famous astrologer who predicted that her husband would die on a certain date which was only a few months away. When she returned home, the lady found the same signs in her husband's horoscope and became dejected. Having found no way to save her husband's life, as a last resort, she came along with her husband to Mother. Mother consoled her and suggested that both of them do certain spiritual practices including a vow of silence every Saturday. She asked them to chant a particular mantra every day in the morning and evening, and also at other times whenever they felt like it. She also recommended that they purchase a calf and raise it. They followed the instructions implicitly. On the fated day, to their amazement, the calf suddenly fell dead. Through their sincere and concentrated spiritual practices, they were able to neutralize the husband's past actions. As a result, the calf died instead of him. Fate had its way, but with an unexpected turn. Mother said that their innocent prayers and pure resolve and faith helped them to transcend their fate.

Young man: If that is so, is it unnecessary to experience the fruit of one's actions?

Amma: Son, faith and alertness will help alot to cross over the many obstacles that might arise in our life. If we are alert, anything can be overcome, in the same way that an object can be prevented from falling by placing it on the ground. Moreover, the very impulse to act is the outcome of the fruit of actions performed in the previous birth.

But the fruit of actions will not affect a sadhak. Many men go to the Arabian countries for five or six years soon after their marriage, leaving their wife in their native place. They go abroad controlling their mind and relinquishing the pleasures of family life for the sake of earning money. Man has the adaptability to alter this life style to suit the necessity. Likewise, what if we give up worldly life in order to attain God-Realization? The old fruits of actions can be transcended by new actions. Actions can be changed by action. Markandeya's life span was extended through tapas, wasn't it? Do you know the story of Markandeya? Mother will tell you.

The sage Mrikandu had no children for a very long time. In order to beget a child, he did severe penance to please Lord Shiva. Finally the Lord appeared before him and asked, "Do you wish to have an intelligent and radiant son who will die at the age of sixteen, or a useless dullard who will have a long life span?" Mrikandu prayed for having the former kind of child.

As was foretold by the Lord, the newborn baby developed into a brilliant prodigy endowed with all qualities. The parents named him Markandeya (son of Mrikandu). All the four Vedas and other scriptures spontaneously dawned in his intellect. Everyone who came in contact with him felt attracted by his good qualities and behavior. But his parents were very unhappy and would weep upon looking at his face, remembering that he would die at the age of sixteen. Somehow they managed to conceal this fact from him.

One day, however, Markandeya saw his parents shedding tears while looking at him and enquired the reason for their sorrow. With choked voices they related the history of his birth and Lord Shiva's prophecy. Thenceforth, Markandeya immersed himself in intense tapas with the strong determination to please Lord Shiva and overcome death.

At last the fated day arrived. When the messengers of Death came, they found Markandeya sitting in samadhi, absorbed in the thought of Lord Shiva. Since they could not approach him, the God of Death himself, Yama, came to take away Markandeya's soul. Waking from samadhi and seeing Yama, Markandeya threw himself on the Shivalinga and embraced it tightly. Throwing his noose around Markandeya and the Linga, Yama tried to pull Markandeya away.

Infuriated, Lord Shiva manifested out of the Linga and killed Yama in order to protect His devotee. The Lord then bestowed eternal life on Markandeya and blessed him that he would remain sixteen years old forever! Then, in response to the prayers of the gods, the Lord brought Yama back to life.

What about Ratnakaran, the forest dweller, becoming the sage Valmiki? Ratnakaran had been a highway robber. Waylaying the celestial sage Narada, he was advised by the sage to give up his sinful way of making a living. Narada asked the robber to go and enquire from his family whether they were prepared to bear part of the fruits of the sinful actions by which he was supporting them. Shocked to hear that they would not do so, Ratnakaran returned to the sage and took refuge in him in order to escape the dire consequences of his evil actions. Narada advised him to chant the Divine Name of "Rama." Ratnakaran was so sinful that the holy name "Rama" would not come to his lips. Narada therefore asked him to repeat the word "Mara" which means "tree" but if reversed becomes "Rama." Taking this advice to heart, Ratnakaran began chanting and became so completely absorbed that he was gradually covered over by an anthill (valmika). Thereafter, he became known as the great sage Valmiki, the author of the epic Ramayana.

Children, these stories are told to show us that fate can be transcended by strong determination and devotion to the Lord. If these are present, nothing is impossible.

Question: Mother, is it possible for a person who has committed many sins in his previous birth to do *sadhana* in this birth?

Amma: Son, even the thought to live for God arises due to the merits accumulated in the previous birth. Such thoughts arise because we have done good deeds. Circumstances also play their role. A person who lives near a workshop from childhood onwards might learn the work which is done there through friendship with workers. A change can occur in one's life owing to association, but merits acquired from the previous birth are needed even for such circumstances to arise.

That is why it is said that merits inherited from the previous birth are needed more than anything else.

Another point to be remembered is this: once one comes to a Perfect Master, all one's sins will be washed away by His or Her grace. After that, one should not waste one's time thinking, "Oh, I am a sinner," but rather one should try to assimilate the Guru's teachings. One should not brood over the past but should start on the spiritual path in earnest when real detachment comes.

Understanding the goal, we should strive hard to attain it. Mother doesn't know anything; She has not studied any scriptures; She is saying all this because you asked. Children, take whatever you want and reject the rest, in the same way that you drink the sugarcane juice and discard the fibre.

We must reflect, no matter how much we have understood these principles. Are we really loving our wife and children? Isn't it out of selfishness? We love others because they give us happiness, or fulfill our desires, or obey or respect us, or have a high opinion about us. Otherwise, we don't. If somebody hates us, feelings of revenge take the place of love. This is the case even with your own wife and children. If they disobey or disrespect you, you will not love them. Where there is real love there is no selfishness. Think of the ways that we devise to make money. We are even ready to kill others to acquire wealth if the circumstances are favorable. In most cases, all these atrocities are done just for the sake of a few people, for two or three members of the family.

Question: Mother, is the form of Kali a Goddess?

Amma: No, son, Kali is symbolic of the divine principle of fierceness which kills the ego. Similar is the case with the other forms of God. When we yell at a cow saying, "Go away!" when it eats the leaves of a young coconut palm, we have the same attitude of fierceness. The cow will not run away if we lovingly tell it to go. It needs a certain show of anger. Likewise, the Mother is roaring and killing the ego through the manifestation of Kali. Through this understanding we can transcend all forms.

Question: Isn't that form of Kali God?

Amma: It depends on our *sankalpa* (conception). We can become identified with that form if our resolve is strong enough. In that state (of being able to identify with an object), whatever we think of, we will become, just as *vettapacha* (a kind of plant) when dipped in ink turns the same color as the ink. If we think of a person, we will feel that we are that person, or if we think of a cow, we will feel that we are a cow. During the course of *sadhana*, there are stages in which we would feel so. From there, we can go to the Attributeless State.

In the beginning of Her sadhana, Mother conceived of God as having a form and attributes. At a certain stage, whatever form Mother would think of, She would become identified with that person; if She thought of a child, She would become that child and even start crawling on the floor on all fours. After some time, Mother heard a voice within Her saying, "Both God with attributes (Saguna) and the attributeless God (Nirguna) are within you. Seek to realize your oneness with the Attributeless." After that, Mother started chanting "AUM" and directly experienced that everything is Brahman, the Absolute. But Mother does not feel that the Saguna sadhana that She did was a mistake. It required much concentrated attention and led Her to the Nirguna Brahman.

Saguna and Nirguna are not two different Realities. Ordinary people like us can reach the Formless Being only through some kind of medium. For those who don't know how to swim, a boat is necessary to cross the river, isn't it? Mother is not saying that you should stay in the boat forever. After reaching the other side, you should get out.

Once there was a disciple sitting on the banks of a river in the Himalayas thinking, "I see God in the form of my Guru but he says that he is not the body. Yet how can I believe him? How can one be with and without form at the same time? Doesn't he talk to me and do all other actions like ordinary people?" While the disciple was brooding over the matter, a block of ice suddenly crashed into the river. As the disciple looked at it, a squirrel jumped onto the ice which floated across the river. Upon reaching the other bank, the squirrel got off and gingerly jumped away.

Seeing this, the disciple thought, "No doubt the ice is only water, but without it, the squirrel could not have crossed the river. The formless water became ice and will eventually lose its form and revert to its original formless nature as water, but the form serves a purpose. Likewise, Nirguna becomes Saguna for taking us across the Ocean of Transmigration. Henceforth, I will look upon my Guru as the embodied form of the formless Absolute."

All forms have limitations. There is no tree which touches the sky, and there is no root which touches the netherworld. This means that all names and forms are finite. We should go beyond all names and forms. Even though God is beyond all qualities and all-pervading, He will come in a form according to our sankalpa.

It was now noon and the Mother told everyone to go and eat lunch. One of the young men said, "Mother, with your permission we would like to stay here until tomorrow evening." "Mother is only too happy to allow you to stay," She replied. As she was about to go, the elderly lady who had brought her grandson for receiving food from Mother again approached Her and said, "Mother, you did not say anything about feeding the child. Please do it now so that we can go before dark." Mother replied, "You will not understand now. You will come to understand only when ..." The Mother abruptly stopped and asked one of the brahmacharins to bring some flowers, sandalwood paste and sacred ash.

An oil lamp was lit and the Mother placed the child on Her lap. She then applied sandalwood paste to his forehead and offered some flowers on his head. She then fed him a little sweet pudding which the grandmother had brought with her for that function.

When everything was over, the family prostrated to Mother and happily took their leave.

Turning to Brahmacharin Pai who was nearby, Mother said, "What a pity, poor people. They will have to bring the child back again."

Wednesday, 2 November 1983

The Ganges river

Last night the *Devi Bhava Darshan* was over at three a.m. The Mother, as usual, spent some more time talking with the devotees after *Darshan*. At four o'clock She took one family to the back of the Ashram and talked with them until five. By the time She went to bed, it was almost six in the morning.

Today at lunch-time some householder devotees came to see Mother. She came to the darshan hut at three p.m. Everyone saluted the Mother and sat down. The young men who had come yesterday were also present.

Devotee: Will God be in the form in which I think of Him?

Amma: That form itself is God, your God. However, it is enough if you realize that both the water in the pond and in the river come from the sea. Through this attitude we can reach God. There is no problem if we consider the power that we see in our conceptualized form as God's power. Everything is one Power. We can reach the Ocean of Brahman through this river of form.

Let me tell you a story. Once there was a group of devotees planning to make a pilgrimage from Kerala in the southern part of India to the holy Ganges river in northern India. When they asked an old saintly devotee if he would like to come, he replied, "I am too old to make the journey. Please take my walking stick and after dipping it in the Ganges, return it to me." When the devotees reached the Ganges, they bathed in it and then dipped the old man's stick in the river. Unfortunately, the stick slipped and was washed away by the river's swift current. On returning to their village, they informed the old saint that they had lost his stick. "Did you lose it in the Ganges?" he asked. "Yes, in the Ganges," they replied. "Then, it's no problem." Going to his backyard, the saint waded into the pond and pulled out his stick! For a Knower of the Self, there is no good or bad, pure or impure. For him there is Purity alone. As far as he is concerned, there is no difference between Ganges water and the water in the pond. But for ordinary people, all these differences do exist.

Question: What is the significance of Ganges water?

Amma: Son, everything depends on one's purity and the strength of one's conception. If Ganges water is not available, a *puja* can be performed, imagining the water to be Ganges water. When we say Ganges, there is a Ganges within us as well. Modern science has proved that the river Ganges, the external one, has the power to destroy germs. Likewise, there is a Ganges within us which has the power to purify our mind. That is why it is said that Ganges flows from the head of Lord Shiva. When we reach Perfection through meditation, we become Him, the Possessor of Ambrosia. The pure Ganges rises up from within. That is what is depicted as the Goddess Ganga hiding in the matted hair of Lord Shiva. Goddess Ganga represents the Kundalini Shakti and its endless flow is the flow of the Ganges. From Lord Shiva, the Perfect One, it flows pervading everything and purifies the whole universe. That is what a *mahatma* (great soul) does. Through intense spiritual practices, he controls and sublimates all his passions, and with his purified vital energy, he sanctifies the whole world. Not that Lord Shiva is concealing His second wife in His matted hair. Some people say that Ganga is His secret wife (all laugh).

The power of faith

Young man: Does ordinary water become Ganges water through *mantra japa* (chanting of a mantra)?

Amma: Yes, it will, but faith is important, not the water. One small boy who saw the priests worshipping a *Shivalinga* in the temple cherished an intense desire to do the same, but he couldn't go into the temple as he was not a brahmin (member of the priestly class). The thought of performing a *puja* to the *Shivalinga* became stronger and stronger in his innocent heart. One day he had an idea. He took some stones and placed them one on top of another. Considering that as Lord Shiva, he started doing the worship. But the poor boy did not have the necessary ingredients to offer to the deity as did the priests in the temple. Therefore he offered plain water, imagining that it was rose water; sand became the food offering, and he used pebbles instead of camphor. After the worship, the boy sat in meditation just as he had seen the priests do, all the while thinking of Shiva. Seeing their friend doing the *puja* to the *Shivalinga*, the boy's friends also sat around him and imitated him, their eyes closed as if meditating. Their parents, not having seen them for a long time, came in search of them. They found the children and saw what they were doing. Taking it only as insignificant child's play, the parents knocked down all the *Shivalingas*. Seeing their parents, the children got frightened and ran back to their homes, all except the first boy. He sat there motionless. When he opened his eyes, he found that his *Shivalinga* had been knocked over. Bursting into tears, he called aloud, "O Lord, what happened to You? Where are You? What am I to do now?" In a few seconds, Lord Shiva Himself appeared before the boy and blessed him. That is the power of conception (*bhavana*) and faith. The Lord was pleased even when worshipped with sand and stones. All those ingredients, though imagined, became real, owing to the *bhavana shakti* of that innocent child, and the Lord was pleased.

The temple in Ambalapuzha

The Holy Mother paused for a while and then continued.

Amma: Children, do you know the story of the temple in Ambala-puzha (a town about fifty miles to the north of the Mother's village)? Priests were invited for the installation and consecration ceremonies of the statue. All of them were eminent scholars who could chant all the four Vedas by heart. In spite of their knowledge, they could not fix the statue firmly on the altar, however much they tried. When the problem remained unsolved, the temple authorities made some astrological calculations in consultation with the priests. According to the calculations, a competent person to do the installation was sitting a few yards away from the temple compound. When they went to the spot revealed in the astrological chart, they found a very primitive and crazy-looking man sitting there chewing betel leaves, having just finished eating fried fish. His name was Naranattu Bhrantan (Naranattu the Crazy). They brought him to the place where the installation was taking place, inspite of the priests' mocking at him and making rude remarks to the temple authorities. They held their noses and spat on the ground to express their disgust. They thought, "What made these people bring this ugly and low caste man here? What is he going to do?" Suddenly, all the priests vomited, but what came out was fish. Then the crazy man who had eaten fish spat on the ground and out came holy basil leaves. Everyone was wonderstruck. Taking some betel leaves, he chewed them and spat on the altar. Placing the statue on the spittle on the altar, he uttered a few words in a scolding tone, "Hey Krishna, sit here!" The statue became firmly fixed thereon.

The name of that town, Ambalapuzha, originated from the word 'tambulam' (betel leaves, when chewed, are usually mixed with three other ingredients, tobacco, arecanut and lime, which together are known in Sanskrit as tambulam). The town was previously known as Tambulapuzha. It was that illiterate layman's spittle and his chiding of God which bore fruit and not the Vedic chanting of the priests. This was because the "crazy man" was a Perfect Soul; whereas, the priests only wanted money. They did not have any spiritual power. Even the scolding of tapasvis (those devoted to the practise of austerities) is beneficial, because they are people who say, "O God, I want neither food nor sleep nor the body nor the intellect nor even You! O God, it is enough if You give me Your qualities, Your heart." Their power is in their concentration and pure attitude.

The sages have declared that there is power in mantras. If they have ordained so, then definitely it is there. Even a wooden plank will move by itself if you ask it to do so after chanting a particular mantra. That is the greatness of the power which they (mahatmas) have acquired. If they ordain that by chanting such and such a mantra, you will get such and such a power, then that will certainly bear fruit.

We will get results only if medicine is taken according to the prescription of the doctor. In the same way, we will certainly benefit if the mantras are used in the way sages have instructed. Scientists and doctors discover medicines and other inventions through experimentation, but their experiments are concerned only with the external world. Even today they are experimenting and the universe still remains a mystery to them. The sages, on the other hand, analyzed their own mind and did intense penance. For them there was no mystery; everything stood revealed to them. The mantras were discovered by the ancient sages through direct experience as a result of their penances. They spoke after having reached the state of Perfection. Therefore, their words will definitely fructify. They had the ability to create anything by mere will. They went beyond everything in this Creation. Therefore, concentration is the most important thing that we must acquire. Without concentration, no work whatsoever will be perfect.

Young man: Mother, isn't it enough to worship God while sitting in our house, or is it necessary to go to the temples in order to worship Him?

Amma: Son, it is all right if you are not going to temples. However, if you go to temples, you will benefit because the vibrations there are entirely different from those of a house or other places where worldly dealings are taking place. In a temple, everyone is thinking of God. The power radiating from the statue creates peace and serenity in the mind. The atmosphere is concentrated and impregnated with the one-pointed thought of the devotees who gather there. Because all are thinking of God in that atmosphere, it is easy for others also to attain concentration. But we should have the right attitude when we go to a temple.

If we have true devotion, we can see the form of our Beloved Deity in the statue installed in the inner sanctum of the temple. Suppose we sincerely love a lady. Whichever woman we see or meet, we will be reminded of our beloved. Sometimes there will be a slight resemblance. At other times there will not be any at all. Even then, we will think and imagine that this girl's nose is like hers, and that girl walks like her, and this girl's eyes are exactly like hers, and that girl's hair is like hers; we will imagine in this way. Likewise, when we see somebody else's child, we will attribute similarities such as, this child smiles like my child. Even if there are no similarities, out of love we will feel as if there were. In a similar manner, one who has sincere love for God will see His form everywhere. If it is not there, he will imagine his Beloved everywhere. That is how real love should be.

Suppose a young man goes to the office. He has a deep love for a woman. He thinks, "She may be taking a bath now. Now she may be having her breakfast, and now she may be going to the college," and so on. Thus his mind will be completely on her. Then he will think, "She will be holding her books like this." Thinking and imagining in this fashion, he holds the briefcase in his hand in the same way as he imagines the girl would hold her textbooks; so much does she saturate his thoughts. Even while sitting in the bus, he may think about her. He will not be aware of the other things happening in the bus, whatever they may be. All of his mind is on the lady whom he loves. For us, this kind of love should go towards God. Because of his thoughts about her, even his ways will become like hers. Eventually he himself will become her, just as Radha became Krishna by always thinking of Him.

Customary observances (achara)

Devotee: Mother, is it necessary to go to Sabarimala carrying *irumudi kettu* (the baggage in which pilgrims to Sabari Hills carry their belongings and offerings to the deity on their heads)? Is it enough if the mind is made pure?

Amma: Son, first of all, we must sincerely enquire whether our mind is pure or not. What you say is correct. It is enough if the mind is pure, but is our mind pure? It is only in the process of purification.

Son, customs are very important. If there is no regular discipline and proper conduct, it is very difficult for those who are still leading a worldly life to control themselves. There is no point in saying that everything is God or Brahman. We have not experienced it. We get angry when we see things which we dislike, don't we? Customs have meaning. People go to Sabarimala with the irumudi kettu on their head. They are carrying punya (merits) and papa (demerits), the burden of ignorance, symbolically in the form of the baggage, and offering it at the Feet of the Lord. Or else it can be thought of as the bag of renunciation. It can also be interpreted as all of our worldly desires and wealth, or the five elements of which the body is composed. This means that we are offering or surrendering everything at His Feet and praying for Ultimate Emancipation. There are many ways to conceive of this custom. Satisfaction arises when we observe customary rites. Then, isn't it good? This is another way to purify the mind. Son, without achara it is difficult to purify the mind. How can a student study in school without a schedule? How will a regular discipline come about?

Question: Isn't love for God enough instead of the baggage on the head?

Amma: Son, the baggage will not be felt as an unnecessary burden if there is devotion. What if everyone goes to Sabarimala waving their hands back and forth? They are remembering the Lord and Sabarimala when they see the baggage aren't they? Ignorant children will pass urine and excreta in the puja room. Likewise, certain disciplines and codes of conduct are necessary to restrain the ignorant from acting willfully. *Achara* is necessary for alertness (*sraddha*). For Mahatmas, *achara* is unnecessary, yet they observe them in order to teach us by example.

Son, you have asked if love is enough and whether it is necessary to go carrying the baggage on the head. Son, it is enough for those who have love to sit in the house. It is not necessary for them to go anywhere. The Lord will come running to a place where there is love for Him.

The achara should not go beyond its limits. You should be careful about that. Some brahmins give too much importance to it, which is not good. This may create a lot of problems. They become bound by too much achara, which becomes harmful for their spiritual progress.

Question: Mother, will there occur a change in Nature through *mantra japa*?

Amma: Son, chanting a mantra with concentration will definitely create a change in Nature. At present, due to man's over-indulgence and evil acts, Nature's harmony has been lost. We have broken the laws set by Nature. Everything depends on the human mind. In the olden days when people were truthful and good-hearted and worked together with mutual love and sincerity, Nature also favored them with prosperity. It rained during the time when it was needed, and only the necessary amount. The sun also shone in the same way. There was perfect balance between Nature and human beings.

Whereas now things have changed. Everything is in chaos and confusion. Human beings act as they like. Morality, righteousness, truthfulness, mutual love, faith and sincerity have all been lost. The balance has been upset. Nature has stopped favoring selfish human beings; now She is reacting. This is a great threat to the human race. The combined forces of human intellect and modern science with all its weapons cannot obstruct Nature's course. We will be saved only if we change. Meditation, prayer, chanting and other spiritual practices are the only salvation. This is not a punishment, but the way which God has provided to make us think, discriminate and act. If we don't change, it is like lying on our back and spitting up; the spittle will fall on our own body. We will be paving the way for our own destruction if we don't change.

Group chanting and prayer is very powerful. It can change anything. The lost harmony of the human mind can be restored only through a selfless attitude supported by prayer, meditation and chanting of mantras. First, the human mind should be harmonized, then the harmony of Nature will spontaneously take place. Where there is concentration, there is harmony.

Question: What should be done if we happen to get caught in the midst of people who discuss worldly affairs?

Amma: You children should try to avoid them. If that is not possible, chant your mantra while sitting with them. Or else tell them frankly but with humility, "My path is different, I cannot do this. I don't have any time to gossip." Another method to escape from such a place is to visualize your Beloved Deity in the person who is talking to you.

Don't give attention to the worldly souls around you even if they protest. This is not a problem for us. Do we keep awake at night because the crickets are chirping? No. In the same manner, consider that their protests and abuses are born of their ignorance. Don't feel hatred or dislike towards them. Pray for them. Suppose a student went to attend his examination. He could not answer the questions properly. Why? Because of his ignorance about the subject. It is not that he knew the answers but refused to write. Likewise, these people. Let them protest; they don't know anything about spirituality.

Our sadhana will not proceed if we go on trying to please others. Nor is offending others our method, for they will do the same to us. Not only that. By offending, we are becoming as ignorant as they. That is not our path. Ours is the path of humility and patience. Therefore, don't act otherwise. If we show humility and patience, this may also create a change in the person who criticizes us. If we get angry, then what is the difference between him and us? In the beginning we will have to bear with the anger of some people. Some will say, "Krishna killed His uncle. Therefore, I also can do the same." It was not because it was His uncle that He killed him. Krishna killed Kamsa because he was the embodiment of egotism. There is only one way to prove the existence of the Truth. Sit quietly and be calm.

Question: It is said that one should always remember God. How is it possible to think of God when one is doing some calculations or other work requiring mental concentration?

Amma: Son, it is possible even though the goal at that moment is something else. Work, whatever kind it may be, requires concentration. Even while working, we can surrender our action and its fruit at the Feet of the Lord. We can remember Him by praying "O Lord, make these calculations correct. You are the power behind my memory. Please help me memorize everything unerringly. My Lord, make me do this quickly. O Lord, why is this taking such a long time?" Thus, you can always remember God while at work. If this becomes a habit, then you can have thoughts of God while doing the calculations.

If you find it difficult, then you should pray before doing the work, "O my beloved Lord, I am going to do this work; please give me enough mental strength to do this as a worship of You. Help me to do this work with the right attitude. This is Yours, not mine. I am doing it with Your power, not mine." Then do the work sincerely, with concentration, and as best as you can without thinking of its fruit. Try to derive happiness from the spirit in which you are doing the work. When it is over, again pray, " O Lord, thank you for Your blessings and guidance. I now surrender both the action and its fruit at Your Feet." When this is practiced daily and constantly, it will become spontaneous.

Once the work is done, having put in as much effort as you can, with an attitude of surrender, then there is no need to worry thinking about the fruit. Fruit is something which will manifest in the future. Worrying about the past or future is meaningless. The former is no more; it has no validity. Even if you go on brooding about things that went wrong in the past, they will not be corrected. The future is also not in your hands. It is controlled by the Supreme. A true devotee who has surrendered everything to the Supreme will not worry about the past or future. For him whatever happens is God's Will. He accepts everything as His prasad.

Ramayana

Young man: Mother, we have troubled you asking many questions. If Mother lets us, we would like to ask a few more. Mother, in Srimad Ramayana it is said that Sri Rama had abandoned Sita. Even if Rama was an Incarnation, was it right for Him to do so?
Amma: Children, before we give an opinion about something, we should see the different aspects of it. Though Rama was an Incarnation, He was primarily a king, and secondarily a husband and father. In those days kings were not like the rulers of the present age. They ruled the kingdom with *dharma* as the basis. They never erred from the path of *dharma*. Rama was a true king. He always aimed at the happiness and peace of His subjects. When there was controversy about His wife, for the happiness and peace of His subjects He renounced His dearest one, Sita. This is real renunciation. Giving

up a thing which is very dear to us is real sacrifice; relinquishing something which is insignificant cannot be called a sacrifice. As far as Rama was concerned, Sita was His heart and soul. In reality, they were not two but one. In order to please His subjects, Rama, a true king, abandoned Sita whom He loved the most.

If you read and understand the Ramayana properly, you can see that both Sita and Rama were Perfect Souls. In that sense nobody could separate them because they were spiritually one. In fact, they had neither sorrow nor happiness because both of them were beyond all dualities. Even then, they suffered like ordinary human beings. That was to set an example of how we should live in this world without deviating from the path of dharma even when we are in the midst of life's problems.

You can see that the same Rama who abandoned Sita, shed buckets of tears the night before the abandonment and also when Ravana kidnapped Her. From that we can understand that He was a loving husband too. Moreover, even if She was renounced by Rama, Sita still adored Him. She never thought or spoke anything negative about Her husband even for a moment. She never thought of another man. That was only because She knew what Rama's duties were as a king and She knew what was in His heart as well. Their conduct makes it clear that Rama and Sita were Perfect Souls. What higher example is needed for us mortal human beings?

Today people never try to understand the scriptures properly. Not only that, they misinterpret them. That is the pity. There are many people who say, "If Rama could renounce Sita, I can also abandon my wife." On the other hand, some women will say, "If Sita could live with Ravana, what is wrong if I live with another man?" What moral degradation! Only renunciates who perform tapas can correctly interpret the scriptures, not others. Sri Rama ruled the kingdom, and at the same time was highly spiritual while living in this world. He was an ideal brother, son, husband, king and friend. He was even a good enemy.

Young man: Mother, that was a really good answer. We have never before heard an explanation like that.

Another young man: Mother, soldiers kill people. Isn't this a sin?

Amma: Son, it is not for their own selfish purpose that they do that. It is for the nation, to protect the country from its enemies, is it not? That is their duty. It is the *dharma* of a *kshatriya* (member of the military class) to fight. There is no sin in it. Sin is incurred when somebody acts solely on the basis of his likes and dislikes, as in taking revenge on someone, hating someone, killing in order to acquire wealth, and other similar evil actions.

Question: Mother, one of my friends has had many different calamities happen to him. He has told me to ask Mother, "Does God need me?"

Amma: Son, God needs everyone and no one. He is in us, but we are not in Him because our mind is attached to different worldly objects, particularly money and property. Therefore, our mind is in those objects, not in Him. That is the main cause of all our sufferings. God created us and the world. He teaches the Supreme Principle and *dharma* through the scriptures. What we experience is the result of living without caring about that. Even if you blame God for your evil acts and experiences, He will not be affected at all, but you will degenerate further and suffer more.

How many different kinds of deformed people stay in Oachira![1] Some are without tongues. So many different kinds of people! Foregoing food and sleep, they call, "Shivane, Shivane (O Lord, O Lord)!" while asking for alms. Wealthy people and handsome people walk in front of them. Even after experiencing all their sufferings, they never think, "O God, we are also living in the same world as

---

[1] A village located about eight kilometers to the north of the Amma's Ashram. A festival is held there every year at which time hundreds of thousands of people visit the temple there. There will also be hundreds of beggars and deformed people present trying to get a little money from the visitors.

these wealthy and healthy people. Therefore, definitely we must have done something wicked in our previous birth or we would not be suffering like this." They don't learn any lessons even though they are laying there begging for their food. They fight and curse each other. Those handsome and wealthy people who walk by also don't imagine that their fate might be the same if they commit evil acts.

Trials and tribulations, ups and downs, are the nature of life. They are unavoidable. When such experiences come, if you leave God denying Him, then you alone and not God are responsible for the consequences that follow. Whereas, if you hold onto His Feet at all times in all circumstances, then He will take care of you. Therefore, tell your friend to proceed with discrimination.

The time was five o'clock in the evening and everyone was sitting quietly with the Mother. The silence was suddenly broken by a scream from the door of the hut. Calling out, "Amma!" the elderly lady who had insisted on the previous day that Mother give her grandson sweet pudding came rushing in like a deranged person. Snatching the child from her daughter, she placed him at the Mother's Feet and cried, "O Mother, please forgive us. Please forgive us for our egotism!" The entire family was weeping aloud. Mother lovingly lifted the grandmother and wiped her tears while consoling the rest of the family. "What's the matter, children?" the Mother innocently enquired. A devotee of Mother's who was also a neighbor of this family and who had accompanied them to the Ashram said,

Devotee: Yesterday they came home by seven in the evening after leaving Mother. I was looking after their house in their absence and was there when they arrived. They narrated the day's events to me, after which I went home and went to sleep at about ten-thirty. Suddenly at midnight I was woken by an uproar in the neighboring house. Hearing their cries, I understood that something serious had happened and came rushing to their house. I was shocked to see the grandchild lying dead in his cradle, surrounded by his sorrowing family. At first, I could not think, but after regaining a little composure, I went about trying to find out if the child was actually dead. I shook him and sprinkled water on his face, but nothing was of any avail. There was no sign of life. An hour passed while the grandmother went on lamenting and crying out to Mother, asking for Her forgiveness. The mother of the child was unconscious on the floor due to the shock.

Suddenly, my wife ran to our house and came back with a bottle of holy water which had been sanctified by Mother and kept by us for use when we are sick. She sprinkled some of the water on the child's face and body. All of us anxiously watched to see any sign of life, while wholeheartedly praying for the child's resuscitation. To our wonder, after ten minutes the child opened his eyes and slowly moved his limbs. After one hour he had become perfectly normal. Realizing that they had committed a grave mistake in forcing Mother to do the feeding ceremony against Her will, they wanted to come here to seek Her forgiveness. Although they started from their house in the early hours of the morning, they could not make the proper bus connections and could only reach here now.

Amma: Do not worry, children. Consider this incident as given by God for your future good. Take it as a lesson to make you more cautious and patient. Do not consider it as a punishment. God will not punish us. Out of His compassion, He will only give us opportunities to think, discriminate and act properly.

Although the Mother knew beforehand what was destined to happen, She did not assert any authority of Her own to prevent it. She never claimed that due to their disregard towards Her the family suffered. On the other hand, She attributed the entire incident to the Will of God. Such is Her egolessness.

14 November 1984

Renounce the ego

A young man: Amma, why does God make us commit mistakes?

Amma: Son, God is not making us do any mistakes. According to which one of God's instructions are we making all these mistakes? Aren't we committing mistakes knowing that they are errors, without listening to the warning given by our own conscience which is God? Son, which God has told you to act egotistically? You drive a car after drinking. An accident occurs due to your careless driving. What foolishness it is if you come out of the car and scold the fuel for creating the accident! Likewise, in our struggle to protect our false pride, we commit all kinds of negative acts. When there is no other way to escape from our misdeeds, we blame God, putting all the responsibility of our shortcomings on His shoulders.

Young man: Mother, if the ego is such a despicable thing, couldn't He have abstained from giving it to us?

Amma: Son, fire has both good and evil effects. It can be used for cooking rice, and also to set a house on fire. A knife can be used for chopping vegetables as well as to kill someone. Good and bad are determined by the use that we make of a thing. There is ego in the attitude, "I am God's child, I am the servant of God." There is also ego in thinking, "I am rich, I am great." However, the former attitude will be for our good; whereas, the latter will lead us into evil. Everything exists in nature; just as there is darkness and light, there is good and bad too. It is our duty to move along the right path, using the discrimination given by God.

However much it rains, the water will not stay on the roof of a house or on the top of a mountain. From the mountain, all the water will flow down to the streams. Likewise, if there is a ditch, the rainwater will flow from all directions and fill it. Nothing will be obtained as long as the sense of "I" remains. grace will flow into us when we have the humble attitude, "I am nothing." The egotist will not make use of the favorable circumstances given to him. He doesn't have the mental strength to do so. We must always have the attitude, "I am nothing."

If the seed has to sprout, it should go beneath the soil with the attitude, "I am nothing." It cannot grow into its real nature as a plant if it haughtily thinks, "Why should I bow down to this dirty earth?" When the button on the handle is pressed down, the umbrella opens. Similarly, if we cultivate and develop humility, when our ego is made to bow low in front of the Supreme and His Creation, visualizing everything as Him, only then will our Real Nature unfold.

People who think, "I am great and something special," are in reality smaller than anyone else. They will always try to project their ego while engaged in any action whatsoever. Just like an over-inflated balloon, they will have to burst one day. The really great people are those who take themselves to be the servants of God and who serve all with humility and simplicity. The Supreme Reality is within us, but we are not aware of It. We remain in the worldly plane of existence due to our ego and this is why we do not know this truth.

Character building

Young man: What then is to be done, Mother?
Amma: Son, first of all, we should cultivate a good character. Suppose you meet a person and say, "Namaste," (salutations) to him. Out of pride he may not salute you back. When you next see him, again say, "Namaste." This time also, he may not respond. Repeat the same the third time. This time certainly he will think, "This man is saluting me whenever he sees me even though I have not responded at all, and he still continues to do it without any feeling of hatred. Now I must salute him back." Thinking thus, he will return your salutation. In this way you can develop a good

habit which will culminate in a refined character in the future, and will help others develop a good character too.

Character building is what is needed first. In the beginning we should deliberately do it. Don't we have to grow? Suppose we have an intense desire to become a doctor. We will study, abstaining from all entertainment, even foregoing food and sleep in order to concentrate on our studies. Why? We want to become a doctor. Likewise, we should intentionally cultivate good character in order to reach the spiritual goal. If we do that, then we won't feel anything as an obstacle. Character building is the first step to spiritual life. Children, try to become good by developing good character.

Skepticism

As the Holy Mother was talking, a serious-looking young man of about twenty-five came in. The Mother gestured for him to sit down. He sat and looked around with a proud expression in his eyes. It seemed that he wanted to make others feel that he was something special. The Holy Mother all of a sudden changed the topic of conversation and said,

Amma: If ten people get peace of mind from a particular place and thereby grow, we should consider that perhaps there is something of real value there. A skeptic is always confused. He has no God, no father and no mother, and maybe he even beats his mother. On the other hand, one who has *bhaya bhakti* (devotion endowed with reverence and fear of God) will not commit any mistakes. In the olden days, the skeptics were those who would serve the world selflessly. Such people are not seen at all today. Mother would say that the genuine skeptics are really thirsting. They are the ones who love God because they are ready to love and serve the world even though they say there is no God. They are always seeing God, Unity or Oneness through others. Therefore, they do good actions. In the olden days, there were such people.

Today one says, "I am a skeptic," and with an inflated ego, kills and beats others. This is what is done today in the name of rationalism. This is not what is needed. A real skeptic is one who lovingly makes others understand the essential principles of life and loves others even at the cost of his own life. That was why Mother said that today's skepticism will cause only degradation. Genuine love arises in a believer when bhaya bhakti develops in him. Those who come near him will also gain peace. This is the benefit that the world gets from a devotee of the Lord. Today's skeptics do not act after understanding the scriptures properly. Those who did in the past, did good to the world. Today's skeptics walk around creating havoc without studying anything, holding on high two or three words taken from somewhere or other.

The rationalistic movement was formed in the olden days in order to get rid of certain evil practices which had crept into religion. However, the skeptics themselves did not really know what was proper conduct and what was evil conduct as based on the scriptures. The scriptures reveal the real purpose of life. That is why their movement has become a failure, synonymous with wickedness and revolution. They have nothing good to contribute to the world. Rather, they make people think perversely.

The child will not make any mistakes when he fears that the father will punish him. Therefore, bhaya bhakti is not something bad; on the contrary, it is beneficial. When children are young, they study well due to bhaya bhakti. Otherwise, we can see them becoming spoiled. We become good without committing any mistakes when we have bhaya bhakti towards God.

When the thirst for devotion and reverence towards God develops, good conduct and qualities like truthfulness, love, compassion and righteousness grow. One will have love and respect for one's parents and (other) elders. One will not tell lies and will try to control anger and other negative feelings. Due to this, the atmosphere becomes peaceful. From obedience arises discipline, and thence follows peace.

In the absence of policemen, thieves will rule because there is no one to fear. If there were policemen, three-quarters of the crimes would be prevented due to the fear of punishment, and the public would live in peace. Similarly, when people believe in the existence of a Transcendent Power which governs the universe and which metes out punishment to the offenders of Its Laws, they will do less evil which, in turn, will result in more peace and happiness for society. Seeing their good example, others will also emulate them.

Some so-called skeptics ask why money should be spent in offering sweet pudding and flower garlands to God in the temple, when there are so many poverty-stricken people dying of starvation for whom the money could be spent. The skeptics do not care to think about how many people benefit directly or indirectly through the temple worship. How many people are employed by the temple in various capacities! The people who grow the flowers and those who transport them, as well as those who make the garlands, and the priests who perform the worship, all earn a living thereby. Finally, the worshipper derives satisfaction after the worship is over. See how many people benefit from mere flowers that blossom today and wilt tomorrow! How can we ignore this fact? Nature also is benefited. The impure air in the atmosphere is absorbed, and pure oxygen is expelled by the flower plants. This is beneficial to all living beings.

Life depends on air, the gross form of prana shakti or life energy. The sages observed that those who breathe quickly have a shorter life span than those whose breath is slow and calm. The pigeon is an example of a fast-breathing and short-lived creature. There is a close connection between the mind and the breath. With the increase or decrease in thoughts, there is a corresponding increase or decrease in the speed of the breath.

Through worship performed with flowers and chanting of mantras, man can attain a long and healthy life. During the worship, his mind will become concentrated and calm, which will result in his breath slowing down. This, in turn, will prolong his life and improve his health. Fast breathing is harmful to the body in the long run.

In the process of worship, thoughts will arise less and less, and the mind will gradually become pure and clear. Such a one-pointed mind will become an abode of virtues and spiritual power. The believer in God who performs the worship conserves energy through concentration, and thereby purifies himself and his surroundings. Is this not a real benefit?

The Ancients knew that in the present Dark Age of Materialism (Kali Yuga) humanity would not be inclined towards righteousness. Greed and the thirst for life alone would reign supreme. Offering sweet pudding and money to God were ways that the Ancients found for developing broad-mindedness, a charitable disposition, and love of God in humankind. It is said that love is sweet, that the thought of one whom we love gives a sweet memory. Offering sweet pudding to God is symbolic of offering our love to Him. But we have never heard that God eats that pudding. The worshippers and the temple employees are the ones who eat it, not God! So then, who benefits by such an offering? Not God, but humanity.

An offering becomes genuine when one gives one's mind and heart along with the offering. See the case of lover and beloved. They offer their hearts to one another and become identified with each other. Similar should be the case with a devotee and God. But how can a devotee truly offer himself as long as he is attached to things other than God? A person's main object of attachment is wealth. A large portion of his mind is occupied with thoughts of material gain. To make such a mind think of God is not easy. When a person offers money to God in the temple, he really offers a part of himself. In this way his attachments gradually decrease, and his love for God and charity increase. One will get the full benefit of any action only if there is complete dedication and self-surrender behind it.

The atmosphere in a temple is also conducive to our well-being. It is an atmosphere of serenity and inspiration. Just compare it to the feeling of a liquor shop. A parrot raised in a temple will repeat the Name of God. If raised in a liquor shop, it will repeat only vulgar expressions.

All this time the young man was keenly listening to the Mother's words. By then his pride had disappeared. He got up from his seat and approached the Holy Mother. Having prostrated before the Mother in a very gentle and humble way, he said,

Young man: Amma, I am a skeptic. I had many doubts about you and the work that you were doing. I came to argue with you and corner you. But, even without asking my questions, you have answered my doubts. What Mother said was correct. I was mistaken.

The Holy Mother smiled and caressed him.

Another young man: Nowadays, isn't it the theists who are making more mistakes?

Amma: Mother was not talking about bogus devotees. Suppose you visit a library where there are thousands of books. Upon opening one book, you find that has no value. Because of this, is there any meaning in declaring that the whole library is worthless? Similarly, if one or two devotees commit mistakes, does it mean that all are doing so? Those who have real devotion will not commit any mistakes. In fact, they are the real benefactors of the world. We often see things from a narrow point of view. That is not good. Be broad-minded. If you go through history with an impartial and discerning eye, you can see that it was devotees and spiritual people who really served the world. It was always they who restored peace and tranquility when there arose a critical period in history. They never accepted a salary for the service they had done to society. They are the truly selfless ones. On the other hand, we become egoistic and arrogant when we say and believe that there is no God. Which is better, to become a devotee or an atheist?

Bhaya bhakti

Young man: *Bhaya bhakti* is blind, isn't it?

Amma: Son, until we become mature, it is the fear of our father and teacher that makes us learn our lessons. When we grow up, the *lakshya bodha* (goal-oriented mind) that we should become a doctor or engineer will develop. Thus, there are benefits derived from *bhaya bhakti* until we can discriminate on our own.

A child wants to go near the pond or well, but he is afraid of his mother because in the past he was spanked for going there. Is this fear blind or a weakness? No, such fear saves the child from falling into the pond and drowning. There will come a time when the child develops proper discrimination. Then no one has to tell him; he knows for himself. Improper discrimination leads to destruction, living as we do without bhaya bhakti. Don't you think so? Therefore, bhaya bhakti will do good up to a certain extent. Afterwards, lakshya bodha is needed.

Son, you have asked whether or not bhaya bhakti is blind. It is bhaya bhakti which protects us when we are living in ignorance. Many children are ruined nowadays because they do not have any fear or respect for their parents and end up in the company of bad friends.

What Mother has to say now is that we should encourage those who give consolation and peace to others, whoever they may be. Children, you must proceed carefully. Mother does not say that you should blindly believe. Think and discriminate, then decide.

Saying this, the Holy Mother got up.

Amma: Children, you are not going now, are you? Mother will come back after some time. Please wait.

The young men came out of the hut and stood in the front yard of the temple. Having told one of the brahmacharins to play a bhajan tape, the Holy Mother then walked towards the southern side of the Ashram standing by the bank of the backwaters. The Mother stood there for a long time looking at the sky. The lines of a song sung by the Mother filled the atmosphere through the loudspeakers.

O Thou Whose form is Power,
While listening to Thy Name,
The mind becomes divinely intoxicated,
The Heart trembles.
O how beautiful is Thy form!

Holy is the tongue that utters Thy Name,
Worthy of attainment
Are meditation and worship.
Invaluable is the intellect that merges in Thee.
Without these, this birth
And all external actions are in vain.

Sitting in front of the temple, the young men silently listened to the song with eyes closed.

Incarnation

It was three in the afternoon when the Holy Mother entered the hut as cheerful as ever. The young men were already seated there expecting the Mother to come. As an expression of devotion and reverence, all of them stood up with palms joined as the Mother entered. With all humility, the Mother saluted them back and sat on the cot after asking the young men to sit down.

The Holy Mother closed Her eyes for a while and became absorbed within. When She opened Her eyes, one of the young men asked,

Question: Mother, will more than one Incarnation appear at a time?

Amma: Yes, son, it can happen. We can understand this by looking at Parasurama, Sri Rama and Sita or Balabhadra, Sri Krishna and

Rukmini. They all lived at the same time, didn't they? There is no such law that only one Incarnation can take place at a particular time and place. Those are misconceptions.

Question: Isn't it also said that everyone is an Incarnation?

Amma: Yes, son, in a sense everyone is, but that should be realized. How many will understand even if told? Perhaps one in a billion, because it is not by intellectual understanding or mere book learning that this knowledge can be gained, but only through pure experience. It requires both human effort and Guru's grace.

Do you know how meaningless it is to say that everyone is an Incarnation? It is like saying that the coconut and the coconut tree are equal. The coconut tree is mature enough to give coconuts but the coconut by itself is not. The coconut may say, "I am also the coconut tree," but is there any meaning in that? A coconut tree is contained in the coconut, but it is not yet ready to bear fruits. The coconut can sprout and grow and become a tree. But now it is only small and cannot produce any fruits; whereas, the coconut tree can give plenty of fruits to others. It is not enough if the coconut merely says, "I am the tree." It should be able to give an abundance of fruits. Similar is the difference between an ordinary soul or person who simply declares that he is an Incarnation, and a Mahatma who is established in the Real. It is not enough to say, "I am an Incarnation." One should be able to shower grace on others and bless them.

Young man: Even then, shouldn't an Incarnation be considered as only a part of God?

Amma: The feeling of being a part can exist only as long as there is body-consciousness. When that is transcended through *sadhana*, the *sadhak* becomes one with the Whole and the veil of ignorance is removed. In reality, part and whole are one. The sense of difference is due to ignorance. Incarnations do not distinguish between part and whole. We should understand the meaning of the "I" which they use. The "I" which they refer to is the Supreme Principle. It is not the "I" which is only five feet tall. "I" means the expansive, all-embracing "I," the "I" which sees everything as one. When an Incarnation says, "I alone am Krishna," which Krishna does He mean? The Krishna which is the Supreme Principle, which is everything. That Krishna is also Rama. When an Incarnation (*Avatar Purusha*) says "I," we will misunderstand and think that He is referring to that small little individual, but He is talking about the "I" which is the Supreme Principle.

Young man: Mother, we have learned that Prophet Mohammed had told those who did not accept his path that they would be subjected to severe punishment. Is this a sensible declaration?

Amma: Son, this can be interpreted in a different way. "My path" means the path which he followed, the path to the Supreme. "Severe punishment" is the suffering that we have to experience created by our *vasanas* when we don't search for our True Nature. When Mohammed said "my path," he was not referring to the "I" which is limited by the body but rather to the Universal or Eternal "I." In that sense, the path he meant was also the path to Eternity. Son, try to have a positive attitude towards all the religions. Take the good aspects from them instead of finding fault with them.

Young man: What form can be attributed to God, male or female?

Amma: (Smiling) Son, God is neither a man nor a woman. He is beyond both. Male and female are within us. Someone or other said, "This is man" and "This is woman." Isn't it only after birth that we make the distinction? What was before that? Mother would say that all are women except the knowers of the Self. There are women among men and men among women. Almost all human beings are women by nature. One who has no control at all over the sense organs is a woman. One who has controlled the senses and mind is a real man. In that sense, how many men are there in this world?

Question: Mother, why then is God being worshipped as Kali? Is this not a female form?

Amma: Son, the sages have portrayed the gods and goddesses with different forms, having given each a particular meaning. Haven't you seen pictures of Kali with the blood-soaked head of the demon Daruka in Her hand? That demon is the demon of *vasanas*, the demon of the ego which Kali has slain. That demon is within each of us and must be killed. Even so, not all deities are just products of the sages' imagination. Some actually lived, like Krishna and Rama.

Question: Does a person who has been a woman in this birth become a woman in the next also?

Amma: Son, the next birth will be according to the thought that one has at the end of this birth. If the desire at the time of death is to become a woman, then you will become a woman in your next birth. At the moment of death, only the unfulfilled and strong desires will decide what you will become in your next life. If they are godly thoughts, then you will become a devotee, but if they are worldly thoughts, you will be again thrown into a world of *vasanas*. That is why it is said that you should cultivate divine thoughts through practice. You cannot think of God all of a sudden, especially at the moment of death. Only if this thought is firmly fixed and established through constant practice will it come at that moment. Son, do you know the story of Jada Bharata? Mother will tell you.

Jada Bharata was a king in ancient times. As the fruit of a life of righteousness, he developed a spirit of detachment and a strong desire for God-Realization. Entrusting the kingdom to his eldest son, he left for the forest in order to do intense sadhana. One day while engaged in japa by the side of the river, he saw a fawn being swept away by the current of the river. Getting up, he rescued it and took it to his hermitage. With great love and care he raised the fawn as if it was his own child. Soon he forgot all about japa, meditation and other spiritual practices due to his preoccupation with and affection for the fawn. Unexpectedly, the time for his death arrived. Even at that time he was lamenting the fate of the deer and died while looking at it. Naturally, he was reborn as a deer, but due to his previous sadhana, he remembered his mistake of the previous birth and remained aloof from his mother and all the other deer. Finally, he was reborn as a man and achieved the Highest Goal through a life of detachment.

Young man: Mother, are you saying that a person who dies thinking of a house will become a house in his next lifetime?

Amma: (Bursting into laughter) Clever boy! He need not, but he might become a carpenter or a mason or a design engineer.

Young man: Can Lord Shiva be called "Mother"?

Amma: Yes, of course, He can be called so. It is said that the "I" has become the father, mother, child, brother, sister and all. Everything is Him alone. You call Him, giving any name. One will say "palu," another will say "milk," and yet another will say something else. Whatever the name, there is no difference either in the color or taste of the milk. God can be called both as Father and Mother. You were told that He is the Father, weren't you? He is the real Father who disciplines you by removing the ego and correcting you, and He is also the real Mother who looks after and protects you lovingly, compassionately and affectionately. Both are two different facets of the same God. Both aspects are unique. You cannot compare That with anything in this universe. That is what manifests through a Perfect Master (*Satguru*), the perfect balance of both Divine Fatherhood and Motherhood. Everything is pervaded by the Supreme Self. He who has realized this can manifest any aspect at any time by self-will.

Steadiness in sadhana

Young man: Mother, some say that we cannot attain the Ultimate State unless we proceed on a particular path.

Amma: Son, a *sadhak* must be steady in his chosen path. He should have an idea about the goal to be attained. Especially in the beginning stages, he should stick to one path and have a Guru who is a Self-Realized Soul. Towards this Guru he should have love, self-surrender and mental affinity. If you go on trying different paths and different Gurus, not only will it not help your spiritual progress but it will utterly confuse you.

Another young man: On their journey to Sabarimala², the pilgrims chant, "Swamiye Saranam Ayyappa" at all the temples they pass on the way. Why is this? Does Mother have anything to say about it?

Amma: That is not wrong. We should see the deity which we worship wherever we go. It is not good to change and worship different deities.

About Sabarimala and the attitude of the devotees during the period of their pilgrimage, Mother has only one thing to say. Cultivation of that attitude was a method found by the Mahatmas to unite people from different faiths in order to give their minds a sense of unity and oneness. Children, don't you know that during the Sabarimala season the devotees call each other "Swami?" They consider everything, even excreta, as "Swami." They call it "Poo Swami." This is the same principle of nonduality, nothing but At-man or God or Swami. This particular period of religious vows and worship teaches the people self-control and a disciplined way of living. During the period of the forty-one days vow, the devotees abstain from all indulgence in drinking, smoking, sex, eating meat, fish and the like. Originally, this was introduced to give them a taste of a disciplined life, and that having tasted it, they might try to maintain the same way of living afterwards. But most people do it mechanically and return to their same old life-style after the vow. Nowadays, even that is not seen. People go to that holy center as if going for a picnic. What a pity. A distinctive feature of the Kali Yuga!

Question: Mother, why is it not good to change deities and worship different ones?

---

² Sabarimala is a famous place of pilgrimage in Kerala which millions of devotees from all over India visit every year after observing various religious vows for 41 days. While traveling to the shrine, the devotees will be chanting "Swamiye Saranam Ayyappa" which means "I seek refuge in the Lord Ayyappa" (the presiding deity of Sabarimala).

Amma: Son, usually people see each deity as a separate entity. They don't see the principle behind it. Mother knows many people who become afraid if they forget to utter the name of one god among the many names of the gods they worship. They think that Vishnu will get angry if they chant Shiva's name while standing in front of a Vishnu temple, and vice versa. This is due to the lack of proper understanding about the principle behind the many gods. There are many rivers; each one has a different name and many branches but all have their source in the mountains. The gods and goddesses have diverse forms, but in reality, they are all One. The various names and forms are meant only to help us in our spiritual practice. Taste and mental constitution differ from person to person. Some like tea, some like coffee and others like drinking only lemonade. In the same way, each one can choose a deity according to his taste and mental make-up, which will serve as a ladder to attain the Supreme.

Once there was a famous devotee. A man from the next village heard about him, and therefore came to see him. The visitor waited outside in the front yard of the house. At that time the devotee was performing his worship sitting in the shrine. The man who came to see him looked in and found that he was worshipping Ganesha. At the same time the visitor dug a hole in the ground. Next, the devotee worshipped the Guru. The visitor dug another hole. Then the devotee offered a puja to Lord Subrahmanyam. Then again the man dug another hole. Then the devotee worshipped Lord Shiva, Goddess Lakshmi and Goddess Kali, each separately. As each deity was worshipped, the man outside continued digging more holes. After finishing the puja, the devotee came out and saw so many holes all over the yard. He asked, "What is this; why are there so many holes dug here?" The visitor said, "I wanted water and so I dug everywhere, but I didn't get any and therefore wasted my time. Had I dug one hole deep enough, I would have found water by this time." The devotee understood. If he had completely surrendered

to any one of those deities, he could have become a Liberated Soul long ago.

Young man: Amma, then what about these different mantras? There are many different ones, aren't there?

Amma: Mantras should be given according to the deity one worships. Anyhow, it is better not to chant more than one mantra. We are trying to concentrate the mind and thereby reduce the thoughts so as to gain peace and purity of mind. Therefore, chanting one mantra is the best. That mantra should be a mantra related to your Beloved Deity. More than one mantra will confuse the aspirant.

Young man: What about a person who has no knowledge about all these things? Suppose one doesn't know how to please the deity using a mantra. What does one do then?

Amma: Child, chanting a mantra is to purify our mind. You don't need to please the deity at all with a mantra. Why does God need a mantra? What benefit is He going to get if we chant a mantra? Does an electric lamp need a kerosene lantern? No. God is Light. It is as if having lit a lamp or candle in front of Krishna's or Christ's picture, we would say, "O Lord, now You can see properly." Is this needed by Them? It is only because They give the power of life that we are able to act. Then we say, "God, I will give You ten rupees for lighting a lamp." What God says is, "There are poor people among My devotees. Serve them and then I will be satisfied and feel compassion for you." What does He need other than that?

The Supreme God is different from the gods (the minor gods or demigods). God is a name attributed to the Supreme Self when It assumes a form and attributes. There are worshippers of minor gods. Their worship is just like raising a dog in the house. If a thief or a stranger happens to come into the house, it barks and alerts us to the fact. It keeps enemies away from us. In the same way, a subtle aura will be around the person who worships with a pure resolve (sankalpa). That will destroy anyone who comes to hurt him. This is why nobody is able to do anything to a sadhak. Just as one who touches an electric wire is thrown off, those who come to injure a sadhak will experience their intention recoiling back on themselves, but they will not know why. Even without the knowledge of the attack, the sadhak will always be protected.

As this conversation was taking place, a snake was seen crawling along the inside of the roof of the hut. It slowly crawled away and disappeared. Looking up, the Mother and devotees watched it. When it was gone, the Holy Mother said,

Amma: Now and then he will crawl around here. He will come to the doorway of the children who light the lamp in the temple if they happen to be late lighting the lamps. Immediately, with joined palms they will call out, "Shiva, Shiva, Shiva, forgive me! I was mistaken and will light the lamp right now." (Smilingly) Do you know how many times they have had to apologize to the snake? (All laugh)

Oblation to the ancestors

Question: Mother, why are oblations offered to the ancestors (departed souls)?

Amma: While alive, every being is surrounded by an aura. At the time of death that aura, along with the soul's inherent tendencies, leaves the body and floats about in the atmosphere, much in the same way that a balloon filled with helium floats. The scriptures say that the departed soul will remain in the atmosphere for two or three years after death. The feelings of attachment, of "I" and "mine" which ignorant souls have towards their relatives, feelings like "my sister," "my mother," and so on, persist even after death. The relatives also continue to consider the deceased soul as belonging to their family. Through this bond, when the relatives offer oblations to the departed soul with concentration, love, sincerity and a strong resolve, the departed soul will feel the effect and be uplifted and will gain peace or perhaps even a better birth. That soul ascends to the higher worlds when the relatives perform *puja* for its sustenance, uttering the person's name and birth star and thinking of his or her form. The relatives' *sankalpa* acts upon the soul similar to the wind blowing a bubble up into the sky. Son, suppose we are living in a small village. However far it may be, a correctly addressed letter will reach us in our house. In a like manner, if oblations are offered in the right way, they will reach the soul for whom they were intended. If it is for our father and if he has taken birth in another place, the benefit of the oblations performed for him will reach him even there. Because we are offering the oblations, thinking of that soul's name and birth star and chanting traditionally prescribed mantras with concentration, the fruit of this action will reach the intended place. Some people continue to perform these oblations even three or four years after the death of their relative, but this is more for the sake of remembrance than anything else. All of the aforesaid applies only to souls who are trapped in the bonds of attachment. Mahatmas who have gone beyond all such feelings can act according to their own wish after leaving the mortal frame.

Question: Mother, are rituals like formal worship (*puja*) necessary? Isn't mental worship enough?

Amma: Son, will hunger be appeased if you merely think of food? Don't you have to eat? In the beginning stages of spiritual life, *puja* and other ritualistic practices are necessary. They are one way to purify the wandering mind. The wandering nature of the mind can be controlled by keeping it engaged in the remembrance of God or Guru. While cleaning the *puja* room and *puja* articles, picking the flowers and making the garland and while doing the *puja*, the mind will always be thinking of the Lord's worship. This one thought will replace the many disconnected thoughts of the mind and give a sense of quietude. A fixed place, time and materials for worship are needed at the beginning. Through constant practice, one will reach a stage where one can perform mental worship at all times and places, but this is very subtle and is possible only after the mind has become subtle through concentration and devotion. After this, one will be able to perform every action as a worship of the Lord.

At this time some householder devotees came to see the Holy Mother. They offered the fruit they had brought to the feet of the Mother and prostrated. The Holy Mother asked them to sit down. It seemed that they wanted to talk to Her privately. Understanding this, the young men got ready to leave. As they offered their salutations to the Mother, She lovingly patted them and nodded approvingly saying, "Namah Shivaya."

27 November 1983

It was eleven o'clock in the morning. A householder devotee living in Bombay, but originally from Kerala, came with his wife and children to see the Mother. The Mother was sitting on the temple verandah with some other devotees. All of them saluted Her and offered the fruit and other things which they had brought.

Amma: Who is this? What brought you children here? Mother sometimes thinks, "Where are those children? Why aren't they coming?" Anyhow, whenever Mother thinks of you, She sees you.

One devotee: (With joined palms) Mother will call us, won't She? Though the body was there, our mind was here.

After a short pause, the devotee continued, "Mother, you asked what brought me here. I know nothing happens without your knowledge." As he uttered these words, both his and his wife's eyes filled with tears. Flooded with emotion, he continued, "Life was going along smoothly and there were not many problems for a long time, but two months ago, all of a sudden my eldest daughter died, and subsequently, in the following month, I lost my job."

For a few moments the devotee became speechless. Then he burst into tears. His wife was also silently shedding tears. The Holy

Mother made both of them lie down on Her lap and gently stroked their hair. After some time, they both stopped crying and sat up.

Amma: (In a very loving voice) Son, Mother knows your sorrow. It is very difficult to overcome such circumstances. Even Mother feels sad about it. Nevertheless, there are certain unavoidable truths which we must face either today or tomorrow. Whatever begins must end; whatever is born must die. This happens in everyone's life. It is quite natural that one might lose his mental balance when such things occur, but think for a moment. Does it make any sense if we go on grieving about it? Mother is not saying that you shouldn't cry at the death of your daughter. Yet if we don't regain our mental balance, then life will become more difficult. Ups and downs are the very nature of life. It is not the incident but how we confront it that is most important. Incidents by themselves cannot influence us. If we are mentally weak, their effect will be worse than if we are strong and well-controlled. The wise ones quickly overcome such situations. A wise man may also feel sad, but quickly realizes that it is all a play, that it is the nature of life. If you go on worrying, it will dissipate a lot of your energy and will make you inactive.

Suppose your finger is cut. If you simply cry while looking at the wound, it will not heal. Wash the wound and apply medicine; that is the only way to cure it. Likewise, brooding and crying over life's problems will not solve them. Try to confront problems and overcome them with proper discrimination and reflection. Crying will take away your mental peace and the problems will ultimately swallow you. But if you confront them with a steady mind, you can conquer them and become their master.

Devotee: Mother, these words of yours give us a lot of mental peace and strength. Mother, now we are in your presence and therefore there is peace. But what are we to do when we are away from you and feel as if thrown into the middle of the ocean?

Amma: Children, God is not confined to a particular body or place. There is not even an atom of space where He is not. Do not think that Mother is only in Vallickavu and is only this body. When you children pray sincerely, thinking of Mother, definitely that vibration will reach Mother and reflect on Her mind. Your prayers and your pure and innocent *sankalpa* will bring Mother to you. Then you will feel Mother's presence and peace.

Devotee's wife: Having received the confirmation from Mother Herself, I feel very happy and peaceful.

The Holy Mother affectionately looked at her beaming face and lovingly patted her arm.

Another devotee: Mother, many obstacles arise in my *sadhana*. No progress is being made.

Amma: Son, suppose we work hard from morning till evening, and with that hard-earned money, we purchase peanuts every evening and eat them. Then at the end of the month, when we look in the cash box, there is no money at all. It was all spent for the peanuts; nothing was saved. Likewise, we do some kind of spiritual practice and then dissipate the acquired spiritual energy by indulging in worldly affairs. Who is to blame if the bucket used to draw water from a well has a hole? There will not be any water left in the bucket by the time it reaches the top of the well. All the water will have leaked out through the hole. Similarly, the power we acquire through meditation will be wasted if we involve ourselves in worldly activities without the proper attitude.

Question: What do you mean by the proper attitude, Mother?

Amma: Do your duties in this world as best as you can while surrendering everything to the Power which is beyond. Understand the nature of life. Act wisely without falling apart when obstacles arise and without getting too overjoyed in favorable circumstances. This world has been created for you. No saint or scripture says that you should not enjoy the pleasures of the world. But you are asked to exercise a certain amount of restraint while enjoying. Always maintain your self-control and be the master of the external objects and circumstances. Do not let anything enslave or control you. When your attitude changes, life's goal also changes, and then your mind becomes more calm and quiet. Take the example of Lord Sri Rama and Ravana. Sri Rama did everything for the welfare and happiness of all humanity; whereas Ravana's motivation was completely selfish. Sri Rama had an expansive viewpoint; Ravana viewed everything from the level of his own ego. Ravana wanted everything for himself; Rama gave up everything for the good of the world. Because of this, Rama is still adored and worshipped. Through Him thousands find solace and succor. Ravana paved the way for his own and the whole nation's destruction and became an evil character condemned by all. This clearly shows their difference in attitude and the effect thereof.

Question: Mother, is it possible for everyone to be like Sri Rama? He was an Incarnation, but we are mortal human beings.

Amma: Son, we always find an excuse when a situation arises where we don't want to blame ourselves. That is foolishness. We never try with determination. We have all the qualities in us, but we never try. We have all the instruments but we never use them.

Take the example of Valmiki who wrote the Ramayana. He was a highway robber, illiterate and primitive. Through constant practice endowed with determination, he became a great sage. He became a benefactor of the world through his compassion towards ailing humanity. How? Through constant chanting. Everything is within us, but our attachments in the name of love always pull us down.

Question: What does Mother mean by that? Do you mean that my love for my wife and children is not true love? Attachment is an aspect of love isn't it?

Amma: Son, only a person who is completely detached can love others without any expectations. Attachment is not an aspect of real love. In real love not only the bodies but also the souls will be united. There will always be the knowledge of the changing or perishable nature of the body and the eternal nature of the Self. Attachment binds and destroys the person who is attached and the person to whom he is attached. Due to this attachment, discrimination fails and discipline will be absent.

In the Mahabharata, Dhritarasthra, the blind king, was overly attached to his eldest son Duryodhana. Therefore, he could neither discipline his son nor make him think or act in the right way. This led to the total destruction of the king, his son and the kingdom. Whereas, Krishna was completely detached and could therefore love the Pandavas and, at the same time, discipline them. The story of Dhritarasthra and Duryodhana shows how the selfishness and attachment of one person can bring about the destruction of an entire society.

Question: Then what should we do?

Amma: Children, the eternal and non-eternal should be known through proper discrimination. Is the love that we get from the world real love? Is it possible for us to love anyone selflessly? In fact, it is not loving but cheating. If it is true love, it should be selfless. We are simply loving in the name of desires.

There was a girl who loved her friend so much that she wanted to buy a beautiful birthday gift for her. She searched and searched and finally found one but didn't buy it. On the day of her friend's birthday, the girl wrote a letter to her friend saying, "My dearest friend, my love for you is inexpressible. I wanted to send a beautiful birthday present to you and I found one but didn't buy it because the price was one hundred and sixty rupees (nine dollars)." This is the kind of love that most of us have.

During weddings relatives and friends sometimes bring presents for the bride or the bridegroom. But each one of them buys a present hoping that twice as many presents will be returned at the marriage of their own son or daughter. Can this be called love? This is business-love.

We love our children. Don't we love them because they were born of our ovum and semen? Do we have the same amount of love for our brother's or sister's child or our neighbor's child? No. Why?

Because they are not ours. Do we try to save our child at the risk of our own life if it happens to fall into a raging river? If the house in which the child is lying is on fire, will we jump into it? No. We know that if we do so, we will die. We don't love even our own child selflessly. Do we love our wife? Aren't we just loving her body, her flesh? Do we love the Self, the Real Being in her? We would even kill her if we found out that she loves another man, wouldn't we? What we want is happiness from her and if we don't get it our love is also gone. Do we really care about her happiness? No, because we always want her to act according to our whims and fancies. We want her to obey us. If not, our love disappears. This is not love. For us, real love is very difficult because we are always selfish and egoistic. Our parents had no thought of creating good children at the time of intercourse. Their minds were full of lustful thoughts only. They wanted pleasure. We are born of them. Then how will we get a good character? There is no need to blame them either. What they inherited was also the same. Degeneration is slowly handed down from parents to children and now that has been transferred from our parents to us.

Now everyone is madly running around looking for peace. Peace should come from within. What is to be done in order to obtain this peace? We should live our life understanding and discriminating between the eternal and the non-eternal. That is the only way. We will get peace only through the knowledge that God alone is eternal. We love everything and everyone with expectation. It is only because of expectation that we hate. Hatred and anger come when our expectations are not fulfilled, when our desires are obstructed. We expect ten rupees from a person, and when we do not get it, hatred comes. Expectation is the cause of all this. Eternal peace and solace will be had only from the Self, our Real Nature.

Have faith in yourself

Question: Mother, what is real faith?

Amma: Real faith is faith in one's own Self. Even when we believe in an external deity or God or Goddess, we are believing in our own Self because that God or Guru is our own Self. If faith is only in an external object or deity, that faith cannot uplift us. With real faith, the worshipper or the devotee will have the understanding or awareness of the all-pervasive, omniscient and omnipotent nature of his Guru or Beloved Deity. Mother has neither told the *brahmacharin* children to have faith in a God sitting up above in the skies on a golden throne nor in Mother. Have faith in yourself. Try to know who you are. That is sufficient. If the grain lying in the granary egoistically thinks "Why should I bow down to this dirty earth? The paddy plant is within me," its real nature will not reveal itself. Only if it goes beneath the soil will its real nature manifest.

Children, in the same manner, only if you give up your aham buddhi (the egoistic mind) will it be possible to know your Real Nature. Otherwise, you will become prey to the rats of desires. If one rat happens to enter into a field, it will destroy the entire crop. Likewise, one desire is enough. It will disfigure the beauty of the Self. This means that you will become a slave to samsara. To get rid of this ego it is said that we must have faith in God because when we believe in God, humility will arise. Real humility comes only when we are able to see everything as God. Humility means to become smaller and smaller. There are two ways to realize God. One is to grow bigger and bigger and become bigger than the world. This means to become aware that "Everything is in me, I am everything." But this is not easy. This will easily inflate the ego because we don't know how to grow big. It is not the ego that should be made big but the real "I." The mind should be expanded to embrace and accommodate the whole universe within it. On the other hand, to become small is much easier. Consider ourselves to be the servants of God. God is not sitting in a particular place or on a throne. He is everywhere, in every object of the world. Therefore, when you think and discriminate properly, you can see that you are the servant of the world. Being a servant of God means being a servant of the world.

Question: Did Mother insist that these *brahmacharins* who are staying here must relinquish their hearth and home?

Amma: Shiva, Shiva, Shiva! Who is Mother to insist? Mother never insisted that anyone should stay here. Balu Mon got a job in a paper mill. There was a temple dedicated to Ganapati near the mill on top of the hill. He would go there and meditate. He wouldn't even eat his lunch. Seeing his indifferent nature, the officer said, "This is not possible. You must discharge your duties properly." This is really what Balu was waiting for. Even before they asked him to leave the job he was finished with it and came here. Having come here, he started crying and said, "Mother, until yesterday I was destroying all my energy for nothing. Should I waste this body and this human birth just for a woman and two children? Mother, don't push me into that world. My father and mother have enough wealth to live on. Then why should I make money and save it? I don't need it. Wouldn't it be better if I could give peace and solace to at least ten people with this body? Not only that, once we come to spiritual life, then we wouldn't think of harming anyone. That in itself is a good thing that we would be doing towards the world, is it not?"

They made the decision and came. Mother never decided for them. They had determination, so Mother accepted them. To give refuge to and guide those who want their life to be dedicated to God is Mother's duty and work in this world. If you go to a thief, he will teach you how to steal things stealthily. A cook will teach you the secrets of cooking. If it is a magician, he will teach you the techniques and secrets of his art. Each one will teach you the art which he knows. Likewise, this is my job. Whoever comes to Mother, She will ask them only to know God and will give the necessary instructions for that. What else can Mother teach them?

In those days the brahmacharins spent their days and nights outside under the trees, come rain or shine. There was no place or room for them to stay. That was good enough for them. There was nobody to give them food and there were no mats or pillows. Seeing their intensity and desire to know God, Mother did not insist that they should go. In the beginning Mother demanded that they all go to work, but they came back, having given up their jobs.

For a short while, the Holy Mother became abstracted. She stopped speaking and sat with Her eyes closed. The householder devotee also meditated until Mother opened Her eyes. She continued,

Amma: Children, none of you should believe just because Mother is saying all of these things. Look at Nature. Nature is a textbook from which we must learn. Each object in it is a page of that book. Each and every object in Nature teaches us something. Renunciation and selflessness are the greatest lessons that we can learn from Nature. Nature sacrifices Herself for humans; whereas, we not only exploit Her, but destroy Her. Yet Nature serves us. The earth is serving us; the sun, the moon and the stars serve us. What do we do in return for their selfless service? Nothing except harm. The unintelligent beings and things of the world have no thinking power, yet they selflessly serve each other and humans. Humans have discrimination and yet they are utterly selfish. They are not even clearing their debts to Nature.

Children, cautiously move forward understanding the subtle nature of whatever object you see. Then you will be able to understand that which is eternal. The well might say, "Could these people take a bath if my waters were not there? Could they get drinking water?" The well is not aware of where this water is coming from. Likewise, I might say, "Would these things happen if I were not here? I worked hard; no one but myself did it." We are not aware of the source from which the power to act emanates. To know the eternal and the fleeting, it is enough if we know that Embodiment of Power. Mother doesn't say that you children should become brahmacharins or sannyasins, but it is not easy to live a detached life while living in the world.

Devotee: Mother, even people who obtain *siddhis* through *sadhana* get into trouble. Don't all of us know the story of Chennittala Siddhan?[3]

Amma: That was not the power which he earned by himself through *sadhana*. They say that somebody bestowed that upon him. If it is obtained from somebody else without doing any *sadhana*, it will perish if misused. It will vanish if one does not maintain it through further spiritual practices. We won't feel like spending lavishly if it is the wealth accumulated by our own efforts. We will remember the suffering which we experienced. We will spend as we like if it is our parents' wealth because we did not undergo any suffering to get it. But we will use it cautiously if it is earned by hard work. *Siddhis* are not the criteria for measuring the greatness of a spiritual person. On the contrary, they are a *sadhak*'s greatest impediment.

One-pointedness

Question: Mother, what should be done to get one-pointedness?
Amma: Children, you should make an attempt and see for yourself. Initially, it is difficult to get concentration. Don't stop your meditation and other spiritual practices because there is no concentration. Constant practice is the only way to achieve it. Until yesterday we were living in another world, the world of illusion (*Maya*). The experiences we had there will trouble us at first. Son, the *samskaras* of so many births are there in our mind. When we start doing *sadhana*, we can see all the negativity coming out and getting exhausted, just

---

[3] Chennittala Siddhan was a man from Kerala who had obtained psychic powers due to the favors bestowed on him by a saint to whom he gave water to drink during the saint's last moments. He became very famous but finally lost all his powers and died of a terrible disease.

as more and more dirt comes off when we wipe the floor using a wet cloth. The mind can be made peaceful by sitting in solitude. Son, concentration will not be attained in the beginning. It is absolutely necessary to have a strong resolve to reach the goal. Suppose we are learning how to ride a bicycle. How many times will we fall down and get injured! Even then, we will not feel that it is a problem because our goal is to learn how to ride. How many shoves do we get at the ticket counter when we go to see a movie! We bear all that because our aim is to see the film. Likewise, whatever impediments come, you children should strive hard to get concentration, constantly keeping up the determination to reach the goal.

Students who have the desire to become engineers or doctors study hard with the intention of achieving their goal. Those who have understood what is eternal should proceed like those students. Time should not be wasted. Discipline arises automatically when the intent to reach the goal is there. Students who really want to learn study even while travelling in the bus. They do not complain that there is no light in their home. They will study even under the street light or go to a neighbor's house to study. Those who have determination are like that. Others will say, "I didn't study because there was no table, no light."

Think and discriminate between the eternal and non-eternal. Then if you children strive, you will get concentration. Whether it is for the body or the mind or intellect, won't you only benefit if there is concentration? We misuse time without knowing its value. Children, how much time is wasted by talking about and criticizing others. Why should we do it? Do we get any benefit out of it?

It is not necessary to meditate sitting with eyes closed in the beginning. Sitting in solitude, you should visualize your Beloved Deity while at the same time looking into the distance. Then cry for the Lord calling out, "O Lord, where are You, where are You? Let me see Your beautiful form and let me merge in You." If this is done, you will gain mental purity.

The twelve-thirty lunch bell sounded.

Amma: Come and eat, children. (Smilingly) Mother doesn't know whether it will be to your liking. Here the dishes are not too tasty. This is an Ashram. It is difficult to maintain *brahmacharya* (celibacy) if we are concerned about taste. This is a place for *tyagis* (renunciates), not for *bhogis* (those immersed in sensual enjoyment). The food given in the Ashram is *prasad* (blessed food).

After serving food to the devotees, the Holy Mother told the devotees that She would return later and went to Her hut.

At two-thirty, some more devotees came to see the Holy Mother. All of them were householders but very interested in sadhana. At three o'clock the Holy Mother again came and sat in the front verandah of the old temple. A few brahmacharins were also present. All the devotees prostrated to the Mother. Mother touched each one of them and saluted back.

That which is proper

One devotee: Mother, you are spending much time for us.

Amma: Mother is here for Her children, not for Her own comfort.

Devotee: You are too compassionate, Mother.

Amma: Mother does not know how to be otherwise.

Another devotee: Mother, what should I do?

Amma: Son, out of twenty-four hours, allow twenty-two hours for worldly affairs. Think of God for at least two hours. *Japa* should also be done for some time while sitting in solitude. It should be performed whenever you have the time, even at work. People spend their whole life thinking and brooding about their family and children. But what is this family and who are these children? Is it we who gave life to the children? They will become ours only if we give life to them. We are only their foster parents. If they really belong to us, we should be able to save them from all circumstances, even death.

Once father Sugunanandan got very angry because Mother called him "foster father" during the Bhava Darshan. He told Devi, "You can go away from here. I want my daughter back." She replied, "If I go, your daughter will become a corpse!" Still, he insisted. Then Mother suddenly fell down and became like a corpse and remained in that state for eight hours. A hue and cry arose around Mother. They even made arrangements for Her cremation. Having called Her "daughter," they were now ready to cremate Her!

The person whom we love so much will be buried or burnt into ashes. That is the end of all relationships. We might remember him or her for a few more days or weeks. Then slowly we will forget all about them until they become a vague memory or dream.

The parents who are in the world are foster parents. Real parents are those who can restore one to life even after death. We should live with this thought in mind, surrendering everything to the Lord. Progress in this way.

When soldiers fight, they know that it is not for themselves that they are fighting. They are only performing their duty. You should live in this world in a similar way. Consider God alone as your true relative. Try to live in an Ashram atmosphere once a week. Slowly control your food and bad habits if there are any. Try to develop an inner detachment while discharging your worldly duties. Dedicate at least one day in a month to doing only spiritual practices like a vow of silence, japa and dhyana (meditation). Spend that day in a calm and quiet atmosphere where you can be away from all the family problems and other worries. You can control your sexual life as well through proper discrimination. Only if we try will we make progress.

Children, you should understand the limitations of the world. The world and worldly objects cannot enslave us if they are seen correctly. Don't give unnecessary and indiscriminate importance to things and incidents. Everything has a place in life but we either neglect it or over-emphasize it. Both are dangerous. There should always be a balance. You can enjoy the world, but over-indulgence is unwise. It will destroy all your virtues making you worse than an animal.

Devotee: Mother, what is the difference between today's society and the society which existed in previous times?

Amma: Son, in the olden days people also had the same requirements such as food, shelter and clothing, but *dharma* existed as the substratum of every activity. There was truth and love. There was cooperation and understanding among human beings. In those days, marriage was not only considered as a physical union of a man and a woman but as an oath taken by both, a joint endeavor to help each other lead a righteous life with God-Realization as the ultimate goal. They had patience, forbearance, endurance, forgiveness and love for God. In other words, they had real love. Real love comes only when there is a thirst for inner development. The husband was ready to sacrifice his life for higher values. The wife too had the same attitude. Their children also were brilliant and righteous. Whereas, today things have changed. The husband loves his wife but only if she dances according to his tune and vice versa. Today's love is not spiritual love but sexual love, love for each other's body. If physical attraction ceases, love is gone.

In the olden days husband and wife were devoted to each other. Through the power of their self-surrender and chastity, they attained Liberation. There is no such thing nowadays. You children should live in the world understanding this principle of dedication to righteousness. Then your children also will become good. Parents should set an example by leading good and righteous lives in order to direct their children along the correct path.

Devotee: Won't we feel like clinging to the good once we come to know what is good and what is bad?

Amma: (Smilingly) It is not that easy, son. One who is totally immersed in worldliness would feel that there is nothing greater than that. When one gets married, then one would feel that there is no other heaven than that kind of life. One will not be able to think about any higher state than that. For him that is the highest thing in the world. Each living being, even a pig or an ant, thinks that its body is the best.

Once Indra took birth as a pig and forgetting everything lived happily in the mud with his wife and children. He thought, "How nice it is to be a pig." (All laugh) That is the power of Maya. Once you come to the world, you imagine that you need a wife, children, wealth, name and fame and position. Therefore, be careful. Perform sadhana.

At this point, the Holy Mother stopped talking and rose from Her seat. She went towards the southern side of the Ashram and walked to and fro along the bank of the backwaters. After some time She went to the hut and came back in one hour or so. It was nearly four-thirty in the afternoon.

Mother went with all the devotees to the seashore for a half hour of meditation. Meditation at the seashore in the presence of the Holy Mother was always very intense. The sound of the ocean waves coupled with the peace radiated by the Mother created a divine mood in the atmosphere. After meditation the Holy Mother sat gazing at the sun while devotees gazed at the Mother. There was an unusually pleasing and captivating smile on Her face.

Whenever Mother went to the seashore, many small children would gather around Her. That day they also came and sat around Her simply looking at Her face. The Mother had some light talk with them and then distributed some toffees to them as usual.

Having returned to the Ashram, the Mother started the evening *bhajan* (devotional singing).

Whose children are we, Mother?
Whose children are we?
What is the purpose of this birth
Which Thou hast given us?

79

I have no one to call my own.
Tell me who I am,
That I may dance in bliss.
O Blissful One, come, come.

O Blissful Mother, when is
The final journey?
That I may dance in bliss,
O Mother, come, come.

This song was composed by the Mother long ago. The power of the song is really inexpressible when She sings it Herself. All the devotees experienced an overwhelming flood of supreme devotion. One cannot help crying to God with intense longing when the Mother sings.

Since it was a Sunday, the Mother's ecstatic singing went on till six-thirty p.m. The Bhava Darshan began by seven o'clock and went on until three the next morning. As usual, She enquired about the devotees once more before going to Her quarters at three-thirty.

28 November 1983

A van full of devotees from Trivandrum came to see the Holy Mother. The *brahmacharins* were meditating and the Mother was walking in the front yard of the Ashram at five o'clock in the evening. Gayatri was also walking just behind the Mother, holding a glass of tea in her right hand and the Mother's face towel in the left. As soon as She saw the group of devotees, the Mother approached them beaming with great love. As She walked towards them, Gayatri said, "Mother, please drink some tea." Without looking at her, Mother replied, "Not now, later is fine."

Amma: (To the devotees) Oh my children, you have come!

One devotee: Mother brought us here.

Amma: It depends how intense your desire is. If you are really desirous of accomplishing something, then you will certainly find a way to fulfill it.

The Mother sat on the sand with all the devotees around Her. They each prostrated to the Holy Mother and placed their offerings of fruit, flowers and other gifts in front of Her.

One devotee: There will not be any time for spiritual practice if one stays in the family. A hundred problems will come up.

Amma: If we have a real desire to know God, He Himself will solve the problems. There are so many such experiences! One should pray to God with a pure and innocent heart.

Once Mother, along with all the brahmacharin children, went to daughter Mohanam's house in Quilon. The next day, when everybody got into the car to return to Vallickavu, her youngest son, who loved Mother so much, also got in. Mohanam was also going to the Ashram, but she would not allow her son to go, telling him, "Tomorrow there is school so you must stay home." The boy started crying and through his tears he said, "My Ammachi, if only God would make me an ant now, I could come with you sticking on to the side of the car." Seeing the sorrow of that child, Mother did not even want to sit in the car. Mohanam would not listen even when Mother asked her to bring him to Vallickavu. Mother then kept quiet but was fully convinced that he would reach Vallickavu if his wish was indeed pure and innocent.

Mohanam was surprised to see her son at the Vallickavu Ashram that evening soon after the *darshan* had started. Do you know how he happened to get there? One of his mother's distant relatives died all of a sudden. The relatives sent a message to Mohanam through one of their neighbors, but Mohanam was at the Ashram when he came to her house. He wanted to convey the message to her in person. Besides that, he harbored a desire to see the Holy Mother about whom he had heard from one of his friends. As he was not familiar with Vallickavu and how to get there, he took Mohanam's youngest son with him as a guide. Whatever be the reason or chain of events, the important point is that Mohanam's son did somehow happen to get to the Ashram to be with Mother on that very same day. That is the power of devotion and surrender.

If detachment arises

Devotee: Mother, my doubt still remains whether it is possible to do spiritual practice if one stays in the family.

Amma: Son, one will understand that all these worldly bondages are nothing if one uses his discriminative powers constantly. Children, do not relinquish your family and family duties all of a sudden. Perform your duties without thinking of past experiences, future expectations or the fruit of your actions. Always live in the present doing your duties as a service to the Supreme. Avoid too much attachment. When you live in this manner, you will feel more peace of mind and one day you will be able to give up everything and dedicate yourself completely at the Feet of the Lord.

Buddha and Rama Tirtha each led a family life in the beginning. But they were always looking, observing and studying the nature of the world. They had so much vairagya (detachment). That is why they left their homes. Once detachment came, then there were no more relationships. No conflict arose for them even if it was their own mother who objected, for they could not attach themselves to anything anymore. That is the point. But children who don't have that much vairagya should not try to imitate this way of renouncing everything.

Question: Does that mean that one should wait until *vairagya* comes?

Amma: Son, what Mother means is that spirituality is not a way to escape from all the problems that confront you. If you run away from your home in the name of spirituality just to avoid the troubles of looking after your wife and children, this does not mean that you have renounced everything. The thoughts about your wife and children will be much stronger in your mind than when you were with them. Therefore, that is not the right way to do it. Perform your duties; at the same time, use your discrimination to avoid the danger of getting trapped in excessive attachment. Mother knows that this is difficult. It is a slow process. One needs a lot of patience.

At the same time, one cannot wait for vairagya to come. It is meaningless to think that one can satiate all desires and then take to spirituality, because desires are endless. They are like the waves of the ocean. They will appear one after another. A person was standing by the oceanside for a very long time. Another person who was watching him asked, "You have been standing here for a long time. What are you doing?" He replied, "Friend, I want to take a bath in the ocean but I am waiting for the waves to subside so that I can bathe peacefully." Desiring to lead a spiritual life after satisfying all one's desires is like that person who wanted to bathe in the ocean only after all the waves had subsided.

Question: Mother, isn't it a sin to abandon one's mother and others?
Amma: It is not a sin if such a state of *vairagya* comes to you. Then their dejection will not affect you because you will be doing a greater good than merely being with them. When real *vairagya* comes, everything falls off automatically. It just happens spontaneously, without any effort. You cannot do otherwise.

A true seeker renounces everything for the good of the world. If one relinquishes his small family to become the servant of the big family, i.e., the world, there is no sin in it. When we make a pit around a huge teak tree to pour water and put fertilizer, many small plants and weeds will get destroyed. That destruction is not destruction. Nobody will care very much because compared to the teak tree, those small plants are insignificant and useless. Likewise, when real longing to realize God comes, one spontaneously cuts off all bondages. He may even give up his wife and children or parents. But he does not incur any sin by doing so because he has done this for the world family compared to which his small family is insignificant. A renunciate's family will be protected and looked after by God. Whereas, aspirants who still have not developed that kind of vairagya must remain in the family and discharge their duties as best as they can, surrendering everything to God.

A bad thing can be abandoned for the sake of the good, can it not? Is it not for the good of our body that we kill a harmful insect? We kill the worms and other parasites in our body. Do you think that it is a sin to kill an extremely poisonous snake? We destroy certain things for our own good and certain other things for the common good. When a true spiritual seeker gives up his family, he is doing that for the common good. One who is attached to the family and other external things cannot serve or love the world selflessly. Only if one is completely free from all kinds of attachments can he do so. Even though attachment and detachment are mental, in the beginning it is good to keep away from circumstances and objects which might do harm to the sadhak.

Family members will not die because renunciates have abandoned them for the sake of God. They will live on. Certainly there are many who have experienced this and survived.

When Rama Tirtha was about to leave his hearth and home, his wife said, "I am also coming." At that time, he said, "All right, I will take you with me, but you must fulfill three conditions. First of all, you should consider your husband as dead." "Agreed," replied the wife. "Secondly, take all your children to the market place and openly declare that these children are God's, not yours." With that she could not agree. "Then how can I take you?" he remarked as he left. He did not even have to state the third condition. However much they may try, mothers cannot develop such an attitude of detachment towards their children.

All of a sudden, Mother went into samadhi.

Question: So then, is it not necessary to perform one's dharma?

The Holy Mother, who was in an abstracted mood, did not reply. The questioner sat gazing at the Mother's face. Some time passed and the Mother opened Her eyes. She understood that he had something to ask.

Amma: What, son?

Question: Don't those who become *sannyasins* without looking after their family need to perform any family duties?

Amma: Son, as Mother has stated before, everything depends on one's mental maturity. *Sannyasa* is not merely clothing oneself in ochre cloth. A real *sannyasin* is one who completely eradicates his *vasanas*. This means that he has no selfish motives at all. He no longer has duties towards his family or his relatives. Only one who has reached that state of selflessness is a real *sannyasin*. One who has attachment to the family is not a *sannyasin*. He must perform his worldly duties, surrendering his feeling of "I" and "mine" to the Supreme. This will enable him to exhaust the old tendencies and no new tendencies will be created. If one has burning *vairagya* to realize God, then he can free himself from the family bondages. In his case, this will happen spontaneously. It cannot be otherwise.

Question: Then one can run away when *vairagya* comes, can't he?

Amma: It is not something which comes one fine morning. In a few it may manifest spontaneously during the early period of their lives, in their youth, but this is very rare. In others, it will take some time. This can also happen when one meets a *Satguru*. By the mere touch, look or *sankalpa* this dormant *vairagya* will awaken. It is not a running away; it just happens. It will become difficult for them to be in the house henceforth. There is no sin in it.

Did Acharya Sankara remain with his mother out of concern for her welfare? They had no wealth or riches. Everything had been given away in charity. Yet Sankara left and took sannyasa. But didn't she get everything? She continued to live and got Liberation in the end too.

The mind should be made ochre. The color of ochre clothes is that of fire, which means the body should be burnt in the Fire of Knowledge. The body is the product of the ego. When the ego is gone, then you become a real sannyasin. But sannyasins of today are like marambu (a kind of wild yam) which closely resembles chembu (a kind of tuber). When marambu is pulled out, there will not be any roots. Likewise, today sannyasins have ochre clothes externally but no spiritual stuff within.

Question: But Mother, Acharya Sankara[4] left with the permission and blessings of his mother, didn't he?

Amma: But how did he get the permission? He had to play a good trick. She might have been afraid that the same or a similar incident might happen again if she didn't allow him to take *sannyasa*. Anyhow, Sankara's mother was not like other mothers. She was a highly spiritual woman. After hearing all this, householders should not leave their homes in the name of *sannyasa*. You must truly have intense *vairagya*. Simply imitating will not work.

Question: What if permission is not given?

Amma: (Smilingly) That doesn't matter. If *vairagya* comes, you can go, that is it. Anyhow, which mother will agree to her son's taking *sannyasa*?

Devotee: So then, does Mother say that there is no sin at all if one abandons his family?

Amma: Yes, if there is real *vairagya*, one can leave the family. Many of the disciples of Sri Ramakrishna did so. There were other people also who came to him after abandoning their wife and children.

---

[4] Acharya Sankara was a great philosopher-sage and exponent of the Advaita philosophy who lived in the eighth century in India. At the age of eight he tricked his mother into allowing him to become a *sannyasin*. He created an illusory crocodile through his mystical powers which seized him while he was bathing in the river. He then appealed to his mother to allow him to become a monk at least during his last moments. As soon as she agreed, the crocodile disappeared.

He made them stay with him. Their family continued living; none of them died heartbroken. If such people have enough wealth for their family to live, then there is no problem. What Mother says is that even if there is not enough wealth, if one has real *vairagya*, no burden of sin will be incurred if he takes *sannyasa*, leaving everything.

Another devotee: Mother, is it beneficial to chant mantras even without knowing the meaning?

Amma: Son, just as one falls asleep if one takes sleeping pills even without knowing that they are sleeping pills, if you chant your mantra without knowing its meaning, it has its own power. Even then, it is better if it is chanted with *sraddha* (faith) and love. Concentration also is necessary. A mantra will have a special power if it is received from a *Satguru*, rather than choosing it oneself.

Once you get into a bus or train, it will take you to the destination even if you don't know who the driver is or which company manufactured the bus or train or from where the spare parts are available. It will drop you at the nearest bus or railway station and from there it will be only a short distance to your home. Similarly, a mantra will carry you to the threshold of God-Realization. From there, you can easily reach the Ultimate Goal.

Question: Mother, you said that a mantra received from a *Satguru* has a special power. How is that?

Amma: A Perfect Master can transmit a portion of his spiritual power to the disciple. That is what he does when he initiates a disciple. There is a natural way to make curd (yogurt). Take the culture and add it to milk and keep it still for a day. Within one day the milk will be transformed into pure curd. Likewise, during initiation a real Master transfers a part of his spiritual power through his purified vital force into the disciple. In fact, the Master awakens the spiritual energy dormant in the disciple when he initiates him. Just as milk turns into curd when a little bit of buttermilk is added to it and allowed to set by keeping it still, the disciple through constant spiritual practice can fully develop this pure vital energy or spiritual power transmitted by the Guru into Pure Essence. He should still his mind through *sadhana*. The Guru always does this transmission of power only after understanding the competency of the student. This understanding includes knowing the spiritual disposition which the student has inherited from the previous birth.

When the Guru initiates the disciple, he sows the seed of spirituality. Just as we create favorable circumstances necessary for the germination and growth of the seed, we must take necessary steps for the strong growth of this spiritual seed sowed by the Guru in us.

Receiving a mantra from a Satguru can also be compared to the transplanting of a wild plant from the forest to the cultivated countryside. The Guru does that, the transplanting of our mind from the material world to the spiritual world.

It was time for the evening bhajan which began at six-thirty.

> *Give me refuge, O Goddess, give me refuge,*
> *O Mother, O Thou Whose divine form is being*
> *Praised by the celestials. Salutations to Thee,*
> *The Primal Supreme Energy!*

> *Salutations to Mother Who is the Cause of*
> *All auspiciousness, Fulfiller of all desires,*
> *Perfection Itself, and the Source of Nature Herself.*

> *Thou art the Cause of creation, sustenance*
> *And destruction. Thou art the Destroyer*
> *Of the wicked. I bow to Thy Feet Who art*
> *Of the form of Pure Existence and Awareness.*

The Mother sang until eight-thirty after which the arati was performed just before nine. Afterwards, the Mother remained seated and the group of devotees one by one came and sat around Her.
Amma: The trinity -- Brahma, Vishnu and Maheshwara -- create, sustain and destroy desires; whereas, human beings create and

nourish desires but do not destroy them. Destruction of desires is what is needed. Absence of that is the cause of all our troubles.

Mother doesn't say that you should not have any desires at all. Without desire, life is impossible. But never let desire control and enslave you. Desires should be under your control.

Question: Mother, is there a God separate from us?

Amma: Even though it is commonly said that God is within us, there is an Infinite Power which exists independent of and transcending every created thing. That Power is God and It is unique. That exists as the source and support of even a Liberated Soul. Which came first, the coconut or the coconut tree? The problem is unsolvable unless one accepts a creative Cause preceding Creation as its Source. That Transcendent Cause is God.

Question: Mother, just see how much this world has degenerated!

Amma: Son, do not look at the world. Look within your own self and remove the impurities from your mind. Practice seeing only the good in others. When all the impurities are removed from your mind, then you will be able to help make others good. Whereas, if you go on blaming the world and finding fault with others, your own mind will become degenerated and you will also become like them. If we try to make the world good before becoming good ourselves, that will do harm both to us and the world. Only one who has studied can teach others; only one who is rich can help others financially; only one who has accumulated can give and only one who is completely freed from sorrow and impurities can free others from sorrow and make them pure.

If you know your own Self, the world will become your wealth, but to know the Self needs constant practice. Mother sees only the Pure Essence in you. One can become like that through practice. When a blacksmith sees a piece of iron, he will not care about the rust covering it. He will think of the object he can make out of the iron after removing the rust. A sculptor, when he sees a rock, thinks of the form he can carve out of it. He does not pay any attention to the moss on the rock. In a similar manner, we should see only the good in others.

Question: Mother, can householders attain Liberation?

Amma: Yes, but they must be real *grahasthashramis*. Living in the house, they must live like Ashramites. That is real *grahasthashrama*. While remaining in the house, they should live for God. It is possible to carry on a spiritual life while living in the world. The one condition is that one must perform actions selflessly without any attachment. One should not worry about the past or the future. Live in the present, surrendering your actions and their fruit at the Feet of the Lord. Perform your duties as sincerely as possible, keeping in mind that all is entrusted by God. Be satisfied with whatever is provided by the Supreme. Anyhow, when we act with an attitude of surrender and devotion, it will bear the best fruit. But do not confuse your mind thinking of the fruit. If you perform your duties in the present, sincerely and wholeheartedly, considering it as your duty entrusted by God, then the future will become your friend. Live today with dedication, then tomorrow will be your friend. Get rid of "I" and "mine" and consider everything as God's.

Question: Mother, who is a real Guru?

Amma: A real Guru is one who kindles and sustains the Light of Knowledge or spirituality in the disciple, destroying ignorance. A genuine Master always works with the *vasanas* of the disciples. He makes the disciple realize his negativities and helps him to eliminate them. A true Master never gives importance to *siddhis*. He has all the powers needed under his sway. Even then, he will always remain simple and humble. A true Master is a Self-Realized Soul. One can see and experience all the eternal virtues like universal love, renunciation, patience, forbearance, endurance, etc., in him. He will have equal vision and perfect balance of mind in all circumstances. There will not be even an iota of selfishness in him. He will have no desires except the good and well-being of the entire creation. He will neither find fault with others nor will he criticize anyone. Peace and tranquillity are his nature. Anger can never overpower him. If you see him get angry, that will only be for correcting and guiding others. His anger is another expression of his love. Such a Master's anger is like a burnt shell. The burnt shell will have the shape of a shell but it will disappear if tapped with a little force. The real Master will appear to be angry but that is only an external show. His mind will not be affected by it.

Question: Mother, what are the signs of a true *Guru-sishya* (Master-disciple) relationship?

Amma: In a genuine *Guru-sishya* relationship, it will be difficult to recognize who is who because the Guru will have more of a servant-like attitude than the disciple. The Guru will have the attitude to transform the disciple by every possible means. The Guru will watch each and every action of the disciple, but the disciple will not understand this. In a true *Guru-sishya* relationship, the Guru will have tremendous patience. Even if the disciple commits serious errors, the Guru will patiently forbear and will give opportunity after opportunity for the *sishya* to correct himself and become flawless. A real Guru will be like a true mother and a true father to the disciple. That means not only will he love the disciple selflessly and wholeheartedly, but at the same time, he will also be a good disciplinarian.

On the other hand, the disciple will serve the Guru with the attitude that the Guru should not even know that he is serving him. That is the duty of a true disciple. Seva or service means obedience. Obedience means self-surrender. Self-surrender means giving up one's own ego, the feeling that "I am doing and I must get the fruit of it." A true disciple will be ready to sacrifice all his comforts and even his body to serve the Guru. A true disciple's love towards his Master will be like the love of the Gopis towards Krishna. The disciple will have no secrets. He will be like an open book in front of the Master. He will always have the awareness that his Guru knows everything. Therefore, he will not commit any mistakes. In such a

Guru-sishya relationship, the Guru will be in the disciple and the disciple will be in the Guru.

A real disciple will eat and sleep only after the Guru eats and sleeps. He will get up before the Guru gets up, and having finished his nature calls, bath and other morning necessities, he will do whatever is needed for the Guru. He will never show impatience or impertinence. Humility will be his trademark. Just as water flows automatically to where the field is low, the Guru's grace will automatically flow into the disciple when he sees the disciple's movements endowed with sraddha (faith) and bhakti (devotion). But today it is very difficult to find such a Guru-sishya relationship.

Question: Nowadays we hear about many *Avatars* (Incarnations), but the *Srimad Bhagavatam* says that there are only ten *Avatars*.

Amma: Son, nowhere is it stated that God will incarnate only during a certain time, place and in a certain form. Nobody can predict where, how or when the glory of God will assume form. All that takes place according to His Will. He can incarnate in any place at any time. He is not bound by time or place. To protect *dharma*, the unlimited and formless Supreme Being accepts different limited forms according to His own *sankalpa* and again makes them merge in His Infinite Self. This is like the waters of the ocean rising up as vapor and returning again to the ocean as rain.

Bhava Darshan

Devotee: Some devotees believe that Mother is the same during the Divine *Bhava* as She is at other times. If this is so, then what is the significance of the *Bhava*?

Amma: During the time of the *Bhava Darshan*, Mother removes two or three veils, so to say, so that the devotees can obtain a glimpse of the Supreme. Even at that time, She is manifesting only an infinitesimal part of Her spiritual power.

Different people have different kinds of beliefs. Mother's intention is to somehow help the people approach God. Some are interested only if they see Mother in the costume of Devi or Krishna. Not only that, very few people know anything about spirituality. Some people find it difficult to believe Mother's words during ordinary times, but if Mother says the same thing during the Devi *Bhava*, they will believe.

Question: Mother, is there any particular time for manifesting this *Bhava*?

Amma: No, there is not. It can be manifested at any time. Mere will is enough.

Question: Mother, why do you wear the costumes of Krishna and Devi?

Amma: They help people understand what *Bhava* is. People have a special pre-conceived idea about Krishna and Devi and Their dress. For example, when we think of the form of Devi, we have in our mind Her enchanting form adorned in a beautiful sari with a golden crown, a nose-ring and other adornments. Similarly with Krishna. When one says "Devi" nobody will think of an ordinary girl. There must be a distinctive quality in the manner of dress. This is what Mother is trying to do. By planting the impression of Devi in the minds of the devotees, Mother is trying to help them to make their faith stronger in order to grow spiritually. By wearing those beautiful saris, Mother makes the *Darshan* more picturesque and thereby instills greater life into the devotees' *bhavana* (attitude). Son, each attire is important in its own way. We were naked when we were born. Later, according to the country and social custom, people adopted different kinds of dress. Whatever is the dress, the person is the same. In this age people give much importance to dress. Mother will make this point clear through an anecdote.

One man was cutting down a tree which was growing by the side of the road. Another man who happened to see him doing this said, "Don't cut down the tree! It is wrong to do so, it is against the law." The first man not only refused to stop but also scolded the other severely. The person who tried to prevent the ruffian from cutting the tree was a policeman. He departed but soon returned in his official dress. Even from a distance, the mere sight of the policeman's cap was enough to make the hooligan flee without looking back. See the difference in the impact created when the policeman came in ordinary dress and later in official dress! Therefore, special attire is needed to teach ignorant people. Likewise, the costumes of Krishna and Devi Bhavas. Some people who still feel dissatisfied even after talking to Mother for hours, will feel fully content after conversing with Her for only a couple of seconds during Bhava Darshan. They feel peaceful after having told all their worries directly to God. The special dress during the Bhavas also helps the devotees to keep the remembrance of the Presence of God. The costumes create a feeling of divine beauty in the minds of the devotees. Beauty is the nature of God, is it not?

Another devotee: Mother, what is the particular speciality of the Krishna *Bhava*?

Amma: Krishna *Bhava* is the manifestation of the *Purusha* or Pure Being aspect. There is no difference between Vishnu who incarnated as Krishna and the Krishna during Krishna *Bhava*. Devi *Bhava* is the Eternal Feminine, the Creatrix, the Active Principle of the Impersonal Absolute. All the deities of the Hindu Pantheon, which represent the numberless aspects of the One Supreme Being, exist within us. One possessing Divine Power can manifest any of them by his mere will for the good of the world. Here is a crazy girl who puts on the garb of Krishna and after some time that of Devi, but it is within this crazy girl that both exist.

Why decorate an elephant? Why should a lawyer wear a black coat or why does a policeman wear a uniform and a cap? All these external aids are meant to create a certain impression. In a like manner, Mother dons the garb of Krishna and Devi in order to give strength to the devotional attitude of the people coming for

Darshan. The Atman or Self that is in me is also within you. If you realize that Indivisible Principle that is ever shining in you, you will also become That.

Question: Should something be done to make Mother known to the world?

Amma: Children, know that Mother is the Truth. Mother needs no propaganda. Does the ever-radiant AUM need any propaganda? Those who have purity of heart and thirst for God will seek out Mother and reach Her.

At nearly eleven o'clock in the night, the Holy Mother got up from Her seat. One devotee said, "You were so gracious to us; you gave a lot more than we deserve."

Amma: (In an excited tone) Oh, what a pity! I am a cruel Mother, none of my children have eaten.

She called aloud "Balu!" He responded to Her call and immediately rushed to the Mother's side. The Holy Mother said, "You know that I am crazy. You should have reminded me about feeding these children!" Balu replied, "Mother, nobody has eaten. Amma said, "Alas, what a pity. I am so crazy that I forget everything. Hurry up, go and get some bananas." Balu brought some bananas and the Mother fed the devotees with the bananas with Her own hands. The devotees said, "Now Mother, we need your permission to leave."

Amma: Now, tonight? So late? You have not eaten anything except a few pieces of banana.

Devotee: We are full, and especially being fed by your hands, we are completely satisfied. We came by car and tomorrow all of us have to go to work.

Amma: No...no...no, don't go today, you can go early in the morning. Have a good rest and go.

Without saying another word, the Holy Mother left. The devotees were in a dilemma. They looked at each other, and one man said,

"The van has to be returned; otherwise, we will have to pay more." Another one said, "Anyhow, it is only a two-hour journey, so let us go." The devotee who had asked most of the questions to the Holy Mother remarked, "If we go, we will be disobeying Mother's words." After a few minutes of discussion, the devotee who asked the questions turned towards Balu who was standing nearby and said, "Please tell the Mother that we had no other choice but to go, and therefore, we left." Balu did not reply as he felt that to do so would be indirectly supporting their wish to go and thereby disobey Mother's words. Even then, they all left within a few minutes.

29 November 1983

The next morning the Holy Mother was sitting in the coconut grove deeply absorbed in meditation. It was eight o'clock and the group of householder devotees who had left the night before against the Holy Mother's wishes entered the Ashram premises. They all seemed very tired and exhausted due to lack of sleep. Seeing the Mother sitting in the coconut grove, they felt more relaxed and related the previous night's adventure to Balu who was standing nearby.

Devotee: Without heeding Mother's words, we left the Ashram and reached the other side of the backwaters around midnight. We asked the driver of the van whether he felt too sleepy or tired to drive but he replied in the negative. Even then, we made him drink some strong tea from a tea stall in the village while going. While proceeding along, all of us without exception fell asleep, even the person who was entrusted with the duty of making sure that the driver did not fall asleep.

One hour or so must have passed when we were suddenly awakened by a deafening sound and a violent jolt. We found to our surprise that the driver had fallen asleep while driving and had crashed into a tree by the side of the road. The front of the van was completely destroyed but none of us got even so much as a scratch.

Had the van missed the tree, it would have gone tumbling into a deep ditch by the side of the road. Even though we had disobeyed Mother, She compassionately protected us from a serious accident. The place of the accident was far away from any houses or shops and it was past one a.m. Although we tried to flag down passing vehicles, none would stop. We simply waited there until five-thirty this morning when someone at last stopped and enquired whether we needed any help. Having reached the next town in his car, we hired another van and returned to the scene of the accident. After talking amongst ourselves, we decided to return to the Ashram to seek Mother's pardon for our disobedience. We have learned a bitter lesson.

After a few minutes, Mother opened Her eyes. As the devotees approached Her, She jocularly remarked,
Amma: My children have learned a good lesson just like the disobedient little goat in the story.[5]

All of them fell at Mother's feet offering their apologies for having gone against Her wishes.
Amma: Children, always remember that when Mother says something it should not be taken lightly. It is the Supreme that makes Her speak. Whatever She says must come to pass either in the near or distant future because Her words are not Her own but are that of the Lord.

After giving the devotees a few more words of consolation, the Mother remained silent. After prostrating to Her, all of them left the Ashram by nine o'clock.

After they left, the Mother went into the meditation hall where the brahmacharins were meditating. She sat there observing their

---

[5] Once there was a little goat who was advised by his parents not to go to a certain pasture to graze as a wolf residing there would eat him. In spite of their advice, the little goat did go there and was eaten by the wolf.

meditation. Soon after that the Mother went to the kitchen and stayed there for a few minutes. She said to the brahmacharinis who were cooking lunch,

Amma: Do you repeat your mantra while cooking? It doesn't seem so. It will be good if you can write on a piece of paper, "Do not forget to repeat your mantra while at work!" and paste it in a place where you can easily see it. That will be a good reminder.

So saying, She left the kitchen and went to the cowshed where She found that the cows had not yet been brought out and were standing in the midst of cow dung. Without uttering a word, She untied all the cows and brought them to the open space and tied them to different trees. Having done that, She was about to clean the cowshed when the brahmacharin who was entrusted to do that work came to the spot. He rushed forward to prevent Mother from doing it, saying, "Mother, I am going to do it. Everyday I do it before meditation. Today I got up late and wanted to make up the lost time. Therefore, I went to meditate before doing this work. Mother, please give me the shovel; I will do it."

Amma: Son, Mother does not consider that a good excuse. A *sadhak* should consider each and every work that he undertakes to be *sadhana*, a means to purify his heart. If it were you, would you lie down in the midst of your excreta? No! These beings, though unable to speak, still have their own pleasures and pains. We human beings, who have understanding and discrimination, should be able to know their feelings. Service is not only serving humans but also creatures, especially cows.

The brahmacharin apologized and promised that he would not fail to do the work again.

Then a householder devotee from Kottayam came with his wife and children to see the Mother. Another devotee, an LIC (Life Insurance Corporation of India) officer, also came with them. Seeing them, the Mother smilingly said, "These children here are very fond of hearing Mother's scolding. They say that Mother's scolding is sweeter than Her love."

As he prostrated, the devotee said, "That is true, Mother. A Guru's manner of disciplining is another facet of his love."

The Holy Mother, along with the devotees, went and sat on the sand near the backwaters. The morning *puja* was going on in the temple. The chanting of the Thousand Names of the Divine Mother was just over and the *arati* was being performed. The sound of the bell echoed in the silent, quiet atmosphere.

The householder devotee: This sound of the bell has a special effect, especially in a silent atmosphere, hasn't it, Mother?

Amma: That is true. When a bell made of bronze is rung, it creates a special vibration. That sound is closely associated with the human mind and impulses (nervous system). In classical Indian music there are many *ragas* (tunes), aren't there? Each tune, when produced in the proper way, creates a certain mood or vibration in our mind. For example, there are *ragas* which can create a sorrowful feeling; there are *ragas* which can create a happy feeling. Those are based on the principles of sound. Sound is vibration, and different rates of vibration affect the human mind and impulses, creating different moods within us.

Question: Mother, I am not getting good concentration in meditation.

Amma: (Smilingly) Son, constant practice is needed. Without this, concentration is difficult to attain. It is not something which you can gain in a day or two. We have been living on the material plane for a long time. *Sadhana* is not necessary if we are constantly aware of the Supreme Principle, but we are not so aware. It has been our habit to think and act any way we like. We never try to discriminate or control ourselves. Now when we try to control our mind and fix it on a certain point, all those past experiences and habits will rise and trouble us. Habits are very strong.

Suppose we have a wristwatch that we wear all the time. It is always on the wrist but one day we sell it. For a few days afterwards, we will continue to look at our wrist to see the time. This is the nature of habit. If this is the case with ordinary and seemingly insignificant habits, what to say of the stronger ones? When we try to change them, our mind will spontaneously turn again and again towards our habits. Only through constant practice can one get rid of them.

Question: Mother, what is real meditation?

Amma: Real meditation arises when the mind constantly flows towards the object of meditation. In that state the *sadhak*'s mind will become firmly fixed on the form of his Beloved Deity during meditation.

Meditation is not simply sitting with eyes closed. It is a state of unbroken concentration like an endless stream. At present, if somebody were to ask if we are meditating, we would say "Yes." Suppose we keep some water on the stove to make tea. If someone asks what we are doing, we would say that we are making tea. Actually, the water is only getting heated up; it is only the beginning. We have not yet added the tea leaves, milk or sugar. Even then, we will say that we are making tea. Likewise, we say that we are meditating, but it is only the beginning. We have not yet reached the state of real meditation. We will get spiritual strength only if we still the mind, which is at present revelling on the material plane. The mind will run around when we sit idle. "Where is my child? How is my wife? Has she gone to the office?" It will wander like this. Meditation is to stop such wandering. In the beginning stages of our spiritual practice, the mind may continue to roam about. This can be stopped only through constant and determined practice.

Children, you have been discriminating between the eternal and the non-eternal for a long time. God alone is eternal. Our life's goal is to attain Him. Son, you should not forget this.

Question: Mother, can one attain God by merely chanting the Divine Name?

Amma: Certainly, why doubt? But concentration is a must. *Kirtan* (singing the Divine Name) is the best way for householders. Having closed the door, one should imagine that one's Beloved Deity is standing everywhere in the room. Then one should pray thus, "O Lord, are You not seeing me? O God, please take me on Your lap. I am Your child. I have no one but You as my refuge. Do not abandon me but always dwell in my heart." Surrender all that we have to *Bhagavan* (the Lord). We will go to the railway station when we travel, carrying heavy loads. After getting into the train, we do not continue to carry the luggage on our head. Having unloaded it, we comfortably sit in our seat, don't we? Once faith in God arises, then surrender everything at His Feet. We should live with the attitude that He will protect us. Everything is His, nothing is mine, He will take care of everything. We have to think this way. A real parent is one who can create children and save them from death. Are we able to create children? If we can, then we should be able to bring back to life those children who die. But, of course, we cannot. Only God is the Giver of life and Creator of the world and all its beings. Therefore, the real father and mother is God. Others are only foster parents.

We have no control over the things or objects that we claim as ours. We have no control even over our own body or existence. Then what can we say about other things? How can we say that a thing which is not under our control is ours? Neither the creation of an object nor its sustenance or destruction is in our hands. Yet, foolishly we think that it is ours. Therefore, dedicate everything to God. We should always feel, "O Lord, I am just a puppet in Your hands. You are the one who gives me power. Even a blade of grass will not move without Your Power." We should pray with longing, "O Lord, where are You, where are You? Wash away my ignorance. Wash away my ego."

Question: Mother, epics like *Ramayana* and *Srimad Bhagavatam* say that the Divine Name has a power of its own, but Mother says that concentration is very important. I find these to be contradictory ideas.

Amma: Of course, the Lord's Name has power. But for everything there must be *bhavana* (correct attitude) or *bhava* (feeling or mood). That is the same as concentration. For example, when a musician sings without feeling, the singing will have no appeal. Feeling comes only when there is *bhakti* or devotion. *Bhakti* towards an object or towards the work that we are doing is important. This feeling comes only when one does the work with concentration. It is a feeling of oneness, of merging in the work. In the same way, although God's Name has a power of Its own, when we chant It with *bhava* or concentration, It becomes more powerful.

Many parents name their children Krishna, Rama, Govinda and other names of God. Everyday they call their children by their names a hundred times, but are they getting Liberation or the Vision of God? The tattwa (the real principle) behind the Names should be properly understood.

This is the Dark Age of Materialism (Kali Yuga). In this age there is a lot of chaos and confusion. Meditation, being very subtle, is difficult to practice. The atmosphere is completely polluted with negative sounds and vibrations. Human minds have become very gross. No one has self-control. Most people think only of objects that will give pleasure. They only think of the body. Since people's minds are very gross, practicing self-control through singing and doing worship is much easier than through meditation, which is subtle. To remove a thorn we need another thorn. Likewise, to overcome the negative sound vibrations we need another sound. That sound is the Divine Name.

There are quite a lot of soot-like stains in our mind. All of that will get washed away when we chant the Divine Name. "You are the All, I am nothing." We should have that kind of love. Otherwise, concentration will not be attained. Son, householders should observe a vow of silence once a week. They should try to get up early in the morning. It is good if they have a regular routine. That will help them to discipline themselves. Until yesterday you were leading a life devoid of spiritual ideals. To get rid of the old habits and replace them with new ones, a regular timetable will be very helpful.

In the beginning you must have love for your daily routine. If you are unable to meditate, try to repeat your mantra. If you find that also to be difficult, then do puja or sing the Divine Names. In whatever way, we must strive hard to attain the constant remembrance of the Supreme. Do not let the mind think unnecessary things. One should meditate by concentrating one's mind on the form of one's Beloved Deity. It is enough to meditate on the feet if it is difficult to meditate on the full form. It is good if meditation is done in dim light. Outside light is a disturbance when we are trying to illuminate our interior.

One should sit gazing at the Beloved Deity's form for two minutes. Then having closed the eyes, visualize the Beloved Deity's form in the heart-lotus. When the form fades away from the heart, one should again gaze at the picture. Though the picture is made of paper and ink, one should imagine that it has consciousness (life). We can attain the Real only through the unreal. Because we are in the unreal, we forget about the Real. We should remember the Real through the man-made picture.

One should cry to God calling thus, "O Mother, where are You? Why did You leave me alone in this forest of materialism? Look, the ferocious animals of lust and anger are coming to eat me. O Mother, take me. Keep me on Your lap. Your lap alone is the safest place for me. Save me from these animals. O Mother, where are You, where are You?"

Our longing to see God should be like the intense desire that we would have to escape if someone were coming to kill us. Our painful longing to see God should be like the pain we would have while dying in the midst of a blazing fire. That much longing should there be to see God. If you are unable to call God the whole day, try at least until noon. You children should find the patience to do this as well.

Question: Is it enough to call God when one is afflicted by some disease or should we go to the hospital?

Amma: Son, human effort and God's grace are both necessary. The Ancients have said, "Half by man, half by God." Self-effort is man's half and grace is God's half; yet, without His grace, nothing is possible in spite of efforts put forth. God and medicine, both are needed. Otherwise, why did the Lord Himself incarnate in ancient times as Dhanvantari, the Divine Physician? A doctor should be consulted if one becomes sick. We should pray to God for the medicine to be effective. Do not dissipate your power by grieving. It will be beneficial if you pray to God when you are afflicted. The Lord will do what is necessary; He will certainly do it.

The Holy Mother stopped for a while and sat with Her eyes closed. It seemed that She was immersed in Her own world. There was a feeling of utter peace and everyone spontaneously slipped into meditation. Nearly fifteen minutes passed by, after which the Mother slowly opened Her eyes. She was still in the same mood.

Nealu brought a cassette tape and played Swami Avadhutendra's "Hare Rama" bhajan. A few minutes went by as the devotees sat gazing at the Holy Mother's radiant face. The Mother was slowly swaying back and forth. Nealu turned down the volume of the bhajan cassette.

Question: Human beings cannot live without expectations but the scriptures say that one should not have any. How can one reconcile both these facts?

Amma: Children, as you know, the desire for happiness will always cause sorrow. It is better if one can transcend both happiness and sorrow. That means to accept them both equally, understanding this to be the nature of life. For ordinary human beings there is no harm in having desires or expectations. But that is not the problem. We are attached to our expectations. That is what brings sorrow. "I expect something" means it is not yet fulfilled, it is in the future. Something in the future can either be fulfilled or can remain unfulfilled, isn't that true? Therefore, always expect that it can either be fulfilled or can remain unfulfilled. That is it. Be aware that something may or may not happen. Take it to be God's Will. There ends the problem.

There should be sraddha (care or attention) in every action of ours. We should imagine that we are removing the stains of our mind while washing clothes and bathing our Beloved Deity while giving a bath to our child. While walking, imagine that the Lord is walking beside you and sitting near you as you eat. Thus we should try to develop the habit of remembering God while doing our work.

Suppose we used to keep the key to the safe in a particular place in the house. We kept it there for a long time. One day we move it to another place. But due to our habit we will look for the key in the original place, even though it has been removed from there. Such is the nature of habits. Habits are very strong, whether good or bad. If we develop good habits, then it will become difficult for us to think or do wrong actions. Even if we want to do evil, good habits will prevent us from doing so. First of all, we must build up a good character. Good thoughts will help us to develop good qualities.

Question: But Mother, the mind is the thing that should be eliminated, shouldn't it?

Amma: Son, the mind is nothing but thoughts. Thoughts, when intense, become actions. Actions, when repeated, become habits. Habits form character. Therefore, to get rid of the mind, first we should change the quality of our thoughts. Good thoughts are useful to fix the mind always on God. Bad thoughts should be replaced with thoughts of the Divine.

Suppose there is some red-colored water in a vessel. If you go on adding fresh water to it, the red color will slowly become less until at last it completely disappears. Likewise, all bad thoughts can be gotten rid of by cultivating and developing good thoughts. In due course, all thoughts should be eliminated by fixing the mind on the Name or form of God. That Name or form will also have to be transcended in order to reach the Final State. The elimination of thoughts is equal to the elimination of the mind because the mind is nothing but a constant flow of thoughts. We will gain Perfection soon if our sankalpa (intention) is to attain the Ultimate Goal.

Suppose a thought arises in our mind to build a house. We will always be daydreaming about it. We will go on thinking about where it should be, how it should look and so on. At first we will build the house through our bhavana (imagination) and then later we will really build it. Similarly, constant bhavana about God will take us to God. We should pray to Bhagavan, "O Lord, please don't let my mind go to the vyavahara (empirical plane). Please take my mind to the heights of God-consciousness." As we rise higher, the things below will become smaller and smaller. When we rise still higher, everything will be seen as one Unity. Those who have reached the heights are able to see everything as One. The diversities of the world will not affect them. Our mind becomes more expansive as we rise higher.

Do not do sadhana with the intention of making it known to others or to please them. We don't stop brushing our teeth, taking a shower or eating food because those are necessities. In the same way, we should remember that sadhana is also necessary for us every day. We will stink if we do not take a bath and brush our teeth. It will be troublesome for others also. We should understand that refraining from doing sadhana is as harmful as this. Sadhana should become a part of our life.

One-pointedness and concentration

As the Holy Mother was sitting conversing with the devotees, one *brahmacharin* came holding a hose to water the plants. However, the water pressure was very little. Mother looked at it and noticed that there were many holes in the hose through which the water was leaking out. Pointing to the hose She said,

Amma: Look at that, children. Because there are holes in the hose, the water is not coming out properly. Likewise, progress will not be gained in meditation if the mind is dissipated through worldly thoughts. At present, whatever spiritual power is gained through meditation and other spiritual practices gets dissipated through indulgence. It is like drawing water from a well in a bucket full of holes. All the water will leak out by the time the bucket reaches the top of the well. As we do spiritual practice, we should take care to control the urge for worldly pleasures. That Supreme Effulgence can be known through intuitive experience only if the mind is made one-pointed without sending it out to the world. Meditation can be done while fixing the mind either between the eyebrows or in the heart. If someone has no faith in God or in a form of God, they can make their mind one-pointed by fixing it on a point or on any part of their own body. One should continue doing meditation with the conviction that one's Beloved Deity is in one's own heart. One may get a headache and pain in the eyes if one meditates on the spot between the eyebrows. Insomnia also may occur. If so, meditation should be stopped temporarily. If restlessness occurs, then it is best to meditate in the heart. In the beginning it is better to meditate in the heart. After having the feeling that the heart is full, it is not so dangerous if meditation is shifted to the spot between the eyebrows. In any case, it is best for householders to meditate in the heart. One will feel a cooling effect by meditating in the heart, whereas heat is experienced if one meditates between the eyebrows.

Question: How should one meditate upon *Bhagavan's* form?

Amma: You should imagine that you are offering flowers at His Feet. When the form fades away, you should imagine that you are mentally embracing the Feet saying, "Father, why are You going away leaving me alone?" Mentally write "OM" at His Feet. Otherwise, repeat your mantra and imagine binding the Beloved Deity from toe to head with the rope of *japa*. Then, imagine that you are undoing this rope. This should be repeated whenever the form fades away. Imagining that the Beloved Deity is standing in front of you, try to see each and every part of the Lord's body. Imagine that you are bathing Him with different things like rose water, coconut water, milk, yogurt, flowers and sacred ash. Adorn His head with a golden crown and put garlands on His neck. Mentally decorate Him with bangles and anklets. Just as the image is decorated in temples, we should adorn our own Beloved Deity. If your Beloved Deity is Devi (the Divine Mother), you should adorn Her with a crown, nose ring, necklaces and other ornaments. She should be dressed in silk clothes. If you do this, the Beloved Deity's form will not escape from your mind. The mind will not get a chance to think about other things. All other thoughts will be restrained. Thus it will become possible to consistently meditate on the Lord's form.

Children, do not forget to always repeat your mantra. In the beginning *japa* should be done in a low voice. Later it can be done moving the lips slightly. Finally it should be done mentally. Thus *japa* should be practiced constantly with each breath. Then *japa* will go on even if we don't attend to it, even in sleep.

While walking, imagine that the Beloved Deity is walking by our side and that we are conversing with Him. While riding in a bus, gaze at the sky and imagine that our Beloved Deity is travelling along with us through the sky. If travelling by boat, visualize the Beloved Deity sitting in a fully blossomed lotus on the water. If sitting alone, imagine that the enchanting form of our Beloved Deity is standing at a distance. Through bhavana we should have the feeling that the Lord is always standing near us whatever work we may be doing. While blowing into the oven to kindle the fire, visualize the effulgent form of the Beloved Deity standing in the fire and blow at His Feet. In this way the mind will merge in the Supreme State through constant practice and our efforts will bear fruit.

Thus when we practice with constant remembrance of our Beloved Deity, we can keep the enchanting form of the Lord shining in our heart lotus. Retention of breath (kumbhaka) happens spontaneously when perfect concentration is achieved through ceaseless devotion just as it is achieved through the practice of pranayama. The path of devotion is enough. You children should not practice pranayama. If you do so without proper guidance, it will be like one who comes to get rid of madness and instead becomes even crazier! If you want to practice pranayama, a Satguru's presence and instructions are absolutely necessary. It is dangerous if one practices pranayama merely from books. One may get constant headaches and pus may even come out of the nostrils; whatever is eaten will not be digested and will be expelled with the feces.

There are people who follow the path of knowledge. They say, "I am a Jnani," (a follower of the path of knowledge) and other similar expressions, but their way of living will be just the opposite of a real Jnani. Bhakti is not different from jnana. Real devotion is itself wisdom. One should put medicine on a cut only after cleansing the wound with disinfectant. Otherwise, it will get infected and become a serious wound. Likewise, having destroyed the ego through devotion, wisdom should be established. Apply the medicine of jnana after cleaning the mind with the disinfectant of bhakti. Only then will there be true wisdom.

Question: Mother, how can one tame the mind?

Amma: Children, that is the most difficult thing in the world. It may be possible to catch the wind with one's hand or to swim across the ocean, but to control the mind is impossible unless one is strongly determined to do so.

In the beginning, the mind will not be inclined towards meditation. It should be subjugated very tactfully. You will not be able to catch a chicken if you run behind it but it will come if you call it after putting its food nearby. In the same manner, do not run after the mind to control it. By slowly questioning and tactfully instructing it, you can get it in your hands. Ask the mind, "O mind, why are you running after these objects? Are you getting any benefit from them? Don't you know that these things are ever-changing?" Thus, the mind should be tamed and eventually directed away from the world of matter to the world of Spirit. Having been distracted by sensual pleasures for a long time, it will not easily yield to Godly thoughts. Children, don't feel dejected, thinking that you have become a slave to the vasanas. Unknowingly we happened to become attached to this world. There will be no problem if we live knowing that God alone is our real relative. Whatever mistakes have been committed in the past owing to ignorance will be pardoned. But once you come to know the right from the wrong, you should try your best to refrain from making mistakes in the future.

Wife and children are only like those whom we meet at the bus stop. All fellow travellers who showed so much love to us will alight and say good-bye at their respective destinations. Your wife, children and all your kith and kin will depart when the time comes. You will remain alone in the end. When we confront the problems of life, we are always alone.

In the olden days even if the husband happened to abandon the wife, she would continue to live, meditating on him always. Such was the case with Rama and Sita, Nala and Damayanti. What about today? If the wife is abandoned by her husband, her next thought is how to kill him. She may even re-marry and proudly walk in front of her former husband with her second husband. Therefore, this is not real love at all. Our own real nature, the Self alone, is our true friend. Somehow due to the fruit of past actions, we happened to come in contact with the world. There is no sense in being miserable about it.

We should live in this world knowing that we are only an instrument in the hands of God and with the faith that He is guiding us. We should try to confront life's problems courageously by thinking, "Nothing can defeat or enslave me. I am God's child." Do not try to run away from the problems. That will only give them more strength to overcome you.

Question: Mother, how should one keep good relations with one's wife and children and with other family members?

Amma: Do not make the wife and children suffer unnecessarily. If their characters are not good, do not dissipate your energy worrying about them. Worrying is not a solution to any problem; it will only make things worse. Discriminative thinking is the only way to overcome life's problems. When we worry, our power of discrimination becomes weak, and then even insignificant problems seem overwhelming. We should pray to God to give our family right-thinking, and we should consider their association with us to be the fruit of our past actions. We will not be miserable if we spend our time in Godly pursuits instead of worrying about our wife and children. Is it possible for us to guide them along the right path? We do not have the power to hear sounds which are beyond a certain range. We also do not have the power to see beyond a certain distance. We are bound by limitations. What can we do? "Take care of everything, O Omnipotent One. I have no power to do anything. I have nothing to say. O Lord, kindly protect us." That is how we should pray. Otherwise, one will only be wasting one's time. Our family, as well as ourselves, will be ruined. In due course, owing to our prayers, God will guide them through the right path. If the husband is the one who is creating the problems, then the wife should have the aforesaid attitude.

In many families only one partner, the husband or the wife, will be good. In such cases, if one of them has patience, forgiveness and forbearance, things can be straightened out to some extent. Children, remember that if we forgive and forget others' faults, God will forgive and forget ours. If the wife is pious and has qualities like patience, love, forbearance and forgiveness, she can also change her husband even though he is uncouth. If she has the right attitude, family life will become peaceful. If both husband and wife are obstinate

111

and unyielding in nature, both should try to correct each other by cultivating and developing patience and forgiveness in themselves.

The family should follow a regular discipline. Try to see God in every action. People blame either God or others for their sufferings but is there really any meaning in doing so? It is our vasanas and attitude that are the cause of our sufferings.

Truth is God. No one except God loves us selflessly. Having closed all the doors and windows, what is the meaning of blaming the sun for not giving light? Who is responsible? Open the doors and windows and the sun's rays will enter the room. We create the veil of ignorance and then blame God for not showering His grace upon us. He is constantly showering grace. Why should we blame God? How can we receive His grace if the mind, which is filled with selfishness, is not made expansive? We should remove the veil of ignorance through sadhana. He does not expect anything from us. An electric light does not need a kerosene lamp.

There is no use blaming God for our sufferings or in saying, "He created me, but did He give me anything? Doesn't He see my suffering?" We have the wealth and property given to us by God, but now there are tenants living on the property. Some people lovingly came and asked permission to temporarily live on our land, and out of compassion for them, we agreed. But they are not vacating, even when we need the space. They are even disturbing us and making it difficult for us to live there. The tenants represent lust, greed, anger, envy, jealousy, and other negative qualities, and the place we gave is our own heart (mind). Is there any meaning in blaming God for this? Was it not we ourselves who gave them permission to live in our place? We live fixing our attention on external things. When we try to go within after understanding what the goal of life is, they come like rebellious tenants waving flags, saying "Go away." It is we alone who give the place for sense objects in the mind where God is meant to be enshrined. Children, do not blame God for the suffering that we have to endure because of our own negative qualities.

What is needed is to evict them as quickly as possible through japa and dhyana.

Question: I wish to do *sadhana* but the thoughts of the past agitate the mind and make it impossible.

Amma: Children, there will be restlessness in the beginning. That is the nature of the mind. We should try to make it one-pointed through supreme love for God. Call God by any name. A father will caress his small child even if the child calls him "da" instead of "daddy," for he knows that it is due to ignorance. But if the grown-up son calls "da," the father will punish him. God will certainly pardon the mistakes which we have committed due to ignorance. The errors which we have committed until yesterday are not errors, because until that time we had no wisdom. But once we know right from wrong, God will not forgive us if we make mistakes. Therefore, children, forget everything which has happened until yesterday. Once you surrender to your Guru or God, the past is like a cancelled check. From today onwards, live with alertness and walk carefully ahead on the path. You needn't feel sad today, thinking about the dream you had seen yesterday. Try to forget everything, considering life to be a dream. Until now, we wasted time just for a few moments of happiness followed by sorrow. However, if we merge in the Supreme Truth, we can always experience Bliss. Even if all the people in the world were to love us, even then, we would not get an infinitesimal amount of the bliss that we get from God's Love. Try for that Eternal Bliss in the time that is remaining.

Gayatri came with a glass of tea for Mother. Having taken two or three sips, She put it down. One devotee distributed the remaining tea among the others as prasadam.

Question: Mother, being a college professor, I have a good circle of friends most of whom are worldly people who talk only about worldly things. How should I deal with them?

Amma: Try to talk less with them, and even then, only if necessary. When they see that you are no longer interested in the things that they are, they will slowly avoid you. Don't think that they will get angry with you; let all of them hate you if they wish. Don't go towards things which will again create trouble for you. You should go towards stillness. Our time is precious. It is not to be wasted by company with others. Whatever time you have, you should be more introspective. Many of the friends come only to gossip and chat, don't they? Lovingly tell them, "We have been talking for a long time. What are we going to gain by talking about and discussing all these things? My goal is to think about God, to give solitude to the mind. You might get angry with me if you don't like it. At present, that is not a problem for me. I can move forward only if I overcome obstacles. I am not angry with you, even if you get angry with me, for I have only love for you. But now I don't have any time to waste." Saying this in a very calm and loving tone, you should withdraw into solitude. Let them love or hate you. Such control is needed in the beginning. We will become good if we make friends with a river. It will make us reach the ocean. On the other hand, if we keep company with a dirty drain, we will also produce sewage, nothing more than that. Good company is with spiritual people or aspirants and will take us to God. Bad company will make our thoughts and deeds evil. A parrot raised in a temple or church will chant God's Name; whereas a parrot raised in a liquor shop will utter only vulgar words.

If friends come, ask them to stop gossiping and give them spiritual books to read. There is also another way to get out of such situations. Visualize your Beloved Deity in the person who is talking to you. While doing so, you will not even hear what they are saying, although they will feel as if you are listening. In this way you will not be wasting any time. All these restrictions are needed for a seeker of God. We are headed for danger when we see faults in others. Children, bear all this in mind and move carefully.

The Holy Mother stopped and asked Pai to sing. Sreekumar played the harmonium while Pai sang a song glorifying the greatness of satsang.

Through association with Realized Sages,
One becomes detached.
Through detachment,
One becomes free of delusion.
Through freedom from delusion,
One becomes free of mental movement.
And through that still mind,
One attains Liberation even while
Living in the body.

The Holy Mother sat completely indrawn. Her hands formed a mystic pose (mudra), Her body perfectly still and Her face radiant with half-closed eyes. After five minutes, She slowly opened Her eyes uttering, "Shiva...Shiva." It seemed that She was struggling to descend from the divine heights. A few more moments had passed when the Holy Mother said,

Amma: Children, *satsang* is good. In the beginning it is difficult to do *sadhana* if we remain at home. Why do we send children to school? Isn't it enough to study at home? No. If they sit in the house and try to study, their minds will go to the kitchen. They may wish to sit on their mother's lap and their attention will be diverted to many different things. In school they will sit and study with concentration, knowing that they can go home only in the afternoon. Not only that, whatever subject is studied is best learned from an experienced teacher. Likewise, in the beginning stages, it may not be possible to meditate and do *japa* while sitting at home. Relatives and friends will come to see you, or your wife and children will disturb you for a hundred different reasons. *Sadhana* should be done in the presence of a Perfect Master or in an Ashram. God cannot be attained by those who are immersed in worldliness, always remaining

115

at home. Temples are built for this purpose. By going there, people who are involved in the world can attain peace and concentration. The concentration that one gets when one goes to a temple will not be gained if one sits in the house.

Even though the breeze blows everywhere, coolness will be felt more if we sit in the shade of a tree. In the same way, although God is all-pervading, His presence will clearly shine in certain places more than in others. That is the greatness of satsang. In the presence of a Perfect Master, one can experience God more than in any other place. Trees and fans are not needed for those who live in the Himalayas because it is always cool there. Similarly, a Guru may not be necessary for those who are highly evolved in sadhana. However, just as the cool breeze in the shade of a tree will give happiness to those who are scorched by the hot sun, the presence and guidance of a Guru is absolutely necessary for those of us who are still in the world. If you want to progress, satsang is necessary. If you feel mentally agitated, you should go to the nearest Ashram and sit in solitude, either reading spiritual books or doing japa or meditation. Constant meditation will not be possible in the beginning stages. You should try to acquire more spirituality without losing what you already have.

Even though we may be in the hot sun, we won't feel the heat if there is a good breeze. Similarly, wherever one may be, one will not feel troubled due to the benefit gained from living in the presence of the Guru.

Children, if you want to fight, you should fight against God. That will make you reach the goal. If you fight with humans, you will become evil like them. Your life will be wasted, everything will be lost, and both parties will be destroyed. If you seek help, seek God's help. Arjuna fought with the help of Krishna and won. Duryodhana fought with the help of soldiers, and although he had much wealth, the result was complete destruction. Therefore, live with complete surrender to God. You can tell your sorrows to God. If you want to quarrel, you can quarrel with God. Children, you should develop this kind of mental attitude.

Without wasting even a single moment, continue your efforts and strive to attain the fruit. Always be aware that God alone is the Truth.

As She completed this last sentence, the Mother stood up. Her body became perfectly still. A benevolent smile formed on Her lips and Her face glowed with spiritual radiance. Both of Her hands manifested mudras; Her hair and sari danced in the sea breeze that blew from the west. She was obviously alone in a world of bliss. The devotees gazed at the Mother's face with unblinking eyes.

Balu and Pai sang a song which depicted the dancing form of Mother Kali, while Sreekumar and Venu accompanied them on harmonium and tabla.

> *Victory, victory to the Mother*
> *Who is the Holy Consort of Lord Shiva*
> *And who is the Bestower of Supreme Devotion*
> *And Liberation.*
>
> *O Ocean of Compassion, who has caused*
> *This world of plurality to manifest,*
> *O Mother, please always dance*
> *In the heart of this humble servant*
> *Who remembers Thee constantly.*

Some brahmacharins meditated while others joined in the singing. After twenty minutes the Holy Mother opened Her eyes and walked with staggering steps. Like one intoxicated, She moved towards the backwaters and sat there for some time. Getting up, She walked to and fro in a bliss-intoxicated mood with both Her hands on the top of Her head.

9 December 1983

God, the servant of the devotees

Today Mother went to a householder devotee's house for evening satsang and bhajan. The house was decorated as if for a festival, and there were many people present. The head of the family along with his wife and children received the Mother in the traditional manner. They washed Her feet and waved a flame of burning camphor before Her, and then they invited Her into the house. Mother first went into the puja room. She sat there for some time and then went into the kitchen. With great love and affection She talked with the servant and tasted some of the food as well. The host, a very wealthy man, said, "It is a shame to talk with the servants like this."

Amma: Son, you see them through a worldly man's vision as having no status. In God's eyes there is neither small nor big, servant nor master. Greatness or meanness is in relation to the heart only. As far as Mother is concerned, everyone is Her child. Mother is also everybody's servant. Children, Mother came when you called, didn't She? Thus, She obeyed you, didn't She? Your servants also listen to what you say, don't they? Son, God is the greatest servant. He must wait for the call of the devotees, then He should immediately come running and grant them whatever they ask. Sri Rama and Sri Krishna were both servants of Their devotees. Mother remembers God the servant when She sees the servants in the kitchen. Both He and they are serving. God serves the whole universe with all its creatures; these servants serve only a few. However, both belong to the same class.

Mother again went into the puja room where there was the well-known picture of Mother Kali standing on Lord Shiva's chest. Looking at the picture, the Holy Mother said,

Amma: Shiva is *Brahman* (the Absolute Reality). The meaning of this image is that Shakti, endowed with the three qualities of *sattva* (tranquillity), *rajas* (activity) and *tamas* (dullness) becomes calm and peaceful by the touch of *Brahman*. The union of the individual and the Absolute is what is depicted in this picture.

10 December 1983

The Holy Mother was in the room above the meditation hall. Although it was already ten o'clock in the morning, She had not yet come to the *darshan* hut. She was giving some instructions to the resident *brahmacharins*. Some householder devotees were standing downstairs expecting Mother's arrival. They could hear Her voice from above and their eyes were fixed on the steps leading to Her room. Just then one *brahmacharin* came down from the Mother's room and said, "Mother is calling all of you." Having said this, he went to the meditation hall. With great joy and enthusiasm they ran up the steps.

Upon reaching the front door of the Mother's room, they looked in. There was a cot against one wall with a dresser by its side and a sewing machine on the opposite side of the room. The door leading to the balcony of the room was open. The stairs leading up to the terrace were visible in the corner. From the terrace one could see the ocean to the west. When desirous of solitude, the Mother would go up there.

Mother was sitting on the floor cutting some cloth in order to stitch something. Next to the Holy Mother Gayatri sat, trying to help Her. Raising Her head, the Mother warmly welcomed everyone with a beautiful smile on Her face and exclaimed, "Oh, my children, come in!" All of them entered and after bowing before the Mother, they sat around Her.

Amma: (Smilingly) Children, do you know stitching? You must know all these things. Mother knows stitching and other crafts.

A woman devotee: Is this a big accomplishment for Mother who stitches the torn clothes of the mind together?

One devotee: Mother, who stitches the world with the cloth of *Maya* (illusion), can stitch anything.

Amma: (Laughing) Shiva, Shiva! What are you children saying about this crazy Kali?

Taking the fruit which the devotees had brought, the Mother cut it into small pieces and fed everyone with Her own hands. They were all very happy and blissful.

Amma: Sometimes, after feeding Her children, Mother feels that She is full. Nobody forgets to eat, but sometimes Mother forgets even to do that. Why does this happen?

Devotee: Mother, please do not play tricks on us. We are already in the quagmire of ignorance. Do not make us sink any deeper into it.

Another devotee: Mother, what should we householders do?

Amma: The mind, which is flying about in all directions, should be gathered together. Only then will it become spiritually strong. The mind cannot be fixed on a single point in the beginning. It should be tuned by doing mantra *japa* continuously. All your attention should be only on that. Do you know what mantra *japa* can be compared to? In kindergarten we learn to write using a slate and to count using beads. In this way the lessons will easily sink into the intellect. Similarly, we can get concentration through mantra *japa*. There are people who attained the goal merely by chanting a mantra. It is not always possible to meditate, but mantra *japa* can be done irrespective of time or place.

A woman devotee: Mother, my mind has no steadiness. My love vacillates between different deities at different times.

Amma: A devotee, if really sincere in his desire to realize God, will have a chosen Deity. There will be a special love or attachment to-wards one of the gods or goddesses, unless one is a *nirgunopasaka* (a worshipper of the Formless). In general, people are afraid that gods or goddesses other than their own will get angry if they are not remembered or worshipped. There is no need for such fear. God is beyond human weaknesses, and therefore, the question of anger on His part does not arise. If God gets angry, He is not God. The apparent anger of God is only for the good of His devotees. When a mother scolds her children, it is not out of anger or hatred that she does so, but only to correct them.

All the different names and forms are, in essence, only one. With the same ingredients, you can make edibles of different names and shapes. Likewise, whatever be the name or form, God, the real Substance, is One. One can draw different pictures, but the paint is the same. Similarly, the power is one although the names and forms may change. Daughter, you received a mantra, didn't you? You should do sadhana keeping your mind steadily fixed on the Deity of that mantra. Understand that all names and forms are His. One must be intent on reaching the goal. A bit of restlessness will be felt in the beginning, but you should hold on tightly. Always think, "O Lord, You are the only one to help me, aren't You? Please be gracious and dwell in my heart always."

The children which you rear are not your real companions. Once the daughter is married, her mother's place is second to her husband's. For the husband as well, the wife comes first and then only his mother. All of them will get off at their respective bus stops along the road of life. Therefore, everything should be entrusted to one's Beloved Deity. Your children also belong to God. What power does a servant have in the master's house? He will be satisfied with whatever is given by the master. The master makes the decisions and asks the servant to execute them. He has no right to question. Similarly, we are the servants and God is the Master. He is the one who gives the remuneration, the fruit; so let us work sincerely and be content with what He, the Master, gives. The Real Self, the Essence, should be known. Children, all power belongs to God, not to us. We are puppets in His hands. If we work with the attitude of surrender, He will protect us.

The well says, "my water," but the well doesn't think about where the water comes from. The spring is the source of the water even without the well's knowledge. In the same way, we also say, "I, I. Is there anything without me?" This is our mental attitude. But do we have any existence apart from the Supreme Consciousness?

A strong resolve to reach the goal is necessary. There is plenty of time to go to movie theatres and hospitals, but there is no time for temples and ashrams. Such is our way of living. Even while living in the world, householders should try to imbibe these principles. Otherwise, the mind will become restless. At least one hour every day should be spent thinking of God, one hour for the sake of the soul.

Real gain is from the Self alone. Only enquiry into the Self is of eternal value, and that is what gives peace. We should know That as the true bliss. What happiness is there in worrying about the family? You should move forward, considering everything as ordained by Him. If one does so, peace will be gained.

Woman devotee: Mother, we are never without sorrow.

Amma: Sorrow is due to desire. We would have attained the bliss of Liberation long ago if desire was the means to attain real happiness. It is said that worldly life depends entirely on the sense organs. Because of this, all our energy is being dissipated through sensual indulgence. Living in the senses will not give us real bliss. Bliss is the same as the one-pointed thought of God.

> Remember, O mind, this supreme truth:
> Nobody is your own!
> Because of doing meaningless actions,
> You are wandering in the ocean
> Of this world.

Remember this song, have satsang and always chant your mantra. Give up talking about others. We find time for every useless and unnecessary thing, yet we say that there is no time to think of God. Do not go to vulgar movies or read novels. Are we not sitting in front of the television or going shopping for hours on end? If you always fix your mind on the Lord, peace will be experienced.

Just then pandemonium broke loose among a group of crows. The Holy Mother suddenly rose and came downstairs. One brahmacharin came, holding a wet crow in his hands.
Brahmacharin: Mother, this crow fell into the water tank.

The Mother quickly took the crow in Her hands. The crow, which was fluttering until then, suddenly became calm. She asked the brahmacharins to chant some Vedic mantras while She blew on the crow's face. The crow died immediately. Having buried it with Her own hands, the Holy Mother again went to Her room with the devotees following behind.

One mantra and one form

Woman devotee: Mother, the mind runs after different forms.
Amma: The fruit (of worship) will be delayed if different gods and goddesses are worshipped from time to time. One will not find water if many small holes are dug in different places. It will be had only if you dig deep in one place. Worship should be done while being established in one's Beloved Deity alone. One should imagine that everything is that Deity itself. Someone says "palu" and another says "milk," but the meaning is the same for both. The difference is one of language only. It is difficult for us who are caught up in Maya to proceed without a medium. Because of this, we call God by different names. Shiva, Shiva, Shiva, Shiva!

The children who have come here from the West are intellectually inclined. Nevertheless, Mother gave them a brass pot of water and a thousand and eight pebbles and told them to imagine each pebble as a flower and offer it at the Feet of their Beloved Deity. Sankalpa is enough.

Children, life is momentary. You should live in this world with this realization.

> *The early part of life is spent in helpless cries*
> *And youth is spent in lustful attachment.*
> *Now old age is coming*
> *And all of your strength will be taken away.*
> *You are going to become like a helpless worm*
> *And without any work, will spend the time*
> *Looking forward to the grave.*

Haven't you heard this song? For how long does this life last?

Question: Mother, is *punya* (spiritual merit) inherited from the previous birth a prerequisite for *sannyasa* (a life of renunciation)?

Amma: Merits inherited from the previous birth are an important factor. But if one has sufficient training and discipline from childhood onwards, one may turn to the spiritual life even if inherited merits are absent. Such people can be properly guided and made into *sannyasins*. But usually parents will not give their children for *sannyasa*; they would even prefer to give them to be killed. However, if the parents give them to God as *sannyasins*, at least they can always see them. Shiva, Shiva, Shiva.

The Mother went into a meditative mood. Uttering Her favorite mantra, "Namah Shivaya," the Mother opened Her eyes after some time and made a swirling motion with Her right hand.

Amma: We think that whatever is wanted will be had from the world. An American psychologist came here. He said, "Mother, thousands of patients come to me. They have no peace of mind and want to know how to get it. I give them some suggestions, but I myself am not getting peace even for a moment. I get solace only from spirituality. That is why I come to see Mother once or twice a year." This is today's world.

Question: Nowadays even *sannyasins* are opportunists.

Amma: True *sannyasins* are beyond fear and scandalizing. Such people never do meaningless things simply to please others. They will not swerve from the path of truth and righteousness. They are not afraid to declare the truth in any circumstances. If a *sannyasin* acts otherwise, one should understand that he is fearful and is only after name and fame. Don't try to reap benefits by pleasing others. Be established in Truth.

Devotee: Mother, we find it very difficult to come here because there is no one to look after our household affairs in our absence.

Amma: Children, God is the real watchman. Many people say, "There is nobody to take care of the house, so how can we come to the Ashram? There is nobody in the house; the children are sick." How many people steal without our knowledge! If we are the real watchmen, we should be able to catch them. What Mother means is, what can we take care of? We say that we want to take care of our children, but can we really do so? After seeing them off to school, are we able to see what is happening to them afterwards? At that time, who is looking after them? Entrust that work to the Lord. Is it possible for us to look after things as He does? Therefore, dedicate everything to Him saying, "O Lord, You look after everything and do what is needed." A thief will not enter, nor will a murder take place if you entrust everything to that Watchman. Other watchmen will do the work only if paid. Therefore, you should come here entrusting everything to God. Have complete faith in Him. Faith can do miracles.

Question: To have absolute faith is not easy, Mother.

Amma: That is true, but think for a moment. When we get into a bus, we blindly believe in the driver even though he is a complete stranger. He might even have caused several accidents. How many bus and car accidents occur everyday! Even then, what makes us travel in a bus or car again? Faith, is it not? What about travelling in an airplane? Usually not even one person will escape alive in a plane crash. Yet, we believe that the pilot will take us safely to our destination. Take the case of a businessman. What makes him start a business? Isn't it faith that he will be able to make some profit out of it? What guarantee is there that all these things will happen as we expect? None at all. So why do we continue to do everything that we do? Faith.

All persons are limited individuals. How can one person save another? Only an Unlimited Power can save or protect us. Now tell Mother, is there any meaning in placing your faith in people? No, but still we do it. Why? Because we neither think about the meaninglessness of it nor of the true meaning in dedicating everything to God.

Effects of former births

Question: Mother, it is said that everything one experiences is the fruit of one's actions, but even people who have not committed any errors suffer. Why is that so?

Amma: Do we remember everything we have done? Do you remember the things that you did when you were young? Do you even remember the hymn which you learned last month? Then how could you possibly remember the actions of a previous birth? All our happiness and sorrow are only the results of our past actions, if not from this birth, then undoubtedly inherited from previous births. Even in the case of twins, a difference in their way of doing things can be seen. It is because of the effect of a former birth. There are people who say that it is due to the difference in the time of birth. Sometimes it happens that among two people who are born at the same time, one becomes a king and another a vagabond. In certain other cases, it happens that one is deformed and the other is without any mishaps at all. Therefore, the fruit of past actions alone is the cause for the differences in experience.

There was a chicken in someone's house. Later another one was purchased and brought home. The hen which was already there started pecking at the newcomer because, for a long time, she alone had been the "all in all" there. The newcomer, however, did not leave. Saying, "I am not so worthless," she began pecking back. This went on for some time until both the chickens had bloody crests. This is the way of the ego, but we blame someone else when sorrow comes. The doctor tells us to observe a certain regimen, but we do not follow it and become ill as a result. Then, what is the meaning of blaming the doctor?

Question: Mother, how can ordinary people know about such things?

Amma: Religious education should be made part and parcel of our lives. Temples, schools and colleges should offer religious studies as well. Parents should take the initiative to impart knowledge to their children from childhood onwards. Like other subjects, religion, its theory and practice, should become an important part of our educational system.

Children, look at the churches of the Christians and the mosques of the Muslims. They give more importance to religious education. They won't allow worldly dramas and films to be shown there. What about Hindu temples? Are they not spending hundreds of thousands of rupees to conduct worldly dramas and other such things? Is there anything else needed to spoil our children's character? Parents have no control over their children. They do not discipline them. The Christians have a rule that they should go to church on Sundays, and they observe that rule. Even householders have a japa mala (rosary to do japa). They know the Bible and teachings of Jesus Christ by heart. Whereas, the Hindus don't even know the meaning of the word "Hindu." How many professors and engineers and doctors are there in our country who do not know even a word of the Srimad Bhagavatam? In the Muslim community, the children are taught Arabic at a very young age. They are taught about their religion. They have very good discipline and etiquette. And what about the Hindus? How many temples are here in the village itself? With the funds raised by going from house to house they conduct vulgar dramas in the temples. In the olden days, children played by making temples in clay and worshipping therein. What do they do nowadays? Donning the costume of a government minister, they canvas for votes.

The Christians teach their children to become priests. Are we teaching our children to become sannyasins? Are the temple authorities doing that? People in the olden days had good devotion. Now devotion is motivated by desire. Our stand is that if God fulfills certain conditions for us, we will give this much money. Giving money to God is like giving a hand fan to the electric fan. Uplifting the community comes only through self-discipline and real surrender to God.

The time was almost one in the afternoon. The Holy Mother took everyone to the dining hall and She Herself served food to all the devotees. As they were eating, She went to Her room.

Ten minutes later, the devotees were surprised to see Mother coming out of Her room with Gayatri. They thought that She had gone to take some rest. Approaching Gayatri, they asked her what was the matter.

Gayatri: Mother is feeling very restless. Some devotees must be praying intensely for Her *darshan*.

Mother proceeded towards the boat jetty on the bank of the backwaters, followed by Gayatri and a group of devotees. After waiting there for a few minutes, one boat arrived and a couple from Bombay got out of the boat and rushed over to Mother. In their excitement, they even forgot to pay the boat fare and take their baggage, but seeing the situation, some other devotees did that for them. Their faces were beaming with joy and devotion as they prostrated to the Mother. Getting up, they said,

Devotees: Mother, we could take only two days leave from our jobs in order to come here. We have come by plane to save time, but we have to return immediately. We are having some urgent family problems about which we wanted to ask Mother. Unfortunately, we could not find any way to inform Mother of our coming and were worried that having come so far, we would not be able to see Her. We have been praying intensely that we would be able to have Mother's *darshan* and talk with Her before returning to Bombay. Mother has heard our prayers!

Having said this, the couple tried their best to control their tears of love and devotion. Taking them to the Ashram, Mother spent some time with them and on receiving Her blessings, they departed with a full heart. The Holy Mother then went back to Her room.

Such incidents are quite common around the Holy Mother. Her ways are always mysterious and beyond ordinary people's comprehension, but She is ever gracious. What can anyone say about those who have realized the Infinite?

19 December 1983

A physics professor from a college in Ernakulam came to see the Mother today. He was a devotee of Sri Ramakrishna Paramahamsa and was very much interested in doing sadhana. He had been doing spiritual practices for a long time but was dissatisfied with his progress. He complained about numerous obstacles and the lack of proper guidance. Having heard about the Mother from one of his friends, he developed a strong desire to see Her and that was why he came.

The Holy Mother sat leaning against the wall in the front verandah of the temple, near the door where She usually sits for bhajan. A few devotees sat in front of Her along with some brahmacharins. With great reverence and devotion, the professor prostrated to the

Mother and sat in front of Her with palms joined together chanting a Sanskrit hymn composed by Adi Sankara.

> *O Goddess Annapurna, the Ever Perfect,*
> *The Beloved and very Life of Lord Sankara,*
> *In order to achieve Wisdom and Detachment,*
> *Give me alms, O Parvati!*

His eyes filled with tears that were about to roll down his cheeks. The Holy Mother wiped his tears and lovingly stroked his forehead and chest. An inexplicable feeling of peace pervaded the atmosphere and was clearly visible on the faces of all those present, especially on the blissful face of the professor. Some devotees spontaneously went into a meditative mood. All the while the Mother sat with a benign smile on Her face. After some time, the professor broke the silence.

Professor: Can I ask a few questions, Mother?

Amma: Namah Shivaya! What does Mother know? You children are very learned. Mother doesn't even know how to write "Ka Kha" (the first two consonant syllables in the Malayalam alphabet). The letters should remain in the memory, shouldn't they? Then you children call me "Mother" and Mother calls you "children." Shiva... Shiva... Shiva.

Having said this, the Mother smiled like an innocent child. That innocent smile was the smile of Universal Love. It was capable of stealing anyone's heart.

Scriptures and the goal

Question: Mother, my spiritual practices are not improving.

Amma: Children, be intent on the goal, that is what is important. Most of the people coming here for *darshan* have to catch the five o'clock bus the next morning in order to be able to reach their offices in time. By force of habit, they will wake up at four a.m. without anyone calling them. If they are not able to get up at that hour they may not get a boat to cross the river. There are also those who come for *darshan* for the first time. They will stay awake the whole night so as to be able to catch the bus. Their determination to reach the goal is what helps them to stay awake. Children, if this kind of *lakshya bodha* (goal-oriented mind) is there to see God, nothing can obstruct your path. Then you will progress by and by.

On some nights the brahmacharins would meditate late into the night. In the beginning, in order to find out who had real detachment, Mother would allow them to sleep only a little. In the day time sleep would come unknowingly when they meditated because of the lack of sleep at night. Then Mother would go and sit in the meditation hall, keeping a stock of small pebbles with Her. If someone happened to fall asleep, Mother would throw a pebble at him. They would meditate with alertness owing to the awareness that Mother was near them. They would be attentive without being overpowered by sleep.

Mother sometimes tells the children, "Your happiness is Mother's health." Mother has no health other than that. Therefore, children, do sadhana without wasting time and attain real bliss. Mother's wealth is Her children. Even if a hundred thousand rupees are lost, they can be recovered. But if one moment is lost, it can never be regained. Your time is precious. Move cautiously.

The brahmacharins do not have any interest in studying scriptures. They say that studying the scriptures will inflate their ego. Their only interest is to meditate. It is not difficult because they came to the Ashram at a young age.

Question: Is there no substantial benefit to be had through the study of the scriptures?

Amma: Yes, scriptures are beneficial. There is one son in Bombay who sent another son here to see Mother. Before coming here, he was given a map and told to take a train going to a particular place and to get off at a certain station. After reaching Vallickavu, there is a ferry for ten paise. All this was written and explained correctly to him. Because of that he came to the Ashram without any difficulty. Nobody could cheat him either because the directions and fares were written down and given to him beforehand. But would he have reached here had he simply sat in Bombay, having read all the instructions? Of course not. Therefore, what we call scriptures are meant to help us travel without getting lost. We can reach a place in one hour instead of wandering around for ten hours. Scriptures are pointers only; they are not an end in themselves. Do we taste sweetness if we write "honey" on a piece of paper and lick it? We should get that through experience. Scriptures were written by the sages from their own experience. We should make the scriptural truths our own. Now they are only in the books and not in the heart. All the great saints and sages and our forefathers as well, did intense penance for years and years. Their renunciation and penance were only to set an example for the generations to come; it was for our sake. We should follow in their footsteps. It is because of their renunciation that both the world and human beings exist even today. If they had committed suicide when they became distressed, we would also do the same, following their example. Didn't Lord Krishna and Christ endure everything? Following their example, can't we also endure? We should also become renunciates like the sages.

There are many who want to make the world good, but to make the world good, shouldn't we become good first? Son, anger cannot be conquered by anger but only through love. Only one who is completely selfless can serve and love the world without any expectations. If there are expectations, service will be selfishly motivated.

Question: What meaning is there in merely sitting with one's eyes closed (in meditation)? Isn't some scriptural knowledge also necessary to serve the world?

Amma: Scriptures were written by those who came down from the plane of intuitive experience. Those truths can be known through experience alone. If one learns the scriptures without first having a certain amount of mental maturity, then one will always be thinking *advaitic* (non-dualistic) thoughts[6] and become egotistical. The children who are here have come with some knowledge of the scriptures. Therefore, what Mother has told them is, "Children, using whatever time that is available, make your mind one-pointed and try to know who you are. Know what your Real Nature is." For the attainment of the goal, *tapas* (austerity or penance) alone is beneficial. The great *Rishis* (sages) said, "*Tapas, tapas* alone." They proceeded forward based on *tapas* alone, not after reading some scriptures. As a result of their *tapas*, the scriptures spontaneously dawned on them. It was not due to studying the scriptures that they could immerse themselves in *tapas*. But scriptures should also be learned. Both are necessary for real progress, but one should not be bound only by scriptural knowledge. One should go beyond the scriptures.

Today people think that studying the scriptures is the same as spirituality. A real pundit is one who is established in the Supreme Self, not one who can give discourses on the scriptural texts like a preacher. Nothing but harm will be received from a person who goes out into the world to teach only after gathering mere book knowledge. That is what is seen in ninety-nine percent of the people.

The intention of the children here is to guide the world after experiencing the Truth through tapas. Let them study their own nature first. Then they will see the Essence behind everything in this world. On seeing a rock, a sculptor becomes blissful beholding the form which he can carve out of it; whereas, an ordinary person sees only the rock. In the same way, the children here will see only God's Form in all the things of the world if they know their Real Nature. They won't even see the externals, the flesh. Having only learned the scriptures, without meditating to gain real experience of Self-Knowledge, how many sannyasins become lecherous upon

---

[6] Thoughts such as "I am not the body. I am the Supreme Being, greatest of the great. There is no need for me to observe any rules of morality or discipline."

seeing a woman? When they see a woman, they see only the flesh; they don't see the consciousness which is responsible for the beauty and vitality.

The bliss which the children here get is Mother's health and wealth. Mother's aim is to make them reach the plane of experience; tapas is meant for this. Let them know who they are. Mother doesn't say that you should believe in Mother or God, but know who you are.

Having made the children sit and meditate, Mother will go and do the kitchen work. Mother will bring and serve food at the place where they are sitting for tapas. What is needed is to develop concentration. The whole world will become ours if concentration is achieved. Just wearing ochre robes will not suffice. What our forefathers told us was to make the mind ochre[7]. Only one who has subjugated his inner nature deserves to wear ochre. Nowadays, people who cannot concentrate their minds even for one minute wear it! Shiva, Shiva!

Question: Why does Mother make these children do hard work like carrying cement, bricks and other heavy things?

Amma: Children, an employer can be seen scolding an employee for walking too slowly while carrying a heavy load. He himself is not in the habit of carrying such heavy loads. It is a great sin if one says, "Hey, run!" without understanding that one is walking slowly due to the weight of the load. If the person who scolds is one who has known the weight of such loads, then it doesn't matter. He will know how fast one can walk with such a load. Only if these children carry such loads today will they have compassion towards the laborers tomorrow and understand their difficulties. Mother also carries the loads along with the children. She will not simply sit idle and make the children do the work. There is no greater or lesser here in terms of people's importance or work. Everything is part of *sadhana*.

---

[7] Sannyasins wear only ochre-colored (rust-red) clothes in India.

Scriptural studies began in the Ashram only after making the children do sadhana for four years. Even now they are doing eight hours of meditation plus one hour for chanting the Thousand Names of the Divine Mother. In addition, one hour goes for practicing yogic postures (asanas), an hour for the study of Sanskrit and one and a half hours for the evening bhajan. On darshan days they sing bhajans till the end of Devi Bhava. Furthermore, there are two hours of scriptural studies. Only twenty days of classes are there in a month. Silence is observed once a week and they must also fast on that day. The children do all the work in the Ashram while chanting their mantra. The mind will become pure through such sadhana.

One brahmacharin went from here to the Himalayas. There is one sannyasin there called "Chiranjivi" (the long lived one) who is more than a hundred years old. He told the son who went from here, "Child, go back and save yourself. Even though it is nearly seventy years since I turned to this path, I have not gained anything because I was unable to develop faith in one Guru. Neither did I get a Guru who could instill faith and obedience in me. Therefore, even today I remain the same as I was when I came here so many years ago. You have Mother to guide you. That is due to the spiritual merits that you have inherited from the past birth. Go and do sadhana in Her presence. Through that alone will you benefit."

Two devotees came to see the Mother. A Westerner of intellectual temperament also arrived. Immediately Mother asked, "Ha, where is Mother's share?" Taking out a small packet which they had hidden in their hands, they gave it to the Mother. It contained some edibles which they had brought to offer to Her. The happiness of the devotees knew no bounds as the Mother opened the packet and tasted a bit. Having tasted it, the Mother distributed the rest as prasad among the devotees.

Amma: Too many sweets are bad for your health. Food influences the character of a person to a certain extent. A controlled diet is very important as far as a seeker is concerned. Eat to appease your hunger and sustain the body. Give up the habit of eating simply when you see food that you like. Eat food but don't let the food eat you. What Mother means is that you can enjoy things, but self-control is always necessary. God created the world for you, not for Himself. Therefore, there is no harm in enjoying the objects, but remember that over-indulgence is always dangerous. Traffic rules are made for our benefit. Similarly, the rules and regulations in a factory or even in one's own house are made in order to instill discipline so that conflicts and accidents will not take place. In the same way, the Ancient Sages set forth certain rules of life which one should observe in order to live joyously in this world.

Westerner: Food doesn't have the power to change the character of human beings. Character is based on mind alone.

Amma: Yes, son, but the body is influenced by the mind and vice versa; they are interdependent. Just try to think deeply immediately after jogging for a long distance. It is not possible due to physical exhaustion. Similarly, one is not able to do physical work properly when the mind becomes weak due to sorrow caused by the death of a near relative or any other similar cause. Because there is a connection between the mind and body, the mind can be conquered if the body is controlled. Therefore, during the period of *sadhana*, food should be controlled in the beginning. Most *brahmins* are *sattvic* and relatively calm. Why? Because they are pure vegetarians. Those who eat meat and other non-vegetarian food are more *tamasic* and rough. Never eat flesh foods. That will make the mind more restless and will create more semen in the body and therefore more passion. Meditation will become impossible. Vegetarian food will not create that much trouble. Look at the cruel nature of a tiger which eats meat and the calm nature of a deer which eats grass.

Westerner: I am not convinced. I must have more proof.

Amma: (Smilingly) Son, you will get it.

The Westerner left after two days. Though he disagreed with the Mother on the point of food, his faith in the Mother had increased immensely during his two day stay. Most interestingly, after two weeks he wrote a letter to the Holy Mother in which he said, "Beloved Mother, I am writing this letter full of remorse. On that day when I disagreed with you about the change that food can bring in one's character, saying, 'I am not convinced. I must have more proof,' you smilingly replied that I will get it. Now Mother, I got it. During my one month stay in India, I didn't take any non-vegetarian food. I reached Germany last week and I ate pork. After eating that, I felt a very strong desire to have sex and my mind became so agitated that I couldn't sleep that night. Having not eaten meat for a long time, I could now clearly feel the difference. Now I know that it was you who taught me the lesson. Mother, you have given me enough proof, I am convinced. Mother, please forgive me for disagreeing with you and thank you very much for teaching me this lesson."

Question: It seems meaningless to follow a regular routine? Can't we live without that?

Amma: Children, if we drink tea for ten days, we will get a headache on the eleventh day if we don't drink it. That is the power of habit. Our character is born of habits. Therefore, a discipline is needed in order to build up good habits. Our present way of living is the result of our past way of living. In order to remove the bad habits and ways of the past we should develop good, new habits. A regular routine is needed for this to happen. In the beginning, we should have love for our routine and strictly follow it. Then only progress is possible.

Even if we are perfect, we should live as an example for others. If we tell a person who is afflicted with jaundice not to eat salt and tamarind, how will it be if we keep it around us? Seeing them available, he will want to eat it since he has not gone beyond taste. His mouth will water and he will break the regimen. Therefore, we should interact with the world cautiously.

Two children of two different houses had jaundice. The doctor told both of them to observe a particular diet. The mother in one house started cooking food without salt and tamarind for everyone. Because of that, the patient in that house followed the diet correctly. The mother in the other house gave the prescribed diet only to the patient but prepared food with salt and tamarind for the others. Do you know what the result was? The patient in the second house broke the regimen by stealthily eating the food which was made for the others. That child's disease increased and he died. Do's and don'ts are not necessary for a Self-Realized Soul. He is beyond all rules and regulations, yet he sets an example by abiding by the rules in order to uplift others. Worldly people can be uplifted only if we act in a disciplined way in front of them.

We are born naked, but because of that, do we walk around with our clothes off? We are wearing clothes for society's sake, aren't we? All these rules are needed for the betterment of society. A regular discipline is necessary.

Question: Mother, I am staying in a hostel. I cannot meditate there due to the blaring of film songs. What can I do?

Amma: Imagine that the hero and heroine of the song are Shiva and Parvati. Previously Mother used to dance intoxicated with devotion and bliss when She heard film songs. The problem arises when you think that the hero and heroine are worldly people. You should see them as Radha and Krishna, as one's Real Nature, the Self (*atmaswarupa*). Everything depends upon one's attitude, doesn't it?

One of the children who lives here now stayed in a hostel while he was studying. Whenever he heard a song, he would imagine that Mother was singing. Others used to tease him if they saw him meditating. Therefore, he would pretend as if he was sleeping while lying down under the mosquito net. When every one had fallen asleep, he would get up and meditate for a long time.

Solitude is necessary. You children should sit in solitude for at least some time. It would be good if you would move away from the hostel and stay in an ashram atmosphere or some similar place.

A devotee: Mother, today I heard one *brahmacharin* reading *Srimad Bhagavatam*. What a fine voice he has!

Amma: Isn't the sound that is produced in a cave special? Similar is the voice of the *sadhak* who is at a particular stage of meditation. The voice of people who have concentration will have a resounding nature. Others will feel attracted when they hear that.

Question: Mother, what is your opinion about seeing cinema films?

Amma: Movies which create a devotional mood are not very harmful, but other types of films should be avoided. Worldly films will create more negative vibrations in us. After seeing such films, people try to imitate what they have seen. One of the causes for the degeneration of our culture is the cheap films that are produced and shown in public. People spend a lot of money, time and energy in seeing them without realizing the tremendously bad effect created by such films.

Long ago there was a film on the ancient king Satyavan and his virtuous wife Savitri. Haven't you heard that story? The husband Satyavan died. The pious and chaste wife Savitri, an embodiment of austerity, followed the God of Death, who was taking away the soul of the husband. Seeing the wisdom, chastity, piety and love of Savitri, the God of Death was pleased and asked her to seek a boon. She asked to have many children. When that was granted she asked, "How can I have children without my husband?" Thus even the God of Death was defeated by Savitri, a chaste wife. He gave back her husband's life.

A tapasvi's (one engaged in austerities) words will never fail. Even if he says something wrong, that will only be to make others good. Even seeming mistakes that he says or does will become correct.

Turning to a devotee who was sitting amongst the other devotees, the Holy Mother suddenly said, "Son, quickly go home." Usually the Mother would never say such a thing. The devotee was about to take leave of the Mother with great anxiety. As he got up after prostrating to the Mother, She said, "There is nothing to worry about. You are going to see something very interesting, that's all."

When the devotee had come to the Ashram that day, he had kept his motorbike on the other side of the river. For the past five days he had found that someone was stealthily siphoning out the petrol. Because of this, he had been having great difficulty getting home when he left the Ashram at night. Considering it a silly matter, he never mentioned anything about it to the Mother. While anxiously leaving the Ashram this day, he could not even guess what would be the interesting thing that he was going to see. Upon reaching the other side of the river, he saw a person sitting near his motorbike siphoning out the petrol. The devotee caught the thief red-handed but freed him after giving a warning. Thus Mother Herself helped him to get rid of the trouble which he had been facing for the last few days.

Question: Mother, how can one gain subtlety of mind?

Amma: It can be gained through concentration which in turn can be attained only by fixing the mind on a point. This point may be the form of one's Beloved Deity. If one does not believe in God, then one can concentrate on an unmoving flame, on the tip of the nose, or on any other point on the body. Whatever the means, the aim is to gain one-pointedness. When concentration increases, thoughts decrease; and when thoughts decrease, the mind and intellect will become subtler. This subtlety will help in having subtle spiritual experience. Spiritual experience cannot be attained through the gross mind and intellect. Reality is subtler than the subtlest. To experience the subtle, subtle instruments are needed. To see the gross objects of the world, the external eye is enough, but to know the soul (Self), the internal eye is needed. When people speak loudly, we can easily hear them, but why? Because the sound is gross. But if they speak softly, we cannot hear them. Speaking softly is subtler than speaking loudly. Our ears are not capable of hearing soft sounds. Similar is the case with all the sense organs and the mind. Therefore, to experience the Self or *Atman*, which is the subtlest of all subtle things, we should develop subtlety of mind.

Question: Is Mother saying that there is justification in wanting to experience the subtle planes of existence?

Amma: One cannot understand everything about life if one stays on the gross, external plane. There are many mysteries in this universe about which one cannot even imagine. To experience all those, one should go into the subtle planes of existence.

How many dust particles are floating inside a room can be known only when the sun's rays enter through a small hole in the roof or wall. Even though the dust particles are everywhere in the room, lack of concentrated light prevents us from seeing them. Now there is no light within you, only dense darkness. You are unable to see the subtle because your mind remains in darkness. When the mind attains subtlety through focusing one's efforts towards God, then all can be seen. What meaning is there in saying, "I don't believe because I cannot see," when one is lacking in subtlety? The effulgence of the Self will begin rising as our mind becomes more and more subtle. In that state we can see every atom of the universe. But this cannot be seen with the external eyes.

Just as the tape recorder records whatever we say without missing even a word, Nature records all of our actions. Each of our words and thoughts subtly exist in Nature. The power born of the penance done by the Ancient Sages is also there in Nature. Even today Mahatmas exist in their subtle plane.

There is a subtle aura around everyone's body. This can be seen very clearly around people who do sadhana. The aura of sadhaks is powerful. Others' auras do not have this characteristic. Ordinary people's auras are dark or cloudy. The aura around a tapasvi is bright like golden rays. If any harm is done to such people, their aura will become destructive to the offenders through the vibrations created by it. It is not necessary that the resolve of the tapasvis should be there for this to happen. They will not have any anger towards the people who trouble them. It is the subtle beings who do the harm. If we raise a dog, it will chase trespassers even if the people in the house are fast asleep. They will not know anything about the things which may happen outside. That is how these subtle beings save the tapasvis from enemies. The enemy gets punished even without the knowledge of the sadhak. That is why appropriate results are reaped by those who vilify a tapasvi. In reality, one cannot even touch him without his permitting it.

The subtle aura around worldly people will retain all their actions. This aura along with the individual soul will travel through the air after death. Eventually that (the soul) will enter into the food of humans. Then it will become the fetus after entering the womb of a woman through the semen of a man. Some souls will remain without getting liberated from that condition for up to three years. The individual soul will advance according to the rituals performed by the relatives for the propitiation of the pitrus (ancestral deities). Some will get Liberation while others will again take birth. All depends upon the fruit of each one's actions (karma phala).

Some yogis enter directly into the womb. They become the soul of a fetus that has died while in the womb. There are other souls who are destined to attain Liberation within a certain number of births. They will depart after becoming the fetus in the womb. Such an abandoned body will be used by yogis for taking a human form. Thus yogis can take birth by their own will rather than as the result of the union of a man and a woman.

The soul will attain Liberation as a result of the proper performance of oblations offered to it and according to its worthiness. Suppose there is a small puddle near a pond. If more and more water is poured into it, it will fill up and flow into the pond. Likewise, the karmas done for the departed help to make them fit for Liberation.

If pitru karma (ceremony done to propitiate the ancestral deities) is done regularly, it should not be stopped. If stopped, harm will result. But there will be no problem if it is not performed at all. Several families came to see Mother who were having problems caused by a break in the offering of oblations to the departed. They said, "There is some evil in the house. Cows don't live long; children are dullards and no children are born to newlyweds." They were always worried. They said that someone had invoked malevolent forces against them. But Mother did not see any such thing. Mother felt that the problems were due to the break in the pitru karmas and came to understand that subtle beings were disturbing the people. Upon enquiry, they said that they used to do pitru karma but had stopped after some time. Mother asked them to begin it again. When they did, everything became all right.

Therefore, the last word cannot be said about everything. There are certain things which are beyond the intellect and ordinary human perception.

23 December 1983

Today the Holy Mother inaugurated an Ashram branch in Pandalam, a village about fifty miles to the east of Vallickavu, the Mother's own village. The Mother and the brahmacharins came to the spot where the small temple was situated on about a quarter of an acre of land. It was an old temple which had belonged to a traditional Hindu family. They could no longer maintain it due to financial difficulties and so they transferred it to the Ashram.

The villagers gave a grand reception to the Holy Mother. They were all very happy and enthusiastic. The Mother purified the inner shrine and performed worship. This was followed by the chanting of the Thousand Names of the Goddess one hundred times, devotional singing and satsang. There was a large gathering and all participated with devotion and love.

Later, Mother came and sat on the front verandah of the temple to give darshan. A charming sight presented itself at that time. A small child came and sat right in front of Mother, followed by a second, third, forth and fifth. Within a few seconds, fifty children were sitting around the Holy Mother. The most striking thing was that they were all below six or seven years old. They sat silently like carved statues in front of the Holy Mother for nearly an hour, gazing at Her face the entire time. They had come with their parents to participate in the festival. Wasn't it a wonder that those children sat silently in front of a person they were meeting for the first time in their lives? The Mother did not speak or make any signs to attract them, except for the never-fading smile on Her face. After one hour the Mother started giving darshan. Even at that time the children were not ready to move away. They sat there until their parents fetched them.

25 December 1983

After spending two days in Pandalam, the Holy Mother came back to the Ashram last night. There was a big crowd for darshan. Many householder devotees came with their children. Like another innocent child, the Mother played and laughed with the children. It was a wonderful feast for the eyes and a joy to the hearts of the devotees to see the Mother playing with their children. Mother even forgot about Her usual afternoon break and went on playing. Sometimes She would say that when She was in the company of children, She would become crazy and forget everything due to their innocence. Eventually the children became tired and sat down. The Mother also sat near them. She asked them about their studies.

Amma: Children, you should sing *bhajans* every day and meditate on God with eyes closed praying, "O God, make me a good and devoted child. Bless me to grow up as an obedient son or daughter. O Lord, bestow on me good qualities like patience, love and forbearance." (Turning to some parents who were standing nearby) Some people doubt whether children should meditate and do *japa* at such a young age. Remember that Dhruva and Prahlada[8] made the Lord appear before them when they were young. The training and discipline which are given in youth will create a strong impression in the mind and play a great role in the building of character. Parents should take care not only to feed and fulfill the wishes of their children but also to discipline them, instilling faith and good culture.

Devotee: Mother, why are some people careless about Godly matters?

Amma: Look at those weeds. Everyone carelessly tramples them. When they become sick, the same people will ingest the weeds with reverence after understanding that they are medicinal. Those who are trampling now are not thinking that some day they may become sick. Now they feel strong and all-powerful. When a disease comes, they will seek the refuge of the weeds. Until then they will step on them. The same is true with the people who do not care now about God. When sorrow comes, they will turn to God and take refuge in Him. Until then they will turn their back on Him.

The Holy Mother asked the children to sing a song. Along with Mother they sang,

> *O Lord, come, come to console me,*
> *A mere atom in this infinite world.*
>
> *O Lord of the Universe Who reigns over*
> *The fourteen worlds, come before me today*
> *And end my sorrows.*

---

[8] Two princes in ancient India who did *sadhana* in order to get the vision of God.

26 December 1983

It was ten o'clock in the morning and the Holy Mother was sitting in Her room. Since there were no visitors, some brahmacharins had an opportunity to talk with Her.

Brahmacharin: Mother says that a *sadhak* should not mingle with worldly people. Isn't everything *Brahman*? Then why is it necessary to differentiate like that?

Amma: (Smilingly) Son, do you have the experience that everything is *Brahman*? Will the picture of a cow drawn on a sheet of paper give milk? Everything is equal only for those who have reached *Brahman*. For others good and bad exist, and they should behave accordingly. Even though the Inner Self of animals such as a cow, dog or cat is one, are they alike? Likewise, even if the Self (*Brahman*) in all human beings is one, their characters differ and therefore one should behave accordingly.

The water in the Ganges River and the water in the drain are both water. But son, will you drink the water from the drain? A sadhak should mingle with someone only after understanding that person properly. A plant should be protected by a fence until it has grown big. After that there is no problem. Now you are like a pond which will become polluted if mixed with drainage water. It would be best for a pond to join with a river. Son, won't you get burnt if you go near fire? If you are immune to fire, then differentiation is not needed. Only then can you say that everything is Brahman. Do not say so while you still perceive diversity. There are people who say, "There is no body, mind and intellect; the Self alone exists and I am the Self." The Self exists in the world of the Self alone. We are still in the plane of individuality. We have a body made up of the five elements which is affected by heat, cold and other dualities. It is in relation to these facts that we live. We have not reached the state of Brahman yet. We will be afflicted with leprosy if we mingle with a leper, won't we? Likewise, if the sadhak mingles too much with worldly people, he will develop a character similar to theirs.

However, why should you children waste your time thinking about how to mingle with others? What is needed is the inner eye; you should become introspective. It is meaningless if one merely makes an external show of being a renunciate. There are some fruits which ripen on the outside first. These will quickly spoil. But those fruits which ripen from within will not easily spoil. What is important is inner detachment and introspection. A good sadhak will behave like ordinary people. In appearance both will look alike, but there will be a difference like that between a real rope and a burnt rope. The latter looks like a rope but will crumble to ashes if you touch it. Similar are the anger and other apparent feelings of a matured sadhak. All his worldly tendencies have been burnt up. They only seem to be there. That is only for the sustenance of the body. We should try to reach that state. On the other hand, don't spoil your sadhana by being too sociable and getting involved in other people's affairs in the name of everything being Brahman. A real Vedantin is the best socializer. But one should attain that state first. It is not enough to just walk around babbling Vedantic sayings.

One brahmacharin had gone to the market to make some purchases and now returned. Coming to the Mother, he informed Her regarding the details of his shopping. There came up the subject of a particular shopkeeper.

Brahmacharin: Mother, that shopkeeper charges more for the goods. That is why we are not going there now.

Amma: That is the way we must treat profiteers. You children are not careful enough when you are buying things. You will pay whatever amount they ask. Therefore, Mother has to pay attention. When you come to know that Mother pays attention, you children will also be careful. Things should be purchased only after enquiring in detail. The shopkeepers also will be careful when they come to know that the customer is attentive. Otherwise, they will cheat us and will try to cheat others too. By our carelessness, we teach them to lie. Do not show sympathy to such profiteers. We dislike their actions not their soul.

Another brahmacharin: Mother, even a small sound distracts me while meditating.

Amma: We do not avoid sleeping because frogs and crickets make sounds in the night. It is their nature to do so. Children, do not pay attention to the sounds. *Sadhana* is not possible if you wait for the entire world to become favorable. Is it possible to take a bath in the ocean if you wait for all the waves to subside?

Brahmacharin: Mother, so many desires come up.

Amma: It is difficult to eliminate desires completely. Therefore, direct them towards God. Develop the desire to do *japa*, to meditate and to have *satsang*. These Godly desires are not wrong. The desire to realize the Self is good. Only worldly desires can be called desires. They will bind us; Godly desires will not. They will liberate us instead. Only if a small fish is used as bait will we catch a big one. It is not wrong to have a small desire in order to gain that which is great. Each step should be made carefully, like the walking of a pregnant woman.

Guru

Brahmacharin: Mother, some say that a Guru is not necessary.

Amma: A Guru is absolutely necessary for a *sadhak*. When a child goes near a pond, the mother points out the possible consequences and calls him back. The guidance of a Guru is similar. One can do *sadhana* without a Guru, but there will be a difference between those who have a Guru and those who do not. It is difficult to raise artificially incubated chickens in the coastal area. Much care is needed. Such care is not necessary for the chickens who have lived with the mother hen. When the chickens grow up unnaturally without a mother, it will be difficult for them to overcome unfavorable circumstances. Likewise, one who does *sadhana* in the presence of a Guru will gain enough mental strength to confront the obstacles that might arise both from within and from the world outside.

It is possible to transplant apple trees from places where they naturally grow. The only thing is that they need to be carefully looked after. Even then, there will be a difference in the quality and quantity of the fruit. The Guru's presence and perfect guidance give the favorable circumstances for sadhana and spiritual progress. Just as the mother hen protects the little ones under her wings, a Perfect Master always protects the aspirant. If there is no Guru, that lack will be seen in the sadhak.

In the coastal area the sand has particles of salt in it. It is therefore difficult to grow jackfruit trees there. But they will grow if you plant them in a hole filled with coconut fibre, soil and other nutrients. Once the roots take hold, we need not fear the salt. Until then, proper care should be taken. In the same way, due to the "salt" of latent tendencies, the plant of spirituality will not grow in the mind of the sadhak initially. It should be filled with love and devotion. Once these become deep-rooted, there will be nothing to worry about from the vasanas.

God-Realization is not possible without sadhana, but nobody has time for that. Keeping awake, factory workers do work during the night shift. They do not sit idle saying that they feel sleepy. If they are not alert, both their hands and the job will be lost. For attaining God-Realization, that kind of alertness and determination are also needed.

Brahmacharin: Isn't a *Jivanmukta* (a Liberated Soul) a person who has attained Liberation? Therefore, are not God and a *Jivanmukta* equal?

Amma: God is higher than a *Jivanmukta*. A *Jivanmukta* who stays in the body has limitations. God has no limitations. Bulbs come in various wattages such as twenty-five, sixty, a hundred and a thousand. Although the electricity which flows through them is one and the same, it shines in varying degrees according to the medium.

Electricity can be compared to God or *Brahman*, the Absolute. The highest and the most powerful medium is an *Avatar*. If God is the ocean, the *Jivanmukta* is a huge wave and the individual soul is a drop of water. God is even beyond a *Jivanmukta*.

Brahmacharin: What harm is there if too much food is eaten?

Amma: Over-eating will increase dullness. A *sadhak* should take only light food.

Cry for the Truth

One *brahmacharin* came to the Mother with a complaint about a silly matter. He started to cry as he was telling the Mother about it.

Amma: A spiritual being should not cry for illusory things. He should cry only for the Truth. One who has to carry the burden of the whole world should not become weak in the face of insignificant matters. Don't cry. No matter how much suffering Mother had in Her childhood, She didn't cry. She shed tears only for the Lord. A spiritual being should be strong.

The Mother noticed a brahmacharin leaning against the wall while meditating. Turning to him She said,

Amma: Do not lean while meditating. Leaning is a bad habit which must be overcome. The mind is a big thief. It is waiting for an opportunity to subjugate you. It is comfortable for the body if you lean but unknowingly you will fall asleep. You should do *japa* walking to and fro if you feel tired or sleepy.

The whole world will become ours if we know the Real Essence. Then we cannot see anything as different from our Self. Only a lamp which has oil can light other lamps and shine by its own light. Only a person who has spiritual power can save himself and others. That oil of spirituality should be acquired through *sadhana*. Then you can go out and serve the world. However, if there is even a drop of water in the oil, the lamp will sputter when lit. Likewise, even a little vice is enough to make the mind agitated and disharmonious.

Brahmacharin: Is it compulsory that a *sadhak* should avoid mingling with the opposite sex?

Amma: Yes. If rain water falls on the ground, it will become muddy. The mind will be spoiled if a *sadhak* or *sadhaka* (woman aspirant) mingles with the opposite sex. The butter which sits near the fire will melt. Similar is the presence of a woman for a man and vice versa. Unknowingly it will create negative vibrations in the mind. This will become harmful to *sadhana. Sannyasins* should not mingle with the opposite sex before reaching the state of Liberation. (Smilingly) But there is nothing to fear for you children when Mother is here. It is enough if you meditate well.

Brahmacharin: Mother, unwanted thoughts come and disturb my meditation.

Amma: Until now we had no knowledge about our property. Only now has that knowledge arisen. The deed of ownership is in our hands but the land is in the hands of the tenants. It is not easy to evict those who have been living on our property for many years. We should argue in the court of God. The present disturbance is caused by deep-rooted past impressions in the mind. It is enough if you discriminate when thoughts come. Have self-surrender and faith. Try to reject unholy thoughts ruthlessly or just ignore them and replace them with good and divine thoughts.

Children, patience is needed to make spiritual progress. Never lose patience. Do your spiritual practices with utmost sincerity and wait patiently. If you are sincere, the results will come.

A person who goes to court will not say to the judge, "I don't have any time. You must pass the judgment immediately." However much time is needed, he will sit in front of the court house enduring heat and rain. Having gone to the hospital, we won't tell the doctor, "I have no time. Diagnose me and treat me quickly." But many people who come here to the Ashram have no time at all.

They have a hundred problems at home. They don't even have the time to bow down in the temple. Such is their lack of devotion and faith. Patience is needed for everything.

About mantras

Brahmacharin: Mother, shouldn't we know the meaning of the mantra which we are chanting?

Amma: When we travel in a bus, train or car, it is not necessary to know who the manufacturer of the vehicle is, what type of engine it has and where the spare parts are available. The bus will take us to the destination; that is, to the bus stop which is nearest to our house. Our whole aim is to reach the destination. Likewise, the mantra will take you to the destination, i.e., the threshold of God-Realization. From there, the Beloved Himself will lead you to the Supreme State, Realization. In the beginning it is not very important to know the meaning of the mantra. It is enough if one is aware of the goal for which the mantra is being repeated. There is no need in thinking, "Maybe the Goddess is sitting and looking to the left or maybe She is looking to the right. She has this quality and that quality." Be intent on reaching the goal, that is what is necessary. Concentrate on the letters or on the sound of the mantra and do *japa*. Otherwise, it is enough to concentrate on the form of your Beloved Deity if you have one. Do not try to do all of these at the same time; it is not possible. The mind can do only one thing at a time. It is quite sufficient if you do any one of these practices.

Brahmacharin: Mother, why are some mantras to be chanted in conjunction with seed letters (*bijaksharas*)? Is not devotional singing sufficient?

Amma: Won't we feel shocked if somebody shouts at us, "Hey you, go away?" Similarly, *bijaksharas* like "hrim" and "klim" have a special power. The Ancient Sages made the resolve that certain mantras coupled with certain *bijaksharas* must have a certain power. That will never prove false.

Brahmacharin: Mother, why is it said that mantras should not be chanted loudly?

Amma: Devotional songs and the Divine Names can be chanted loudly. But that is not the case with the mantras which the Guru utters into the disciple's ear. The Guru will be giving different mantras according to each *sadhak*s competency. It is not possible to give the same mantra to everyone. If chanted loudly, there is a chance that others will hear the mantra and repeat it resulting in negative consequences. The Guru initiates according to each one's spiritual path, power of assimilation and physical and mental constitution. It is better not to chant the mantra loudly in order to avoid such problems. Mental chanting is the best.

27 December 1983

It was the Christmas holidays. As instructed by the Mother, the birth of that great soul, Jesus Christ, was celebrated in the Ashram also.

Today before coming to the meditation hall, the Holy Mother went to the temple where Brahmacharin Sreekumar was performing the daily worship in the absence of Brahmacharin Unnikrishnan who usually did it. Having finished the chanting of the thousand Names of the Divine Mother, Sreekumar was sitting in meditation. Mother gazed at him for a few seconds and said, "Be attentive. The mind is getting distracted." Saying this, the Mother touched the spot between his eyebrows with Her index finger and said, "Here, concentrate here."

The morning meditation was about to end. The Holy Mother came to the meditation hall from the temple and sat down. She reminded the brahmacharins about maintaining their daily routine and doing the physical work that was allotted to each of them. The Mother suggested that some work be given to those who did not have a particular job to do. It seemed that some of the brahmacharins felt displeased about having to do the work which they were asked to do. The Mother did not heed their objections but rather insisted that they continue with the same work.

Amma: Children, you must find satisfaction and happiness in any work given in any circumstance. You should not have a special interest in doing a particular work and dislike in performing some other work. This is how you can go beyond likes and dislikes. Everything should be considered as God-given. Try to be a perfect instrument in the hands of God and accept whatever He gives happily. Otherwise, what is the difference between us and the worldly people?

Children, don't think that Mother is condemning the world and the people who are immersed in it. The world is created by God for us to enjoy and we must do so. But there are certain rules and regulations for everything. While you are in a court or police station or hospital, you have to abide by certain rules and regulations. Likewise, as you live in the world enjoying sense objects and utilizing natural resources, you must follow the rules put forth by the scriptures, teachers and Mother Nature. If not, you will have to suffer. But children, as far as a serious sadhak is concerned, he must always try to withdraw the senses from the outside world.

With regard to the sadhana of the brahmacharins, the Mother would never allow them to make decisions on their own and because of this, they would sometimes feel a little upset. Even then, She would be unyielding and if necessary, would even refute the points which they would bring forth to justify their stand.

When the conversation was over, the Holy Mother asked all the brahmacharins to sit for five minutes in a contemplative mood. She said, "Let your minds become peaceful and calm." Everyone obeyed the Mother. After that, She sang along with them,

> *O Thou to Whom the celestials bow down,*
> *Whose tale is wonderful, grant us the strength*

To be devoted to Thy Feet.
We offer Thee all our actions done
In the darkness of ignorance,
O Protector of the distressed.
Forgive us for all our impatient utterances,
O Ruler of the Universe.

The Mother became fully absorbed in the singing. At times like this, one could see the different facets of Her devotion pouring out one after another. Sometimes She would laugh boisterously and at other times She would shed tears of ecstasy. With both hands stretched forth towards the heavens as if appealing to the Divine Mother, She would sing with all Her heart. This, in turn, would open the floodgates of devotion in the hearts of the brahmacharins who would also sing with overflowing love towards God.

After the satsang and bhajan, the Holy Mother went to the hut to receive the devotees. The darshan went on until a little after one o'clock. Getting up, the Mother was about to step onto the staircase leading to Her room when She suddenly turned and said, "Alas, my son, I forgot!" Without uttering another word, the Mother ran to the temple followed by some of the brahmacharins and devotees.

Inside the temple they saw Sreekumar sitting in deep meditation. Already more than three or four hours had passed since the Mother had left him there meditating. The Mother sat near him, slowly and gently rubbing him on the chest. After a few minutes, Sreekumar opened his eyes but closed them again. This happened a few more times until he became his normal self. As instructed by the Mother, a thick blanket was spread on the floor. With the help of the devotees, the Mother made Sreekumar lay on it. Having said, "Now he is all right. Let him relax here for some time," She came out of the temple and closed the doors behind Her. As She slowly walked to Her room, the Mother commented, "He has gone up."

In the afternoon Brahmacharin Balu had an opportunity to be with Mother. She was lying down in Her room with Gayatri and Kunjumol sitting near Her. Balu prostrated to the Mother and sat near Her. The Mother stretched forth Her clenched fists towards the sky. Shaking them vigorously and making a grinding sound with Her teeth, She called out, "Kali...hey, Kali!" Pointing Her index finger upwards towards some unseen object, She produced some seemingly meaningless and bizarre sounds. She remained in that position for some time and then slowly became Her usual self. Balu asked,

Balu: Amma, what is the meaning of all these mysterious gestures and moods?

Amma: (Abstractedly) Oh...I don't know. They just come like that. (After a short pause) Do you know how much I am struggling to stay here in this world in the midst of all of you? It is really very difficult. But when Mother remembers the sorrows and sufferings of the people, Her mind melts and becomes compassionate. That is what keeps Her mind down here.

Balu: What was the experience that Sreekumar had this morning?

Amma: He was intensely desiring that Mother should come to the temple and give him some spiritual experience. Mother gave him a bit of just that.

All was silent. Balu gazed at the Mother and wondered at the mystery of this complex personality, who in appearance was just an ordinary village girl, but in actual fact was a storehouse of infinite spiritual power. He sighed and put forth another question.

Balu: Mother, how can one escape from evil thoughts?

Amma: Evil thoughts start coming up when we try to remove them. Previously we did not know that there were so many evil thoughts in us because we were completely immersed in them alone. That is all. We feel that they are evil thoughts after we have developed a different attitude from before and now want them removed. Bad thoughts might arise during meditation. Then you should think, "O mind, is there any benefit in cherishing these thoughts? Do these have any value?" By thinking like this, you should reject unnecessary thoughts. Complete dispassion must come. Detachment should arise. The conviction that the sense objects are equal to poison should become firmly rooted in the mind. Always tearfully pray to God, "O Lord, please let me see You. You are my life; You are the Eternal One. Mind, why do you crave all these silly and meaningless things? They cannot give you the happiness which you thirst for. These are not the things which I asked you to seek." Change will slowly come about through prayers to God and through questioning the mind.

Children, this is only the beginning. You should try hard. Cry to God while sitting alone under a tree or in any other solitary place, "O Father, O Mother, why am I thinking about such things? Isn't sensual pleasure equal to a dog's excreta and a mere illusion?" In due course, evil thoughts will go away.

Different paths

Question: Are many different paths needed to know God? Why are there the paths of knowledge, action, devotion and yoga?

Amma: Some people like to eat fried jackfruit. Others like to eat the ripened fruit. Yet others like to have it cooked as *aveel* or *toran* (two different vegetable preparations). For some it is not good for their stomach if they eat it ripened. Some others will become sick if they eat it fried. Even though the aim is to appease hunger, one type of food is not suitable for all. According to the taste and bodily constitution of the child, the mother gives food. In the same way, the Guru instructs the disciple in which path he should choose and gives advice according to his character or nature. The sole intention is to reach the goal.

Different paths will suit different types of people. Concentration of mind is what is important. Some people will not get devotion. They will strive by controlling their breath while they meditate on the kundalini. Others who are very dynamic and creative will walk in the path of karma or action. Bhakti yoga or the path of devotion is the path wherein the devotee will have the attitude that everything belongs to God. Nothing and no one is one's own. In this path we are humble. The attitude of a servant, of being a nobody, will be there. Thus there are different paths.

There are many who talk about the path of knowledge. Mother has observed plenty of them. One sees no practice in action, only mere talk. They will say that everything is Brahman, the Absolute. If that is so, shouldn't they see others as one with themselves? But that is not usually the case. Those who are fit to walk in the path of knowledge will have a strong spiritual disposition inherited from the previous birth. The practice of knowledge is spontaneous for them. Others, in the name of knowledge, do nothing but babble and inflate their egos. They do harm to themselves and to others as well.

Whatever the path, a Perfect Master is a must, especially if practicing the path of knowledge or the path of yoga. Doing sadhana based on mere book knowledge is dangerous, especially if following either of the above two paths. Mother cannot approve of those people who walk around saying that they are practicing the path of knowledge. Their knowledge is only verbal. That is not what is needed. He is a real Jnani who is born with such a spiritual disposition inherited from the previous birth. Other than such a one, nobody will become a Jnani just like that.

Question: It is said that one can see light in meditation.

Amma: *Sadhak*s who follow the path of devotion might not see it. That is mainly for *raja yogins*. For those who follow the path of yoga, that will happen when the mind becomes one-pointed. *Bhakti yogins* cannot see it so easily. They meditate on a form, don't they? Children, you need not pay attention to such things as seeing light. If you do happen to see it, do not give it too much importance. The Truth is far beyond all such things. Therefore, try to transcend light and reach the Truth.

Question: It is said that those who meditate on Mother Kali will get Her *darshan* quickly.

Amma: Do you know why that is so? Our mind will easily get fixed on Her *rudra bhava* (fierce aspect). (Smiling) That is predominating in our character, isn't it? Most of us are *rajasic*. Kali's form is suitable for a *rajasic* mind. Once the mind gets fixed on the form, if the *sadhak* continues with the same intensity and sincerity, the Deity will appear before him. Concentration of mind is all-important. Once the mind is conquered, everything else will become easy. All forms are only for gaining concentration. Among those, the form of Kali is special in that the mind will quickly get fixed on it. But Ultimate Realization is possible only through the eradication of *vasanas*.

Question: Is there any relationship between the form of worship that we are doing in this birth and that of our previous birth?

Amma: The Deity which we loved and worshipped in our previous births will become our Beloved Deity in the present birth. A real Guru will give only the form of the previous birth to worship in the present one. Even if the disciple is meditating on a different form, the Guru will give the correct one instead. The tendencies of the previous birth will subtly remain in a person. It is our experience that in accordance with our past tendencies, we will spontaneously exclaim, "Oh, my Krishna!" or "Oh, my Devi!" or other Divine Names when we accidentally fall down.

Question: Does the form have any significance other than as a support for concentration?

Amma: Some forms are products of devotees' imaginations. Yet other forms are of Divine Personalities who actually lived in the past like Sri Rama or Sri Krishna. They are not simply imaginary forms meant only for concentration. As you know, Lord Buddha, Chaitanya Mahaprabhu and Jesus Christ were great souls who lived at one time. Likewise, Sri Rama and Sri Krishna were Divine Incarnations who lived on this earth. They were not mere mythical heroes. Perhaps Devi might also have incarnated to slay unrighteous people. The story of the Ramayana takes place not only within us but it also happened externally. Krishna's story also is actual history. Thus, all these have historical importance in addition to being forms of meditation. But these forms are not enough for a *tapasvi*. He should give up the form and go beyond. That is why Mother says,

> *There is no tree which touches the sky;*
> *There is no root which reaches the nether world.*

All forms have limitations and possess only certain defined qualities. We should go beyond them to God, who in truth, is *nirguna* (attributeless). However, we can reach there only by clinging to a form.
Question: What about meditation on a light?
Amma: Different people resort to different means in order to get concentration. All methods are there in Hinduism. God is there in whatever you see. If you think of Him as a blade of grass, He will give you *darshan* even in that form. For gaining concentration, you can use any prop, but you should have faith in it. We are the ones that give life to the form.

Suppose someone has a piece of his girlfriend's sari. When he looks at it, he will remember her. The value is not in the piece of sari but in her whom he sees through it. Therefore, it is priceless; it is not mere thread for him.

Depending upon one's individual capacities, the Guru will advise whichever path will enable one to reach the goal easily. However much Advaita (Non-duality) you talk, without concentration and a pure resolve (suddha sankalpa), no spiritual achievement is possible. For that, sadhana is needed.

There stood a hollow tree by the side of the road. A passerby said, "That is hollow, it is good for nothing." Another person said, "Not so, various things can be made from it." The first man ignored the second and walked away. The second man, however, cut the tree and removed all the decayed portions from the good wood. Though it needed a lot of effort, he could make what he intended. While the first man carelessly walked away saying that the tree was useless, the second man acquired the furniture which he made out of it. He gave life and form to it.

There is a son in Chettikulangara (a village about thirty kilometers from Vallickavu) who brought some very nicely made small desks to the Ashram one day. They were ideal to use as writing tables for brahmacharins and would have cost more than a hundred rupees if they had to be purchased. He made them by using pieces of waste iron which he found by the side of the road that had been thrown away after some construction work. He also found some pieces of pressed board and rusty hinges which had been kept in a heap by the side of the road. For those who had thrown these things away, they were just trash. But this person saw the desk in those objects. When an artist sees a piece of waste paper, he sees the flower which he can make out of it. He doesn't see it as waste. In a similar manner, those who have reached the state of Pure Consciousness will see That alone in whatever they see. Because we haven't reached that state, we see only the chaff and not the Essence. We see only faults and drawbacks in others.

It was four o'clock in the afternoon. After saluting the Mother, Balu left Her room and went to the meditation hall. The brahmacharins were getting ready to chant the Bhagavad Gita. Having finished Her bath, the Mother came downstairs. Her resplendent form and benign smile filled the devotees with joy. They all stood with palms joined in reverence. A few of them had not had the chance to see the Mother during the morning darshan. The Mother took them to the hut. Amongst them was a very young bank officer who was a good sadhak as well and very interested in becoming a brahmacharin. As an inquisitive young man, he always would ask several questions to the Mother. As the Mother was giving darshan, he tried to clear his doubts.

Young man: What attitude is indispensable for a *sadhak* in the beginning?

Amma: Humility. The *sadhak* should always try to cultivate and develop humility. This is the first and foremost quality that is needed. Humility means obedience, surrendering one's ego and leading a life in submission to the Divine Will, that is, implicit obedience to the words of the Guru. The Guru is all-pervading, and therefore, a *sadhak* should try to consider everything that happens to him as his Guru's wish. When that attitude comes, humility will manifest spontaneously.

Children, when the seed is sown beneath the soil it should feel, "I am nothing, I am nobody." With the dawning of that attitude, the seed germinates and the seedlings sprout. Humility is needed if you want to know the real "I." First you should cultivate that.

I do not care whether others love me or not. But what I want is to have a selfless attitude towards each and every person and thing in this world. Sadhana is done to attain that. We will not get this attitude in the beginning, but we should try constantly.

Children, always try to chase away the "I." It is a customary rule that a peon should show respect to his superior officer. That is his duty and there is no greatness in it. But an officer's greatness is seen when he respects the peon. Children, likewise, your progress lies in showing humility even towards a beggar. Mother does not see any greatness in your showing respect only towards Her. What Mother looks for is whether you children respect others or not, whether you children are selfless, or whether your attitude is egoistic towards others, whether you have humility or whether your attitude is, "I cannot bow down." These are the things which Mother cares about. Sadhana is for destroying the vasanas, but many people are nourishing them instead. This is not good. In the beginning, you should develop a good character. That character will guide you afterwards.

Question: Mother, which *asana* is the best?

Amma: Any *asana* in which one can sit comfortably is the real *asana*. You can sit in any way that suits you. In the circus there are those who work hard to learn tightrope walking. Later they can perform feats while doing so. They can even dance while standing on the tightrope. The same is the case when learning to ride a bicycle. First we carefully learn to ride. Even though we might fall down several times, we still continue to ride. In due course we can show any feat. In the same way, in the beginning you should practice any one *asana* and attain perfection in that. Later there will be no problem in whichever *asana* you sit. Then you can meditate even lying down. But first you should reach that state.

With a hesitant look on his face, one brahmacharin approached the Mother. For some reason he wanted to go home.

Amma: Children, it is not good to mingle with the family and other worldly people. In the beginning we should avoid worldly people. Otherwise it will not be possible to progress spiritually. Those who want to learn to ride a bicycle go to an open ground. Nobody would try to learn to ride a bicycle in a crowd. You don't want to hit somebody in the back. You should keep away from crowds in order to avoid accidents. Here Mother sings devotional songs, sits in *Bhava Darshan* and does different spiritual things without a moment's rest. All these make the people think of God. The *brahmacharins* chant the *Bhagavad Gita* and Vedic mantras. Even at that time we are thinking of God, aren't we? We may not have the patience to always sit and meditate with our eyes closed, which is difficult in the beginning. Slowly the mind will get established in God through these various means. When we practice in this way, we are not away from God for even a minute.

Chant your mantra always, even while taking bath or sitting on the toilet. Do not mingle too much with worldly people. The family people do not have the same amount of attachment towards you which you children have towards them. Their attachment ends when they understand that there is no benefit for them to be gained from you. Then why do you go there and intrude on them while expressing your love?

Children, try to do sadhana without wasting time. Once you have tied the cow, how can it get up and walk even if you shout, "Hey cow, walk!" Similarly, one cannot reach God while being in bondage. Do not try to row the boat after you have tied it to the shore.

Many people are destroying themselves by robbing and murdering for selfish gains or simply for harming others. Children, Mother is raising you to lead these people to the Supreme State. Show them the correct path, even if you have to sacrifice your own comforts.

Question: Some argue that *grahastashrama* (married life) is good while others say that *sannyasa* (renunciation) is good. Which is the best one to accept?

Amma: Children, each is great in its own way. A householder who leads a life of sacrifice, abandoning all selfish desires and performing all his actions dedicated to God, is undoubtedly great. A monk who gives up all sensual pleasures and leads a life of self-surrender and renunciation is also great. But today no one leads a married life correctly in accordance with the scriptures.

Here in this world there are many ditches and stagnant ponds wherein harmful germs flourish. A sadhak's aim is to unite all these ponds of individual souls which are so harmful to the world and make them flow into the Ocean of Brahman. This world is filled with wicked actions and mutually opposing attitudes. A sannyasin should make human beings attain the realization of the Supreme Essence and thereby destroy all wickedness. That is what we come to spiritual life for.

Oh! How many people are in anguish! So many kinds of suffering exist -- no sleep, no food. During Devi Bhava and even at other times, Mother's clothes will get soaked with the tears of the worldly people. Almost every person bursts into tears when they come near Mother. What for? They say, "Mother, I don't have any children," "I am not getting that money," "I cannot go there," "They are scolding me." Thus they have hundreds of sorrows. We have to look after their affairs. A spiritual being's aim is not to get married and look after a family. The whole world is in us. We should have a feeling of responsibility like a king has towards his subjects. We should have the attitude, "These are all our subjects; they are suffering. We must save them." Rama abandoned Sita for the good of the world. Why can't we renounce our small selfishness? In due course we may be able to give up bigger things. Only then can we look after the world. How can selfish people make the world good? Ravana was destroyed because he lived for himself. Rama protected the world through His selflessness. We should imitate that. We should always imitate the Mahatmas. Even in His last moments, Jesus Christ prayed, "O Lord, forgive them for they know not what they do." Krishna bestowed Liberation on the hunter who shot Him with an arrow. Such selflessness is needed. A sannyasin selflessly serves others. How will a householder who is himself suffering and immersed in selfishness be greater than a sannyasin? While a householder supports just one family, a sannyasin is obliged to support the whole world. Brahmacharins and sannyasins are the people who give peace and consolation to the world.

Moreover, a sannyasin is not a bhogi (one who indulges in sensual pleasure) like most householders, but is a tyagi (renunciate). Some people will say that such a life is too difficult. Let them say so. Our prayer is, "O Lord, give me the anguish caused by a life of renunciation so as to help me merge in You. Give me the longing to call You. Then only can I see you everywhere and serve You in everyone.

If one is a grahasthashrami (one leading a householder's life strictly in accordance with the scriptural injuctions) he will be a tyagi, but a mere grahastha (a married person who cares not for the life of a real householder) will never be so.

Whatever action one engages in, the mind should be in God. Haven't you seen "Ammankudam Tullal" (an ancient folk dance in India connected with Goddess Durga in which the dancers move rhythmically with decorated brass pots on their heads)? Whatever gestures they may make, their mind is fully on the pot which is on their heads. In the same way, our mind should always remain on God. God is the only object which always gives bliss. But in the beginning we should exert ourselves a little. Mother makes the children suffer a little here. Do you know why? These children have never known what life's sufferings are. They have all led comfortable lives before coming here. They must know what suffering is, what sorrow is. Only then will they be able to understand the sufferings of others. Only then can they serve them selflessly and wholeheartedly and know the gravity of the situation.

Do you know why the parents fondle their children? Because the children were born as a result of the parents' moments of pleasure. They have many expectations. Whereas, Mother got these children (the brahmacharins) as the fruit of Her suffering. Mother had done years of severe penance without even drinking water. That is why these children are coming to Mother now. Mother has no expectations except to take them to the Ultimate Goal. But that is not possible if they don't work hard. Children, you should love all. Only then will God love you. The state of equanimity is the real God.

It was Devi Bhava day. There were many people, so it was four in the morning when the Bhava Darshan was over. At the end, Brahmacharin Pai chanted a Sanskrit hymn composed by the great sage Sri Adi Sankara.

> *O Mother, I do not know the mantras or yantras (mystic diagrams) which reveal Your greatness. Nor do I know Your hymns and invocations, nor the stories of Your glory or the way of Your meditation. I do not know Your mudras (hand poses) or the way of worshipping You. O Mother, I know*

only one thing: if one chooses Your path, one will be saved from the miseries of life.

One could see that Pai was singing with his whole heart. As he sang he became overwhelmed with devotion and burst into tears. It became difficult for him to complete the chant. Brahmacharin Rao also shed tears of bliss. The young bank officer was also in rapture. On the previous day Pai had complained to the Mother, "Nowadays I don't have the longing of devotion." It was obvious that Mother had showered Her grace on him this day.

In the Mother's Ashram quite often one could see the brahmacharins shedding tears of devotion while singing bhajans. The Holy Mother Herself has said several times that in this dark age of materialism there will be a band of youths who would relinquish all worldly pleasures and, fortified with the zeal of spirituality and love for God, would disseminate spiritual light throughout the world.

28 December 1983

It was afternoon when several young men came to see the Holy Mother. The brahmacharins welcomed them and after showing them around the Ashram, brought them to the front verandah of the temple. Soon the Mother came and sat in Her usual place where She sits during bhajan time. The young men, not knowing how to show respect to the Mother, remained standing. The Mother asked them to sit down and added, "Children, it is enough if you respect yourself." Having said this, She smiled graciously.

Amma: Children, where are you from?

One young man: From Trivandrum.

Amma: Did all of you have your lunch?

Some time passed in silence while the Holy Mother sat in an absorbed mood with eyes closed. The young men closely observed Her. After a few minutes the Mother made a whirling motion with Her right hand which formed a mudra and chanted, "Shiva, Shiva..." Then She opened Her eyes.

One young man: We believe in scepticism and Marxism. We would like to know and understand the activities in this Ashram.

Amma: Son, each person's experience is his guru. Scepticism, Marxism and other similar philosophies are good, but are you actually able to live up to those principles? If you can, you do not have to accept anything else. People talk a lot but do very little. Talking and doing are two different things. Anybody can go on talking about the high ideals of life for days together, but if you observe their life, it will not have any connection with what they say. Such people cannot do any real service to society. The impact which they create among the people will be short-lived. Nobody will remember them after their death.

Take the case of Rama, Krishna, Buddha, Christ and other such great souls. They lived aeons ago, but even today people remember them and worship them. Why? Because they lived the ideals which they spoke of. They could bring about great transformations, both in the minds of the people and in society. Even today thousands are inspired by them. They were not mere talkers but doers as well. They were not receivers but givers of everything that they had. They were the real leaders, real thinkers and real reformers. Whereas, we are neither leaders nor thinkers nor reformers but mere receivers. Mother does not claim any greatness. You are intelligent. Observe what is going on here and come to a logical conclusion. Mother wants you to think; She does not want to impose any ideas on you.

Therefore, children, what Mother says is that whatever may be your political party or principle, try to live by those ideals. Mother does not criticize the ideals; they are good. But live them; that will save both you and the country.

The young men were tongue-tied. Their intention was to corner Mother by presenting their ideals very logically, proving everything else as hollow and meaningless. Now what could they say when the Mother Herself supported their point of view? They seemed to be thinking something but did not utter a word.

Amma: If somebody happens to scold us or quarrel with us, we will hate him and might even beat him due to our enmity towards him. Sages have no enmity towards anyone. They have no political party. They love those who oppose them. That is what the sages and other noble characters of our epics did.

One devotee: Mother also does the same.

Amma: Namah Shivaya! Mother is your servant.

Young man: Mother, will you show *siddhis* (occult powers)? Are they not all fake?

Amma: (Smilingly) Mother does not have any *siddhis* and She never shows *siddhis* either. *Siddhis* have nothing to do with spirituality. Materializing things is against Nature's law. That law should be respected. If they want, great souls can break this law, but usually they will not unless an emergency arises. Nobody can create what does not exist. Only things which are already existing can be materialized. After all, why should anyone do that? Such things as a watch or ring or necklace are available in the market.

Self-Realization is a state of perfect mental balance by which one can face all the situations of life without weeping over the painful and rejoicing over the pleasant. Welcoming both pleasure and pain while abiding in peace, and going beyond them considering them as the very nature of life, this is Self-Realization. This is not the same as showing siddhis in the way you are thinking.

Young man: But what about the general talk going around that many people had divine experiences when they came here?

Amma: That is their faith. One will be benefited through faith. Faith in the doctor is needed even for the success of the treatment. If we see certain powers in others that we do not have, is it sensible to say that they are false? Try to understand what that is. That is what is needed, is it not?

169

Children, accept what Mother says if you find it agreeable. Where there is concentration, there is power (shakti). Those who have it will show many things. If you want, you can call that power illusory. A river which flows through many branches will not have a powerful current. If the branches are redirected and the river is made to flow only through the main stream, the force of the current will increase greatly. It may even be possible to generate electricity from such a strong current. Similarly, at present our mind is flowing out towards hundreds of sense objects. If the mind is controlled and focused on one point, tremendous power will be generated which can be used to do wonderful things. What is the secret behind the powers of a magician or hypnotist? It is their power of concentration. They have developed it partially; spiritual beings develop it fully.

Siddhis are shown due to the desire of the people to see them. The Real Gem is within us. People are after siddhis, the imitation gold, instead of knowing and understanding that Real Thing. We are walking around begging without knowing this fact.

Once Mother had been invited to a certain place. The hosts and other devotees there started singing bhajans, but all of their attention was fixed on the sacred ash which was pouring out of the Deity's picture. What a pity! Mother told them, "You are wasting your time looking at ash which is available in the marketplace if you pay ten paise. You will be benefited more if you look at the Deity's Feet."

Try to live according to the principle of real spirituality. If you are after siddhis, your desires will go on increasing, resulting in bondage. We came to this world to free ourselves from these bondages, not to get more and more entangled. Mother is here to help remove desires, not to create them.

People who crave to see siddhis do not even need a Beloved Deity. They want only the things which the siddha creates. They will always be thinking, "Now he is going to create this, now he is going to create that!" They are even ready to give up the siddha for his siddhis. Do not go after those unworthy siddhis. Know the

Self. Know who you are. That is what Mother has to say. There is nothing to gain by showing siddhis.

It was obvious that the young men were quite convinced. They also seemed to be very taken in by the Mother's simple and lucid explanations.

Amma: Children, everything will be known spontaneously if you do *sadhana*. Understand who you are. Know the Self. Then you can lead a life without attachment to anything. Such a state of mind will come if you do *sadhana* sincerely. Even modern science accepts spirituality and the benefits gained by the world from a real *tapasvi*. A hypnotist will hypnotize people. But later, he himself will collapse. He is like a battery; he will have power only if he charges, not otherwise. Both a *tapasvi's* and hypnotist's power is gained through concentration. But the *tapasvi* always has that power. Other people use it for base things and will lose the power. They gain it only through unnatural means. The *sadhak*, on the other hand, acquires that power through severe and constant penance. Other people cannot sustain such austerity, but the *tapasvi* constantly lives in it. A hypnotist's power will go on diminishing and finally will get destroyed. But a *tapasvi's* power never decreases; he is always full. A hypnotist hypnotizes another person by looking at him and instructing him. But he can do this only to a person whose mind is weaker than his own, not to those with stronger minds. A *tapasvi* becomes the very Self of everything. His will is universal. He can do anything and everything if he wills it so. Through rigorous spiritual practices, he becomes an unending storehouse of spiritual power. His battery will go on charging, not diminishing. The power of other people will easily be lost due to the inability to re-charge their power through concentration.

Even though the whole sugarcane is sweet, we will not eat the entire thing. Having swallowed the juice, we will throw away the stalk. Likewise, children, you do not have to accept everything that spiritual science says. Accept it only after observation.

171

Question: What about characters like Sri Krishna in the epics; aren't they just mere fictional characters?

Amma: We cannot say that Sri Krishna never existed and that He is a fabricated character. Everything about His birth and life are clearly delineated in the *Srimad Bhagavatam* and *Mahabharata*. The time and star of His birth and the incidents which occurred during His life up to the time of His leaving the body are described in detail. Even today people celebrate His birthday. Hundreds of thousands of people have been and even now are inspired by Him. They praise Him and worship Him. How can a mere character born of the imagination of a poet create such an impression in the minds of people to even transform their lives? In addition to this, there are many things which give proof of Sri Krishna's birth and His activities in this world. Many places connected with His life still exist. We know those places where He lived and reigned. Sri Krishna was born, lived in the world and led a kingly life, yet showed us the path to Eternity, setting an example in every way. Is this possible in the case of a mere romantic character? Krishna is both within and without. At the same time, He is the Supreme Self. He did live in a human form but a *sadhak* should turn inwards and try to see Him there.

When worldly people look at subtle truths with their gross intellects, they cannot see anything. Do not say that a thing does not exist simply because you cannot see it. Most of us have never seen our forefathers; yet, isn't it meaningless to say that they never existed? Our own existence is the proof of theirs.

If you look at a map of Kerala, you can see a place called Oachira. In our part of the country Oachira is considered as a very important place. But in a map of India or a world map, it may not be visible. Because of that, is Oachira non-existent? It is foolish to think so.

Question: What is the benefit of *sannyasa*?

Amma: Children, do you have the patience to understand those things if Mother tells you? If so, Mother will tell you. Everything necessary will come to the place where a *tapasvi* sits. He doesn't have to go out searching. Worldly objects are not a problem for him. He always experiences bliss in the vision of the Real Gem. He is blissful even in the dirtiest place. Circumstances cannot enslave him. He is the master of them. Because he has overcome all sorrow and is completely peaceful, he is capable of giving peace and happiness to others, eradicating their sorrow and disappointment.

A real sannyasin is a real servant of the world. In fact, he is the only one who serves and loves the world without receiving anything in return. For a genuine sannyasin, the whole world is a garden and each individual is a flower therein. He belongs to the whole world. He has no particular caste, creed, sect or religion. Everyone has equal rights to him.

How many people can get a job if there is a factory? Likewise, how many people can get peace of mind if there is a real sannyasin? How many people get transformed, inspired and become aware of the higher values of life because of him? The question, "Why sannyasa?" will not arise if you understand the great things done by sannyasins.

A lover will always think of his beloved. Spiritual beings also have this nature. They will imagine, "My Lord is like this, He is like that..." Thus through bhavana (imagination) the Lord's nature will dawn in them. God will say, "I am attributeless, I am all-compassionate, I am Love, Truth, I reside not in a particular world, I am all-pervading, I am in all of you." To imbibe and imitate these qualities, a medium is needed. Therefore, accepting the sages or Mahatmas as models, we should try to imbibe their qualities. Trying again and again, we will become That Itself, just like the plant "vettapacca" which becomes ink-colored when immersed in a bottle of ink. Do not think that we can understand the spiritual world without striving hard.

Householder and sannyasin

Question: Isn't a householder who looks after his family greater than a *sannyasin*?

Amma: No, that is not correct. A householder who looks only after his family is not greater than a *sannyasin*. But a householder who leads his life in a spirit of renunciation is. Both are great if they are observed in the correct spirit. Attitude is the important thing. How you do a thing is more important than what you do. A *sannyasin* is one who renounces everything and sees everything as equal to a blade of grass, be it a princess or the whole world and its pleasures. He tries to free himself from the sorrow caused by *samsara*. He even helps others in that. No dexterity is needed to enjoy pleasures, but mental strength is needed to cast away pleasures regarding them as equal to a blade of grass. Spirituality is for a courageous person. A householder is equally great if he leads a detached life surrendering everything to God, accepting all his experiences, both good and bad, as His blessed gift. But for most people it is difficult to lead a detached life while living with the family. Somehow or other one will get bound. Otherwise, one needs to have a tremendous amount of mental strength and detachment to lead such a life.

A real householder should be able to renounce everything whenever he wants to. He should be like a bird sitting on a dry twig. The bird knows that the twig will break at any moment. Therefore, it will be ready to take off at any time. Likewise, a householder should always have the awareness that worldly relationships are momentary and may break at any time. Therefore, like the bird, he should be ready to cast off all bonds and leap into spirituality. He should have the firm faith that all the actions in which he is engaged are just temporary work entrusted by God. Like a faithful servant he must be able to do everything without the sense of ownership. Whenever the Master, God, asks him to stop, he must be able to do so. God is the employer and we are the employees. The employee does the work entrusted to him with sincerity, but at the same time, he knows that nothing is his. Whenever the owner or employer asks him to quit the job, he does so without any objection. In the same manner, a householder should be ready to give up all pleasures and worldly comforts whenever he wants to do so. He should do his duty but as a sadhana, as a worship to the Lord.

God is one

Young man: Many troubles are created in the name of the gods! Do you have anything to say about that?

Amma: Gods? There are not many gods. There is only one God. The different forms are only to enable people to adopt and use the form which they like, according to their mental tendencies. In this way the goal is attained easily. People in different countries call Him by different names. God is not many because of that. Sometimes in movies the same person will enact the role of Krishna, Bheema and Arjuna. The person is one, but the costumes are different. In the same way, God is one but is known under different names and forms. The same girl is looked upon as a sister by her brother and as a wife by her husband. The younger brother sees her as his eldest sister. There is no change in the person; she is the same girl. In a similar way, the Power is one but the names differ.

Now about the troubles. God is not needed for that. There are enough trouble-making evil vasanas in human beings. In fact, all troubles are created by our own ego and negative tendencies. These evil tendencies will create problems in the name of property, wealth, women, politics, false prestige, competition for greatness and the like. It is the nature of human beings to quarrel in the name of something or other, most of the time in the name of silly and meaningless things. They quarrel even in the name of God. Those who do not have faith in God will create trouble in the name of something else. Thus the aim of having faith in God and real spirituality is to remove the evil tendencies which cause these troubles in the first place.

Therefore, it is not God or our faith in God which is the cause of the existing troubles in the world, but rather our non-belief in God. Our own ego is the troublemaker. Real believers in God and spiritual people are peace lovers. In fact, they are the messengers of peace and love. Do not see other people's faults.

The young man sat there silently immersed in thought. Then the Holy Mother continued,

Amma: Children, you will see only faults if you are keen on that. If you search for the good, you will find that. We can see people who lead an extremely evil life, walking around, saying evil things about good people. It is more difficult to see good in others.

It seemed that the young men were a bit humbled. They had nothing to say and simply listened attentively to the Mother's words of wisdom. Their prejudice might have made them think that they could have handled this "uneducated fisher-girl" easily. After a short pause, the Mother continued,

Amma: There were two women who lived in neighboring houses. One was a munificent lady and the other a prostitute. The prostitute was a poor lady and had no other way of making a living. However, each time she committed a sin, she prayed to God with great remorse for forgiveness. The other lady, although she was munificent, always spoke critically of her prostitute neighbor to anyone who came to visit her. Having given something in charity, she would tell them, "Look, that woman is a prostitute. Don't go there." She would say this even to beggars. Having heard of this criticism and the fact the the neighboring lady had talked about her manner of making a living to all the visitors, the prostitute's mind was always filled with repentance. She sincerely prayed to God for forgiveness. Years rolled by and both of the ladies died. As she was very charitable in nature and was respected by the people, the munificent lady's dead body was cremated with reverence and honor, but there was not even one person to attend to the corpse of the prostitute. Somebody took it and threw it in a graveyard where it was pecked at and eaten by vultures and dogs. However, interestingly enough, the prostitute's soul ascended to heaven and the munificent lady's soul went to hell. Children, do you know why? Because although the first lady was munificent in nature, her mind was always keen on finding fault with the other lady. Therefore, her body which did all the charity was cremated with all honors, but her soul, which was only keen on finding fault with the other lady, went to hell. In the prostitute's case, with her body she did wrong things, but her mind was always intensely repenting and praying. Therefore, her body was treated befittingly and her soul went to heaven as a reward for her pure mind. This will be the result if we sit looking at other people's faults instead of correcting our own wrong attitudes.

The Mother sat silently with eyes closed uttering "Shiva, Shiva." After a few seconds, She opened Her eyes and continued.

Amma: Children, what is the benefit in walking around looking at the faults of others and talking about scepticism and other "isms"? Day by day you will be spoiling yourself, that's all. It is said that as you think, so you become. How can one make others good when he himself has not become so. Even if we intend to, it is not so easy to become so. When such is the case, how will it be if we try to make the world good? Is the world so small that it can be made good just by thinking? God will look after all that. Without abandoning selfishness, no one can make the world good. Even great souls who were completely selfless could not make the whole world good with all their power of penance. Then what can be said about powerless, limited human beings who are completely under the sway of selfishness and ego? Children, instead of looking at others and criticizing them, try to correct yourselves first.

The young men gazed at Mother's face with wonderment. Again there was a pause followed by another question.

Question: There are more than thirty *brahmacharins* here. How are the expenses of this Ashram met?

Amma: That power which sent them here is looking after them. The help extended by the devotees is due only to the inspiration of that power. Not only that, those who stay here are people who are satisfied with what they have here. Even if they do not get certain things one day, they do not complain. But the Lord has never created such a situation. If something is needed today, it will somehow come. In this Ashram Mother has never asked anything from anyone, yet everything has come; everything was sent by Him. This is a place for *tyagis*, not for *bhogis*. Contentment in every circumstance, in all situations, is the trademark of a spiritual seeker. Only food sufficient to appease hunger is given here. Those who want something more need not come here.

Question: Is spiritual life necessary at such a young age? Wouldn't it be enough a little later in life?

Amma: That is left to them. Everyone has the freedom to choose their own path. Another person has no right to question it. Why did you children choose the path of scepticism and Marxism? Because you have a natural inclination for that, haven't you? Each person has a different *vasana*, and it is that *vasana* which determines his field of action. There are others who like to drink only lemonade or fresh water. We should not be adamant, saying that everyone should like tea. These children accepted what they liked; that is their *vasana*. Even in worldly life among members of the same family, some become doctors while others become engineers, scientists or even peons. Everything depends upon one's predominant mental disposition.

Also one should remember that the strength to do sadhana and search for the Truth will decrease as we get older. Then where is the time to think of God? Only those who have strong spiritual tendencies inherited from previous births will take to the path of spirituality while they are still young.

Question: Is there any benefit in *sannyasa*?

Amma: Nobody becomes a *sannyasin* for some benefit. The meaning of the word "*sannyasa*" is to give up even the thought about benefit. If there is any benefit, it is not personal. It is benefit for the whole world. It is a natural evolution of compassion and an attitude of renunciation alone. The world is really benefited only by devotees.

Mother would say that those who have enmity towards Mother actually love Her more than the devotees. Do you know why? Because their only thought will be, "Somehow this girl should be destroyed. She must be killed, do you hear, killed!" They think more about Mother and have more concentration than the devotees do. Kamsa[9] attained Liberation because of his one-pointed thought of killing Sri Krishna. Devotees will not have the same intensity of concentration in meditation which a thief gets while stealing. Therefore, even those who oppose Mother are benefited by Her.

At this point the young men who boasted of themselves as sceptics were really humbled. They were convinced. The young man who asked the question said, "Mother, although we were misinformed, we now thank the person who told us about you because if he had not said anything we would have not known about you. We have never heard such clear and simple explanations to clear our doubts. Now we take leave of you. We will come and see you with our other friends." The young men saluted the Mother who affectionately patted them on the back chanting "Namah Shivaya." With palms joined in reverence, they took their leave.

Mother was invited to a devotee's house in Quilon, so the father of that family came in advance to bring Her. Sitting in the hut, the Mother was talking to him. It was four o'clock in the evening. Some of the brahmacharins came with questions.

Amma: Do not waste your time always asking questions. Concentration on your *sadhana* is what is needed. Mother gave a mantra to everyone. Do not be puffed up because of that and think, "I am Mother's disciple." Do not feel proud thinking, "I have the ticket" after getting into a bus or train. If you do not show the ticket when the ticket collector comes, he will immediately make you get off. He

---

[9] Kamsa was the king of Mathura in Sri Krishna's time. After hearing a prophecy that Sri Krishna would kill him, he was always thinking of Him and the way to dispose of Him before himself getting killed by Him.

will let you alight at your destination only if you use your ticket for the proper place and in the proper way. Otherwise, you will have to get off before your destination.

Until now, everyone has been entrusted with selling only peanuts. Those who succeed in that will be put in charge of a general goods store and if successful, from there to a wholesale shop. If successful there, they will be employed in selling gold jewelry. Next, you may be made the owner of a department store if you succeed in all the previous endeavors. After that, you do not have to do any work at all. Mother has no responsibility in the matter of those who fail in the business which would give supreme happiness forever.

Leaders

Now the Holy Mother started talking about discipline.

Amma: Mother has entrusted each one in the Ashram with a responsibility. Others should respect what they say. That is a sign of spiritual humility and discipline. Even though there are teachers in the school, a leader is necessary to enquire whether the students are talking unnecessarily or doing other things against the rules and regulations of the school. That is needed in spirituality also. In the Ashram, Mother may not be able to sit near Her children always. You should not be defiant towards them.

Brahmacharin: Mother, can one discontinue *yogasanas*?

Amma: *Yogasanas* can be performed in two different ways, as a technique of meditation and as an exercise for the internal organs. In both cases it is not good to stop completely. Especially in the beginning stages, you should keep a regular time for doing them without fail. If they are done properly as a meditation, your power of concentration will increase. As an exercise they will give strength and balance to your internal organs. If you want, you can reduce the number of *asanas* in due course, but do not stop completely as it might create physical discomfort.

Devotee: Mother, why have you incarnated in this nasty place?
Amma: There is no such thing as clean and unclean for Mother. The lotus flower grows in the mud. If there is no mud, there is no lotus. Therefore, can we say that mud is bad? Mere manure is used as fertilizer for beautiful flowers, is it not? Looking at the manure in this way, can we say that it is dirty? There is no good and bad for people who are spiritually thirsty. They will come here whatever the surroundings. Besides, in the last five hundred years there has been no Ashram in this coastal area. That lack also should be removed, should it not?
Devotee: Whatever be the matter, some people will always oppose. That is the nature of the world.
Amma: Son, opposition is absolutely necessary. Only if there are black goats in a herd can the white goats be recognized distinctly. The beauty of the white sand is seen because black sand is there as well. The darkness of black reveals the lightness of white.

After the usual evening bhajans, Mother went with some of the brahmacharins and brahmacharinis to Quilon in a hired vehicle. When the driver increased the speed, Mother said, "Son, drive slowly." Mother instructed everyone to sing bhajans when the people started talking. She Herself sang,

> *O Divine Mother, Mother of the World,*
> *O most courageous Mother,*
> *Giver of Truth and Divine Love...*
>
> *O Thou Who art the Universe Itself,*
> *Courage, Truth and Divine Love...*

As the singing went on, the driver increased the speed again. In the midst of the singing, the Holy Mother loudly said, "Son, stop the car." After slowing down, the car came to a halt and veered a little to one side. After getting out of the car to enquire why the car had veered, the excited driver found that one of the wheels was about to slip off. Everyone sighed and looked at Mother with joined palms. What if the car had still been going at a high speed?

Later when Mother reached the devotee's house, She said, "It was a very bad time for you children. Your devotion and faith in God saved you." With tears in his eyes, the father of the family said, "It was all your grace, Mother."

29 December 1983

After returning from Quilon, the Holy Mother lay down on a mat spread under a coconut tree to take some rest. The brahmacharins who could not accompany Her to Quilon seemed like people who had been separated from Her for a long time. They came and sat near the Mother after prostrating to Her. A trace of anger was also seen on one brahmacharin's face. Understanding what was in his mind, the Mother smiled and said,

Amma: The flowers of the coconut tree will remain near the top of the tree until they become larger and then bend low. In the same manner, we must also bend low (become humble) as we mature. Many flowers will bloom on a tree from which all the leaves have fallen, making the flowers notably visible. On those trees which retain their leaves, flowers will be seen only here and there. The flowers of Godliness will diminish if the leaves of ego, jealousy and other negative qualities increase. The full Vision of God is possible only if all the evil qualities of the mind are removed.

Usually there are no waves in mid-ocean. The waves are only by the shore because there is no depth there. A Jnani will be calm. It is people who have read only two or three books who make a big noise. They have no depth.

Question: How can one see God in everything?

Amma: Children, you have faith in Incarnations like Rama and Krishna, haven't you? Thus, if you can visualize God in human forms, why can't you see Him in other objects too? Is not God all-pervading? If not, He is not God. He is in each and every atom. In the beginning one should cultivate this attitude with deliberate effort. As you progress with your *sadhana*, this feeling will become natural. Practice is needed to attain perfection in anything. When such is the case with mere worldly arts, what to say of the Ultimate Knowledge? All this will be understood if the mind is made one-pointed. Electricity is produced from flowing water. A river which flows in different branches is first obstructed by a dam. From the resulting powerful combined flow, we produce electricity. Likewise, the Vision of God is possible with the power which is gained through concentration of mind. At that time we will come to know that God is everywhere; everything is God. Do not make a fuss now. Be calm; wait patiently and do your *sadhana*.

Question: Mother, what is the benefit of *satsang*?

Amma: Students who study engineering take the help of various instruments. Above all, they seek the guidance of an experienced teacher. For realizing God, we must utilize the *Mahatmas* as a means; they are the guides. Without their help it is very difficult to travel on this path. They will protect the *sadhak* like a mother hen protects the chicks. In their presence, we can feel God. They are the only ones who desire nothing except the well-being and spiritual progress of the students. Now we are in the scorching heat of worldliness. Their presence is like the cooling breeze in the shade of a huge tree. *Mahatmas* are like the Kalpataru (wish-fulfilling tree). Therefore, take refuge in them. That is the benefit of *satsang*.

Brahmacharin: Mother, my past frightens me. Is there no way to escape it?

Amma: While travelling on a river, nobody racks their brains thinking of where the source is. There is no need to do so. Several failures might have occurred in your past. There is no meaning in wasting your time thinking about that. What has happened is over. What is needed is to mould your future. For that, live in the present. Do your actions in a better way, surrendering everything to a higher goal and seeking refuge in God. Do not grieve thinking of the past; that is foolishness. You are wasting both your energy and capacities by doing so. By worrying about the past your mind becomes weaker and weaker and you lose the strength to deal with the present. Remember that you are God's child and that He will protect you. In that way you will gain the strength required to face the difficulties.

Brahmacharin: Those who abuse Mother have no sense of shame and Mother will simply sit there smiling. How is that possible, Mother?

Amma: Shame and disgrace are there only as long as you think that you are the body. Once the body-consciousness is transcended, then all differences disappear. Then there is only Oneness. The feeling of Oneness arises from the realization of Pure Consciousness. In that state who can tease or abuse whom, what disgrace and what shame is there? Not only that. Mother grew only because of such abuses. Therefore, how can She feel sad when somebody speaks against Her, whoever they may be? Mother can only love them.

Japa and dhyana

Question: Sometimes during meditation, *japa* and *dhyana* happen simultaneously. Sometimes the form alone remains; *japa* becomes impossible. At some other times, both cannot be done. What can I do, Mother?

Amma: In the beginning stages of meditation, *japa* and remembrance of the form are both necessary. *Japa* should be done even if the form is not retained. After some time, one will reach a stage where one can focus on the form alone, at which point *japa* is neither necessary nor even possible. Now and then, some may feel that the mind has become blank. That is only a feeling. The mind will not become blank so easily but that feeling will lead to sleep. At that time, either remembrance of the form or *japa* should be done with alertness.

The mind cannot do two things at the same time. Therefore, while chanting the mantra with your lips, you can either concentrate on the form of your meditation or on the sound or on the letters of the mantra. Otherwise, focus your attention only on the form without chanting the mantra. Do not try to focus both on the form and the mantra. That is impossible. There will come a stage when repetition of the mantra will happen spontaneously at all times.

30 December 1983

The brahmacharinis were sitting in the dining hall chopping vegetables. A few women householder devotees were also helping them. The Holy Mother also joined them and began cutting vegetables. As far as Mother is concerned, no work is low. Sometimes She can be seen cooking in the kitchen. At other times one can see Her carrying bricks and sand with the residents. She will be seen sweeping the Ashram premises or doing other work. It is wonderful to watch the Mother on such occasions. She could do any work most beautifully within the shortest possible time that others might make a mess of even if they tried for hours on end. Understanding that some of the devotees present were not chanting their mantra, the Holy Mother, as if to a brahmacharini, said,

Amma: Any work, especially cooking, should be done while chanting the Divine Name. Cutting vegetables and thinking about worldly things, is this what should be done by people who wish to lead a spiritual life? Many people will eat the food cooked by you. If you let your mind wander while cooking, that will affect those who eat it in a negative way. On the other hand, if you chant your mantra while cooking, that food will spiritually benefit those who eat it.

One of the householder devotees seemed to be perplexed. She felt that Mother was talking about her because she was not chanting her mantra. She started chopping vegetables chanting her mantra and said to the Mother, "Mother, please bless me to chant my mantra always."

Mother smiled. Another woman devotee asked, "Mother, it is said that women should not do japa and dhyana during menstruation.

Amma: There is no meaning in that. One can do *japa* and *dhyana* at any time. Not only that, it is especially at that time that it is needed in order to maintain mental purity. During menstruation there will be an increase in negative thoughts and feelings. Therefore, always do *japa* and *dhyana* at that time.

It was nine o'clock in the morning. The Mother came out of the dining hall where many householder devotees were waiting to see Her. Going to the coconut grove with all of them, She asked them to sit down. As it was time for meditation, the Mother said to the devotees, "Let us meditate for some time. Children, sit closer." The Holy Mother closed Her eyes and entered into samadhi. Sitting near the Mother, the devotees also tried to meditate. The Mother opened Her eyes after half an hour or so. The devotees were anxiously waiting to be called by Her so they could each unburden their sorrows and sufferings at Her feet. The Mother called the devotees one by one. Some of them asked Mother to clarify their doubts.

Attain the state of desirelessness

Question: Mother, it is said that another birth is needed in order to enjoy sensual pleasures if one becomes a *sannyasin* before fulfilling the desire for enjoyment. Is that correct?

Amma: This is applicable only to a person who has many unfulfilled desires. There are many such people who take *sannyasa* due to the excitement of the moment. Later all their spirit and enthusiasm diminishes and the predominant *vasanas* will start manifesting one by one. Such people will not have the determination to do any *sadhana.* In due course, they will come completely under the sway of their *vasanas.* At the moment of death, such people will be thinking of their unfulfilled desires and expectations. They will have to take another birth according to their *vasanas* in order to enjoy the pleasures for which they longed.

Question: Suppose one became a *sannyasin* after reaching *bhogantya* (the end of sensual pleasures). He has burnt his *vasanas* through *sadhana.* In his case, is another birth needed?

Amma: No, but such people will be only one in a million. A general statement cannot be made using them as the criteria. Generally speaking, one will have to be born again if he does not reach *bhogantya.* Anyhow, one cannot satisfy all one's desires and then become a *sannyasin.* It is like standing on the seashore waiting to take a bath after all the waves have subsided. It is also not possible to become satiated by satisfying our desires one by one.

Question: Mother, you said that satisfaction will not come through the enjoyment of desires. It is also seen that once people immerse themselves in pleasures, they get more and more drowned in them. If so, how is it possible to take *sannyasa* only after all desires end?

Amma: Children, you should discriminate while enjoying worldly pleasures. Through constant discrimination, you will reach a mental state where you can give up everything. Relatives, riches, sensual pleasures and the like can only give temporary happiness. They are all non-eternal. It is not the external objects which give us happiness. There are many people who have all material pleasures but are still unhappy and discontent. Many commit suicide even while living in air-conditioned rooms. If the air-conditioned room was the source of their happiness, then why should these people commit suicide in it? Therefore, even if we have everything, if there is no mental peace, we cannot lead a happy life. If you go on craving for worldly pleasures, happiness cannot be gained. Understand that objects are ephemeral. Search for the eternal; that is the real source of happiness, the Self. Be satisfied with what you have. Renounce greed, selfishness and jealousy. If you can do this, in due course you will reach the state where all desires end.

We will not get much of the taste of the food if we eat while holding our nose. Also there is no taste once the food goes down the throat. Therefore, taste is only a sensation of the tongue. If we think and discriminate in this way, we will get the ability to eat without caring about the taste of food. In this way, by removing delusion through discrimination between the eternal and the non-eternal even while enjoying worldly pleasures, it is possible to renounce everything, attaining the state where all desires end. Only a sadhak will understand this. Others will think that these are things which are impossible. There are many worldly people who argue that pure celibacy is not possible. They are speaking for themselves, that is all. It is impossible for them to think that there are higher stages beyond their own. Those who do proper sadhana can observe perfect brahmacharya (celibacy).

In the evening, the Mother went to the seashore with all the devotees. The sun was about to set, its red color spread over the horizon and reflected in the vast ocean. Having prostrated on the seashore, everyone sat down for meditation. The ocean waves chanted the sacred syllable "AUM," and a cool, gentle breeze blew from the West. The seashore was very silent. It was an ideal atmosphere for meditation. The Holy Mother told the householder devotees,

Amma: Children, meditate fixing your minds on the sound "AUM" produced by the ocean waves. Or meditate imagining that your Beloved Deity, sitting on a lotus on the surface of the ocean, is beckoning you with Her or His hands.

Having said this, the Mother closed Her eyes in meditation. After half an hour, the Holy Mother got up and walked along the seashore by Herself. It was dusk. Sitting on a rock which lay a few yards away from the spot where the devotees were seated, the Mother started singing loudly. Hearing the song, the devotees slowly got up from their seats, went near the Mother and sat behind Her. Absorbed in Divine Love, the Mother sang,

> *Aren't Thou my Mother, O aren't*
> *Thou my dear Mother Who wipes away my tears?*
> *Aren't Thou the Mother of the fourteen worlds,*
> *The Creatress of the world?*
> *For how many days am I calling Thee,*
> *O Thou Whose nature is Shakti!*
> *Won't Thou come?*

An unearthly Divine Presence pervaded the atmosphere. The devotees became inspired by the Mother's cries and they too sang loudly. It seemed that they even forgot where they were sitting.

It was seven o'clock by the time the Mother returned to the Ashram with the devotees. As usual She distributed toffees to the fisher-children who would wait for Her along the way whenever the Mother went to the seashore.

31 December 1983

It was four o'clock in the evening. A group of college students came to see the Mother, having heard about Her from one of their friends. They were very curious to know and understand more about Her. It was clear from their demeanor that they were not the arrogant type. The Holy Mother was sitting in front of the temple and happily welcomed the young men, inviting them to come and sit on the temple verandah. They all sat a little distance away from the Mother. The Mother's natural way of enquiring about their names, native places, studies and other details really impressed them. When the light talk was over, one among the students humbly asked,

Question: Mother, young men who are almost our same age are living here as *brahmacharins*. Is this not escapism? Is *sannyasa* necessary at such a young age? Is it not enough to take *sannyasa* after leading a worldly life? Mother, please do not think that I am asking this simply to argue. I am having this doubt.

Amma: (Smilingly) Children, what makes you argue for worldly life?

The students looked perplexed.

Amma: Children, you have attachments to your family and to many other things. Is that not the reason you give importance to worldly life? We won't argue for things which we are not interested in, for objects which we hate, will we?

Student: That is right.

Amma: All right, children, what is the nature of this love which binds us to the life of the world. Children, have you ever thought about it?

The students remained silent, keenly listening to what the Mother was saying.

Where does happiness come from?

Amma: Children, all the love which the world offers will ultimately lead us to sorrow. There is no selfless love in this world. Is our life to be destroyed just for the sake of a woman or two children? We feel that we will get happiness from those, yet happiness is not in any object. It is from within us. Happiness is experienced when the sense organs are concentrated. Suppose there is a nice song on the radio. Only if we concentrate on it will we derive any happiness from it, not otherwise.

Student: Of course.

Amma: Such is the case with everything. Suppose we put a *laddu* (a kind of sweet) in our mouth. It tastes good only if the mind is on that sweetness, doesn't it? Therefore, happiness is derived from concentration of the mind. We feel that happiness comes from a woman or other objects. If happiness is derived from concentration, it follows that it is not dependent on any particular object. Momentary happiness is experienced when we concentrate on momentary objects. What then will be the amount of bliss gained if concentration is attained on the Lord, the eternal repository of all glory? In truth, there is no greater or lesser bliss if it is observed with a subtle intellect. Bliss is only one.

Happiness comes from within. The dog will bite the bone and think that the energy it gets from the blood of its own wounded gums is from the bone. We are also similarly deluded when we think that the bliss we get, in truth, from within, is coming from an external object. What the Rishis (sages) want us to do is to think, "What is this birth for? Why all these sorrows in the world? What is real peace? What is eternal?" One should think about all these questions. The objection that you raise about sannyasa being escapism is due to your thinking that the world will give you happiness. In reality, is there happiness in worldly life? It is true that we wander about for happiness. But is there any time bereft of agitation? Is there peace? Where is happiness without peace? How can Mother recommend that one should embrace the worldly life which gives only agitation ?

Student: The human race should exist, shouldn't it?

Amma: (Smilingly) Ah, to think about the preservation of the world by us who came yesterday and will go tomorrow! Shiva, Shiva! We ourselves do not have any existence. We will die today or tomorrow. Then how do we sustain the world? Is the world such a small thing for us to protect? God will look after that. Children, concentrate on the elimination of your own sorrow. Even that can be gained only through hundreds and hundreds of births. When such is the case, how are you going to sustain the world? Will the world continue to exist only if we get married and have children? The world will exist even if none of us are here. To find a way to protect oneself is more intelligent.

Student: Will one be saved if one believes in Mother or in God?

Amma: (Smilingly) Mother will never tell the children who come here to lead a spiritual life to believe in Mother, or in a God sitting up in the sky. Have faith in yourself. Know who you are. Who am I?

What is the sense of individuality? What power do I have? What can I achieve? One should know one's Self first. For that, one should live understanding what is eternal and what is transitory. To understand, through an analytical study, the true nature of the world in which we live, is discrimination between the eternal and non-eternal. Do not say that it is unnecessary. One who is serious-minded should think about what is the substratum of oneself and the world. Erroneously considering the visible world to be its own substratum, don't make a meaningless uproar.

Experience transcends reason

Amma: We will come to know that there is God when we ourselves search and understand the difference between *nitya* (the eternal) and *anitya* (the transient). With the eyes of ignorance, we can see only up to a certain point. Having looked with such eyes, we say that there is nothing beyond the point where our eyesight reaches. The external eyes cannot see things which lie behind a wall or a tree. When it is very dark we cannot even see a person who stands right in front of us. The sense organs are undoubtedly limited. We can see more when we become subtle.

Student: Sceptics blabber alot.

Amma: It is good if it is real rationalism (scepticism). But what if the sceptics are people who believe blindly? When they say that there is no God, are they saying so after having searched for Him properly? Experience is beyond reasoning. For each subject there are people who are well-versed in it. The words of such people are the valid means of knowledge. Likewise in the spiritual field also, there are people who have experience. It is their words which are the most authentic source of knowledge about that subject. They have seen God and also prescribe ways to see Him.

Mother has seen the sceptics giving a picture of their leader to the people when distributing his books. They will keep the leader's picture even after his death. Is this not blind faith? Why do they keep the picture? Because they love and admire him. In the same way, we love God and so we worship His picture.

A sceptic became Mother's devotee. That son brought some books. In one of the books it said that Christ and Krishna never existed. In another one it was written that Christ was a revolutionary. Just think, a person who wasn't born was a revolutionary! And to think that they worship the pictures of the people who write such unworthy words. Spiritual people worship the pictures of pure souls.

Today's sceptics cannot be properly called sceptics. Only a person who has eaten a thing can say whether it is tasty or not. What does it matter if one states an opinion about God, without having searched for and attained a proper knowledge about Him? Who would consider the denial of chemistry of one who has not even studied the subject? And what value is there in the denial of the science of physics by one who has not studied physics? What benefit is there in such so-called scepticism? Some people say that the attainment of God's Vision is the experience of a neurotic patient. This implies that, according to them, all the great saints and sages of the past and even their followers were all neurotic. What a nonsensical statement that is! All these "patients" had some visionary experience, some extraordinary universal revelation beyond individual neuroses. Mother is sure that those who think a little will not blabber nonsense like this. Those who have common sense will not believe their words either.

In the same way, what sense is there in saying that they (sceptics) will believe only in things which they can see? The ancient Rishis said that there are many suns and moons in space, not only one sun and one moon and modern science has proved it. But we cannot see them. Would these people say that these suns and moons do not exist because they cannot be seen by the naked eye? The Rishis proved the validity of all their experiences in their own laboratory. Whatever is said in the Vedas and Puranas is being proven true.

Modern science agrees with these ancient texts. Still these so-called sceptics go on talking like tape recorders.

There is a Power beyond words, an Inexpressible Power, and that is God. Everyone says that it is within, but it is not enough merely to say so. It should be known through intuitive experience.

Didn't A. T. Kovoor (a famous rationalist) say, "My eyes should be given to the medical college after my death?" When one says "My eyes," or "This is mine," it is implied that the object is different from "you." When he said "My eyes," it was quite clear that he must be different from his eyes. Therefore, when he said, "Donate my eyes after my death," it should be understood that A. T. Kovoor was not the corpse. The real "he" was other than the corpse. There was a consciousness which existed in that body. That consciousness is God.

Student: Some lead a pleasant life, some others a sorrowful one. Why is God's Will such?

Amma: God does not differentiate. It is our *bhavana* (conception) that projects a sense of difference on Him. Using God's own power, we abuse Him or we say that there is no God. It is like saying with our own tongue, "I have no tongue." We are not looking into ourselves. We are looking at other things. We don't think at all. We stand ready to kill those who tell the real principles of spiritual life. How did they kill Jesus? How did they act towards Nabi? Weren't there people who threw stones at Sri Narayana Guru when he was alive? Now they worship him. But those great souls did not have even an iota of bad feelings seeing all this injustice. They are the ones who took birth to set an example for the world.

Without showing partiality to anyone, the river flows at all times. Having made a dam across it, we will say, "Look at the partiality of this river. It doesn't flow this way." Having blocked the flow of the river, why should we blame it, saying that the river is not giving water? Having consciously rejected God's grace, we say that He is partial and shows differences. That is due to our ignorance. We do not observe things subtly.

Question: Why should we offer various things to God? Is it not to please Him?

Amma: God is Light itself. He does not need our wax candles and other material offerings. Lighting a lamp for God and offering food to Him is for our satisfaction and expansion of heart. All that we see is God's. Then what can we give Him? On the other hand, it is we who steal that which belongs to Him. The *Rishis* showed us the way of devotion based on knowledge, but we do not care about that.

Devotion based on knowledge

Question: Mother, what do you mean by that?

Amma: Practice devotion while knowing and understanding the essential principles of spirituality. The devotee's attitude should be that God is all-pervading, omniscient and omnipotent. All that we see is God. We should love God for God's sake, for devotion alone. We should love God selflessly. We should have pure devotion, loving for love's own sake without having any worldly desires. He who really loves God will worship Him, seeing everything pervaded by Him and serving others as His forms. These are the ways of devotion based on a knowledge of the essential principles.

Seeing God only in a particular form without understanding the real nature of Godhood is not true devotion. If God abides only in a particular form or place, being limited, He is no longer God. Many people who are devoted to temple worship have this kind of faith. They think that God is only in the inner sanctum of the temple. This kind of faith is harmful and will not help us progress spiritually. If Hinduism is viewed from the point of devotion based on spiritual principles, it is neither a religion nor a cult.

If we want mental peace, we should understand the difference between the permanent and the transitory and act accordingly. All our relatives will depart some day and we will be alone. Therefore, we should think about the real goal of life. If we live with that understanding, we will not even fear death. Our forefathers showed us that path but we do not follow it.

We should somehow gain concentration. Meditation and other spiritual practices are meant only for that purpose. Scientists make discoveries through concentrated investigations while sitting behind closed doors, don't they? Concentration is needed even for that. Everything will be spoiled if there is no concentration.

Children, all of us are searching for Eternal Bliss, but we will not get it from perishable objects. We should search for the Imperishable Self. That alone is eternal. It is that effort which goes on in the Ashram[10]. The children who stay here have enough wealth in their homes for their parents to live. None of them have to earn money for their families. Mother has forcibly sent those children whose families were not well-off, back to their homes. Let them look after their family affairs first and simultaneously do sadhana. At present, they can only do that much. Otherwise, what will the family do?

Solitude and regularity in one's routine are necessary in the beginning. Otherwise, it will be very difficult to achieve anything spiritually.

Question: Are there any servants in the Ashram?

Amma: No, there are no paid servants in the Ashram. The *brahmacharins* themselves do all the work while repeating their mantra. Before one scolds a laborer, he himself should know the laborer's sufferings. Therefore, the work in the Ashram should be done by each person. Life in the Ashram is difficult. How much difficulty is there in learning to ride a bicycle! How many times will one fall down in the beginning! When such is the case while learning worldly skills, is it possible to gain the bliss of the Self without undergoing difficulty? Suffering is not a problem for those who are intent on reaching the goal.

---

[10] This is a play on words. "That effort" in Malayalam is "â shramam." Mother is saying the "â shramam" takes place in the "ashramam (Ashram)."

Advaita Vedanta

Question: Mother, do you teach Vedanta here?
Amma: First let us learn the alphabet. Then we can move on to compound letters. Is it enough to say, "I am *Brahman?*" We should express the nature of *Brahman* in our actions. Even if someone scolds us, we should be able to remain calm without getting angry. We should discriminate thus, "I am not the body, I am the Self. If I am the Self, then there is no need of sorrow." A person deserves to be known as one who has reached *Brahman* when he has an attitude of non-hatred. In that state he does not have the feeling of inferior or superior. Everything is within us. We are the Absolute Self. But it is not enough to merely say so. The feeling of being the Absolute should arise within us. Both the jackfruit and the seed of the jackfruit are *Brahman.* The jackfruit is capable of giving sweetness, but the seed is not. It must sprout, grow, become a tree and then bear jackfruit. Until then, the seed is not the same as the tree or the fruit. The tree is within the seed but it is in the dormant state. If properly cultivated and looked after, the seed can also become a tree. Likewise, we can also reach the state of *Brahman* if we try.

What sense is there in calling ourselves Brahman, we who run after food and clothing while considering the body to be eternal? Look at great souls. They have no hatred toward anyone. Smilingly they mingle with everyone. They lead the world looking upon everything with an equal eye. That is what we must follow as an example. First we need a regular discipline. The fence of regular discipline is needed to protect the young plant of spirituality from the animals of worldliness. Advaita (Vedanta philosophy) is not something that should be told or taught by another person. It should be experienced through sadhana. What you see here in this Ashram are those disciplines which will lead one to that understanding through experience.

The brahmacharins must do six to eight hours of meditation a day. They must do all of the external work in the Ashram. They must cultivate humility and a service mentality and develop love for each other. Unlike worldly people, they cannot go to the movies, nor can they go to the market and eat whatever they like. They have a strict diet. Sometimes the food which is served here will not be tasty. At other times there will be only rice without any side dishes. They sleep very little. Most important of all is sadhana. Intense sadhana is needed in order to get rid of the fascination with the world. It is not enough merely to speak of Advaita.

We are immersed in an illusion thinking that that which is, is not, and that which is not, is. We see the world through the eyes of ignorance. We must know the difference between what is eternal and what is changing. At present we are asleep but the goal is to reach a sleepless state. As we do sadhana, there will come a state where there is no sleep. At that time we will remain conscious even during normal sleep. The body will rest but the mind will remain awake. To reach that state we should advance a great deal in sadhana. When we awaken to God-consciousness, we will realize the world to be a dream. But now we tend to look outwards. The Ancient Sages, on the other hand, looked inwards and became omniscient. How many aeons ago did they write about today's happenings!

Uttering "Shiva, Shiva," the Holy Mother entered the indescribable state of samadhi. Her countenance became beautifully radiant and there was a gracious smile on Her lips. Everyone sat silently around Mother while looking at Her face, like honey bees surrounding a fully-blossomed flower.

Having returned to Her normal consciousness, the Mother smilingly asked the students, "Children, didn't you get anything to drink?" The Mother then called Gayatri and asked her to make tea for them.

Image worship

Question: Since God is everywhere, is it necessary to worship a stone?

Amma: What is wrong with that? We remember the real apple when we see the artificial one, don't we? Likewise, the images of different gods and goddesses remind us of the Ultimate Reality. When a devotee beholds an image of Rama or Krishna, he is reminded of the real Rama who lived in Ayodhya and of Krishna who lived in Dwaraka. Since God is everywhere, He is in the stone as well. Our minds become concentrated when we worship a stone with the attitude that God is within it. It is not the stone, but we who receive the benefit thereof. It is we who get peace of mind.

Children, when you see a handkerchief given by your beloved, do you think only of the cloth and its price? You remember your beloved, don't you? Therefore, it is more a reminder of your beloved than it is a piece of cloth. Bhavana (attitude) is more important than anything else. When we worship a stone, it ceases to be a mere stone. The resolve (sankalpa) that the stone is God is behind the act of worship. It is that sankalpa which is important.

Question: It is said that the Ganges River has certain medicinal powers and that it won't get spoiled.

Amma: Son, modern science has proven it to be so through research and experimentation.

Question: Some disagree.

Amma: Without duality there is no world. Even a coin has two sides. A full day is comprised of day and night. The sun neither rises nor sets, but only seems to do so. It is said that only if there is opposition will there be growth. Different people will say different things. We should not pay attention to them.

> *What is told will not be seen;*
> *What is seen will not be told.*

This was said by the Rishis. We always talk about the world. When this world disappears, we will behold the eternal Brahman, but we will not be able to say what It is. We should see That and directly know what It is. At the same time, do not believe what is seen in the newspapers or what is heard on the radio or television. We ourselves should analyze and study the matter. Modern science has discovered through experimentation that the water of the Ganges River has the power to destroy germs.

Question: Why are there so many castes and religions?

Amma: Son, there is only one God. Mother does not care about caste and religion. People from all castes and religions come here. That Supreme Essence, the Self says, "In whatever way you conceive (of Me), I am there." There are not many gods. Ultimately everything depends on one's faith.

The world becomes the wealth of him who knows Reality

Question: Some people become *sannyasins* after renouncing everything. But even a *sannyasin* needs money, doesn't he?

Amma: For one who has known the Reality, the world is his wealth. He has nothing else to gain. A real *sannyasin* is beyond all worldly needs. He is beyond happiness and sorrow. If you give him something he might accept it. However, even if he doesn't get anything, he is still happy. No power can conquer him or his mind because he is beyond body-consciousness. In our country no *sannyasin* has ever starved to death. The Lord Himself will directly look after the needs of a true devotee and renunciate. If anyone doubts this, let them come to Mother. She will prove it from Her own experience.

Question: Even devotees experience sorrow, don't they?

Amma: It is God Himself who makes them sorrowful. God will make the devotee suffer using egotistical people as instruments. Those who are sorrowful will call God with more concentration. In this way, God Himself will make a bridge and by means of that bridge He will come down.

Once the sage Narada went to see some Rishis. They said, "We have performed sacrifices for a long time but we have had no results."

Then Narada replied, "You have performed fire sacrifices but was there any selflessness and love while doing so?" Narada continued, "I know a fisherman who had an intense desire to see the Divine Mother. He approached a sannyasin who told him, "The Goddess will appear before you if you call Her with as much longing as a person being held under water would long for air. If you call the Mother like that She will definitely appear." Having complete faith in his Guru's words and without caring about his body, his life or his house, he plunged into the water saying, "I will come up to the surface only after I have seen the Mother," and with that he whole-heartedly called out "Amma!" Immediately Devi appeared in front of him. The Mother asked, "Son, why did you call Me? What do you want?" The fisherman said, "Amma, I don't want anything. Make everyone in the world good, and bestow happiness upon them. My only request is that Mother should come and eat at my house whenever She feels hungry." Here again Narada continued, "The power of innocent love is obvious. If you call the Divine Mother with love and longing as that fisherman did, you also can receive darshan."

But however much they tried, no love grew within the Rishis. Thinking about this, Narada decided to correct them. Approaching a demon of those days, Narada told him, "The Rishis are doing penance in order to kill you." Hearing this, the demon angrily set out in search of the Rishis in order to kill them. Reaching their abode, he approached the Rishis, and catching them by their hair and beards, dragged them out and tortured them. In the struggle between life and death which ensued, the Rishis used all their powers and fully surrendered their minds to Devi, with the one thought, "There is no refuge other than Mother." They called out loud, "Amma, Amma!" and at that moment Devi appeared in front of them and killed the demon, thereby saving the Rishis. It is the Lord alone who gives sorrow to the devotees, for only then will they call to Him whole-heartedly. However much worship and other spiritual practices you do, there will be no benefit if there is no love. If one is really a devotee, one will look upon sorrow as a blessing which will act as a bridge to the Lord.

It was nearly six o'clock in the evening. With much humility, all of the students except for one prostrated to the Mother and took leave of Her. This student remained seated in front of the Holy Mother. He said,

Young man: Mother, I am interested in taking *sannyasa*.

He seemed very inspired. The Mother smilingly consoled him saying,

Amma: Son, everything will happen according to God's Will. Enjoyment which is gained from worldly pleasures is like the enjoyment which one gains by scratching a scab. It is a pleasure when you scratch, but later it will become infected. It will itch again and become infected with pus. You may feel some temporary happiness while enjoying worldly pleasures, but later they will become the source of tremendous sorrow. The wound will not get cured if it is treated by merely applying medicine externally. The external wound is only a symptom of the disease which you have within. The inner germs should be killed; inner cleansing is what is needed. If that is done, *sannyasa* is possible. But if that is not done, you simply walk around in ochre clothes making a show of renunciation. Taking up spiritual life is not an easy thing. It requires great mental strength and courage. Therefore, think well before deciding.

Mother will yield to good character, but not to wealth

Very recently a branch of the Ashram started functioning in a nearby place. A devotee who joined in the activities there was disliked by a group of devotees who hailed from the same village. There were conflicts and protests concerning his coming to the Ashram branch. They counted on Mother to side with them in ousting the devotee and his family. Some of the devotees approached the Mother with this in mind and told Her, "Mother, you should keep him away from the activities of the Ashram for some time." When Mother asked why, they said, "If that one man is kept away, many others will favor Mother and the Ashram." Hearing this the Mother retorted,

Amma: Would you give one child among your children to your neighbors if they told you that they would give seven or eight of their children to you instead?

Devotee: No.

Amma: Then how could Mother discard one son?

Everyone was silent.

Amma: Mother will yield to good character but She will not yield to money and pride. Mother is free to do as She likes. She will not allow anyone to obstruct that freedom. Mother is ready to yield to Her children's good character. All are children to Mother. She cannot show favoritism.

The next time the Mother visited the Ashram branch, the first house She visited was the house of that particular devotee who was opposed by the others. Most amazingly, Mother had never been in his house before. No one had ever told Her in which area the house was situated. After getting into the car, She instructed the driver to go in a certain direction, and when the car reached a particular house, asked him to stop. Indeed, it was the house of the dejected devotees. When Mother came to their house, all of them were crying before Mother's picture which was installed in their shrine room. They were very dejected thinking, "Today Mother will come to the Ashram but we cannot go and see Her." They were afraid that the opposition would create problems if they came. They told Mother that they had strong faith that She would come to their house in response to their heart-felt call. Later the Mother commented about this incident saying, "It was their innocent call which brought

Mother to them." The family burst into tears when they saw that the Mother had come. She lovingly consoled them and sang a song,

I will worship until the end of my life,
But rid me of my sorrow today.
O Goddess, Primal Supreme Power,
Bless me and remove my grief.
How many sufferings am I bearing.
Why art Thou delaying to cast
Thy gracious glance?
O Mother, drown me not in Thy Maya.
I bow to Thy Feet always.

Listening and understanding the meaning of the song and realizing how the song was connected with their lives, all of them wept before the Holy Mother again and again. The Mother once more consoled them by putting each one on Her lap like a mother does to Her children and wiped their tears with Her own hand.

1 January 1984

A group of householder devotees came to see the Holy Mother. All of them were newcomers. They had read an article about the Mother in a newspaper and out of curiosity wanted to see Her. A few among them had a little spiritual background. It was nearly nine o'clock in the morning when the Mother, who had been observing the brahmacharins' meditation, came out of the hall and happened to see them. With a smile on Her face, She approached the visitors and welcomed them in Her own natural and spontaneous way. She asked, "Children, where do you come from?" It took a while for the visitors to realize that it was the Mother Herself who was standing in front of them. They never thought that they could see Her so easily and without any mediators. They could not even speak for a few seconds. Slowly one of them said, "We come from the North and this is our first visit."

The Mother again spoke, "Come on, children," and walked towards the darshan hut, the visitors following Her. First the Mother took a mat, spread it on the floor and asked the visitors to sit down. Then She said,

Amma: Shall Mother sit on this cot? It is just because Mother can see all of you easier and you children can see Mother without any difficulty. In reality, Mother does not like to sit higher than Her children.

The Mother's simplicity, humility and utter naturalness had a great impact on the visitors. A few moments passed in silence. For a while Mother was transported to Her own plane of awareness. She sat with eyes closed in meditation. After sometime She opened Her eyes uttering, "Shiva, Shiva," and made a circle in the air with Her finger. One man among the visitors asked a question.

Visitor: Many great souls and Incarnations have taken birth in India. All of them have tried for unity and integration. In spite of all their efforts, there are still many problems; chaos and confusion reign both in the lives of individuals and in life as a whole. Why is this so? Doesn't it mean that those great souls have failed in their mission?

Amma smilingly but penetratingly looked at the questioner's face and spoke as if from a different plane of consciousness.

Amma: No, it is not that they have failed but rather, that you have failed to apply their instructions in your life. You have read many books without understanding how to apply their teachings to your life. You have continued to beat your wife, you have punished your children without any reason, and have quarrelled with your parents without any cause. You have failed to discharge your duty as a husband, father, son and official. You have wastefully spent your money on intoxicants and other such things and are full of hatred and anger. Who is to blame, *Mahatmas* or people like you? When people like you live in society, how can life improve? First try to correct yourself. Let each individual try to do so. Then you can see the nation growing as a whole. The *Mahatmas* revealed the path. It is up to us to discriminate and walk on that path. Having arrogantly committed all kinds of prohibited actions, what sense is there in blaming the *Mahatmas*, our great ancestors?

Beholding the Mother's extraordinary mood and sharp words, the visitors were taken aback. The man who had put forth the question sat with his head hung down. Even the brahmacharins who were present became a little confused on seeing the gravity of the situation. But in a few moments everything became clear, as the questioner threw himself at the Mother's feet crying loudly, "Forgive me, forgive me!" The Holy Mother gently lifted him, put him on Her lap and stroked his back with love and affection. Still he went on sobbing. The Mother said, "Son, don't worry, don't worry, everything will be all right. Now you have come to Mother, don't worry." Unlike Her previous expression, the Mother's face now radiantly shone with compassion and love. Later it came to be known that what the Mother had said about this man's personal life was true, that he had been leading an utterly unrighteous life. When Mother pointed out one by one his faults and weaknesses, he was astounded and, at the same time, filled with remorse as he recalled the evil actions which he had committed towards his wife, children and parents. Later he said, "I never dreamed that the question which I asked was being directed towards a person who was aware of all my thoughts and actions. When the Mother suddenly retorted, I was really shocked." Thereafter there occurred a great transformation in his life and his whole family became Mother's devotees. He even helped his friends and acquaintances to change their lives by bringing them to Mother.

After their friend's experience, the others were quite convinced of the Mother's omniscience. They did not ask Her any questions but reverently prostrated before Her and took their leave, each having experienced Her motherly love and ubiquitous vision. Before leaving the Ashram they spoke to one of the brahmacharins.

Devotee: Actually we wanted to ask Mother many questions when we came here, but She has cleared all of our doubts by Her actions. One purpose for our coming was to seek the Mother's blessings for bringing about a change in our friend. Without expressing anything to Her about it, She has graciously fulfilled all of our wishes. Now we can go in peace.

When they had gone, the Mother rose from Her seat and went into the temple. When She came out, it was ten o'clock and She found some young men waiting to see Her. The Mother sat on the verandah and asked them to sit near Her. The young men, though seemingly educated, were not very polite. They exhibited a tendency to argue with the Mother.

Amma: Children, there is no meaning in mere dispute. Arguing must be for the sake of knowing the real nature of an object, incident or experience. *Tarka* (the science of logic) is not the mere juggling of words. The subject matter should become an experience. Would you get sweetness if you write the word "sugar" on a piece of paper and lick it? Will you get a bitter taste without chewing the leaves of the margosa (neem) tree? Children, what made you want to come to the Ashram?

One young man: We heard about the Ashram and felt like coming. We would like to talk to Amma.

Amma: What is there to talk about? All are in *samsara*[11] alone. What Mother says is how nice it would be if this *samsara* stopped. Children, however much rain water falls on the mountain-top, it will not remain there. It will flow down to the river below. The low-lying ditch receives the water from all sides. This is the greatness of humility. This is what is needed. Everything will come running to

---

[11] A pun on the word "samsara" which means both "talk" and "the wheel of birth, death and rebirth."

the place where there is humility. We should know that everything is within us. For that, humility is needed. Nothing can be gained if you egotistically walk around challenging others thinking, "I am great, omniscient, I have nothing to learn from anyone. I can win a dispute with anyone." Only after we ourselves have become good can we advise others.

The young men looked at each other. There was a sigh.
Question: Why is it that many people spend their time simply criticizing the Ashram?
Amma: That is their nature. Let us follow our nature. Why should we look at others and criticize them? A person from Tamil Nadu came and asked for a commodity in a shop in Kerala. The word which he used to name the goods was a vulgar one in Malayalam, the language of Kerala. The shopkeeper was about to beat him. Only when another person interfered and explained could he understand the meaning. It was the linguistic difference which created the problem. Likewise, we cannot find any fault in those who oppose us when we understand their nature. They have only that much knowledge and therefore they protest.

Some will write praising the Ashram, while others write with abuse. We are affected by neither. Look at our forefathers. How much Krishna and Christ had to endure! Mother has said that we do not need any advertisement in the newspapers. Truth will spread even without that. Didn't news spread even before there were newspapers and printing presses?

To know and experience something requires effort. To simply express an opinion about a particular thing does not require any effort at all. Move your tongue up and down and different sounds will come out. To say that the Arabian Sea does not exist is easy. Any fool can say that. But to go there and experience the vast expansiveness and to feel the breeze from the sea, effort is needed. Children, an intelligent approach to a subject is important. Penetrate it. Then you can realize its real nature. Otherwise, you will see only its superficial nature which will always misguide you. Trying to find out the real nature of an object is real tarka.

The young men seemed stunned. They could not open their mouths for a few seconds. The Holy Mother lovingly smiled at them while they gazed at Her face. There was a short silence. Then Mother continued.

Amma: Children, Mother wants to ask you something. Young men like you always have a questioning nature. Mother likes that. But at the same time, Mother always wonders why young men like you will not try to do something which is useful for yourselves as well as for society. Can't you practice a little bit of meditation or other spiritual practice and see how they work? How can you label something as not good without experiencing the truth of it? Try, and if it doesn't work, then discard it or express your own opinion about it. Otherwise, it is unintelligent and illogical to criticize something without properly understanding it.

Young man: We accept what Mother says. Still, doubts always gnaw at us. After all, we are ordinary human beings, aren't we? Everyone speaks about God. Is there any clear proof that He exists? How is it possible to believe in something which cannot be proven?

Amma: All right, if there is no God, let it be so. Do we ever say that we do not exist? No. What evidence do you have to prove that your grandfather existed? Isn't it your own and your father's existence? Similarly, the existence of the Universe proves the existence of its Creator, God. Therefore, study yourselves first. Mother does not say that you should believe in Her or in a God who dwells up above in the sky. Have faith in yourself, in your own Self. You think that only that which can be seen and understood is you, that is, the body, mind and intellect; but you are something more than that. To know or to study yourself is not merely to have knowledge of your gross body and other things associated with it. That which gives you power, vigor, strength and the effulgence of life is something different. Modern science calls it energy and our Ancient Sages called it the Self, or God. You cannot deny "*Shakti*." In reality, it is there that your real existence lies. That is the real "you." To study yourself means to know that Self without which you have no existence, power or vigor. But that is very subtle. You cannot perceive it, but you can experience it. As you go more and more into it, you will get the power to understand that Self. But if you revel on the gross level, the subtle level cannot be understood. We reach God when we go in search of ourselves.

Question: The *brahmacharins* are very young. Is it necessary to take up *sannyasa* at such a young age?

Amma: One spontaneously renounces everything and takes to *sannyasa* when one has had enough of worldly life. It is a natural process. Nobody can become a *sannyasin*. It just happens. There is no special time for it.

Question: To become a *sannyasin*, why is an ashram and a Guru needed?

Amma: Why are doctors and hospitals needed but for the treatment of disease? If the disease is to be cured, the rules and regulations as instructed by the doctor should be observed. Likewise, a *sadhak* also has to observe certain disciplines. As he is imperfect and his understanding and discrimination are undeveloped, he needs a Perfect Soul to guide him and make him walk in the correct path. The real *vidya* (knowledge) is to make the mind one-pointed. That is difficult if one stays in the world. The mind will get dissipated. But it can be easily controlled if one comes to an ashram and lives under the guidance of a *Satguru*. The atmosphere in an ashram is conducive to spiritual practice. The mind is like a monkey whose rope has been untied and let go. Agitation is the result if there is no mental control. Where is peace and tranquillity for worldly people? A spiritual person has peace. Those who imitate him will also get peace. It is to gain external happiness that we struggle to get into a cinema theater to see a movie. That happiness is only temporary. In spiritual life also, there is struggle, but that is for gaining spiritual bliss which is eternal.

Question: Are there different stages in meditation?

Amma: Yes, there are. But you will not understand such matters even if Mother were to talk to you about it. There are things which should be told to *sadhak*s alone. Proper understanding and assimilation are necessary in order to know such things. Anyhow, concentration is the basic factor. When concentration increases everything will be all right. Therefore, children, try to acquire concentration.

In the beginning one will not get real dhyana (meditation). What we do in the beginning cannot be called real meditation as it is just a practice or exercise to attain the state of dhyana. Even then, we will say that we are meditating. Results will be gained if you try constantly. Suppose we place a pot of water on the stove to cook rice. If someone were to ask, "What are you doing?" we would say, "I am cooking rice." In reality the rice is not being cooked, only the water is being boiled. Even then, that is what we would say. So even in the initial stages of dhyana we would say that we are meditating.

The different stages in meditation are subjectively experienced by the sadhak. Initially one will have to strive hard to focus one's mind on one's Beloved Deity. In the beginning it may not be possible to visualize the full form. Even then, one should not get depressed but should continue one's practice by trying to visualize only the feet of the Deity. In due course, one will be able to visualize the full form. Through the power of persistent practice, the form will become clearer and clearer. As meditation becomes deeper, the form will become full of life and may move and talk to the sadhak. The Beloved Deity may even appear before one whenever requested. This is real "Darshan" or God-vision. One's own spiritual power solidifies by the force of one's resolve and manifests as the Deity. Following this stage is the merging of the sadhak with the Beloved Deity through intense love brought about by constant remembrance of God and the renunciation of every other thought. From there, the Deity Himself will lead one to the final state of Non-dual Experience.

One of the young men: We have conversed with many scholars but none of them could give us very satisfactory or convincing answers. Mother has really opened our eyes. We are grateful to you, Mother, for clearing our doubts.

Amma: Suppose a person who is not a doctor teaches medicine and methods of treatment. The students would prefer to listen to a doctor. Similarly, classes for *sadhak*s and those who are spiritually thirsty should be given only by *sannyasins* and spiritual people; scholarly householders are not enough. Even after studying so many spiritual books and scriptures, they are still worldly people, aren't they? How can worldly people properly teach that which is beyond worldliness?

Mother is not here for dispute. Mother has spoken this much because She feels that you children have the inquisitiveness (jijnasa) to really want to know. The children here who are brahmacharins would prefer to do what is seemingly bad, having given up bondage, rather than to do what is seemingly good while remaining in bondage. Giving up bondage means giving up attachment. Once attachment and aversion are gone, there is only love. Attachment binds you and makes you a lustful person; detachment uplifts you and makes you selfless. Doing apparently bad actions after giving up bondage does not mean doing things like plundering and murdering but rather making a show of anger and other passions for the good of the world. Even when a spiritual person who has attained the state of Perfection makes a show of anger, his mind will be filled with love. He is like a burnt shell, a shell in appearance only which will crumble into powder if you touch it. His anger is only an external show which he displays for the good of the world. He will be a good disciplinarian, a perfect lover of the human race. Even the seemingly cruel actions which Krishna did were for the good of the world. The general good of the entire human race is the

Enlightened One's motto. He is not attached to a particular class, creed or religion. Whoever takes refuge in Him will be uplifted.

One cannot love and serve while remaining in bondage. There will always be some kind of selfishness. What a pity it is for people to remain as slaves to the world and worldly objects! Still, what false pride such people have! They think that there is no one greater than themselves. A cup of tea or a bottle of liquor is enough to enslave these "great men." The love which is experienced within the family is not selfless love. God alone loves us selflessly. We are saved if we become convinced of this.

The young men offered their salutations to the Mother and wished to take leave of Her. They were very contented. The Mother asked them to have their lunch in the Ashram before going, to which they happily agreed. The Holy Mother and the young men entered the dining hall. The chanting of the Bhagavad Gita was in progress as the food was being served. A few of the residents had not yet come. Noticing this, the Mother said,

Amma: Everyone without exception must come and chant the *Gita* and the other mantras while the food is being served. This is the best time to test one's patience. Doing actions while remembering God will become a habit thereby.

Again, having noticed some of the brahmacharins sitting in a haphazard way without keeping their backs erect, the Mother said,

Amma: The spine is our center. We should always be aware of it. While sitting or standing, the spine should be kept straight.

Lunch was over. The Holy Mother lay down in the dining hall itself. Devotees had already started coming to the Ashram as it was Bhava Darshan day. Many of them sat around the Mother, including Lutz from Germany.

One devotee: Is not *Advaita* the Supreme Truth?

Amma: For whom? Those who have reached that state can say that everything is One. Even then one cannot say that there is no duality.

There is duality even when we think, is it not so? One who has experienced that everything is One becomes silent. Then there is no one to speak. When you start speaking, there are two, or *dvaita*. *Dvaita* is needed to make people good. Mere speaking of *Advaita* will make people egotistical. *Advaita* is not something to be preached; it is an experience which one should live. Only through *dvaita* can one progress spiritually.

Question: On which point should one meditate?

Amma: Meditation can be done between the eyebrows and in the heart as well. Meditation in the heart is much easier. Sometimes meditation between the eyebrows can cause headaches and pain in the eyes. Tears might come from the eyes and the body may also become heated. Meditation in the heart will have no such complications.

Lutz: The breath stops during meditation.

Amma: (Laughing) The breath will become still when we get concentration. We may even feel that the breathing has stopped. Oh, son Lutz, if your breathing stops, you will die. Let us try to die first. (Laughing) Nobody has died because of meditating. If you die while meditating, it would be such a death that you would not take birth again. Meditation will save us from all kinds of agitation. One need not be a believer in God to do meditation. One can imagine that one is merging in the Infinite just as a river merges with the ocean. This method will certainly help one escape from being agitated.

Question: Spiritual institutions give importance to visiting hospitals. Why is this so?

Amma: It is good if spiritual people visit hospitals at least once a month, particularly hospitals where lepers are being treated. This will help make the mind stronger and softer as well. Increasing ones *vairagya* (dispassion) will give more determination to the mind. The heart will become soft due to compassion. It will help us understand that those people are suffering as a result of wicked actions performed in their previous lives. We will think, "This experience should not happen to me. For that, I should tightly catch hold of God. I don't want to stay in this world, O Lord, I only want to merge in Your Feet." We will feel compassion towards those who are suffering and be ready to help them, while also thinking that this disease should not happen to us.

Question: Scriptural studies are also necessary, aren't they?

Amma: There is a kind of game played with stones. You, my son, may know it. Previously, Mother knew a girl who used to play this game. It was really funny when she first played it because she did not know how to play it properly. Even without learning the game, she always wanted to play it. But she always played it incorrectly and foolishly. Therefore, the others would not even allow her to play with them. Only later did she learn it properly. If she had learned the game properly in the beginning, she would not have committed the mistakes, would she? That is why it is said that scriptures also must be studied. Only one who knows the path can travel correctly without getting lost. Scriptures will show you the way. They are pointers.

One brahmacharin: Mother, is *hatha yoga* good?

Amma: In the beginning *brahmacharins* should not learn *hatha yoga*. It is just like teaching them to lie. However, *hatha yoga* is good for householders for increasing their mental strength and to sustain their body. A *sadhak* comes to realize the Self by cultivating the attitude, "I am the Self, not the body." If he practices *hatha yoga* to make his body last longer, that will only help him to become more and more conscious of his body and this will pull him down from the path of Self-Realization. One can practice *hatha yoga* after the state of merging in the Reality. Thereafter, it is beneficial for the world if the body is sustained. *Hatha yoga* will be helpful at that time. In the beginning, pure love and devotion alone are needed. Bliss is gained when the sense organs merge in the mind through concentration. It is not obtained from exterior objects. Therefore, if you want bliss, try to acquire concentration. There is no point in running after *hatha yoga*.

2 January 1984

Vow of silence

Last night the Darshan was not over until four in the morning and the Mother went to bed at five. Neither lack of sleep nor irregularity in matters of food are problems for Her. All that She wants is the happiness of the devotees who throng to see Her. Every moment of Her life is dedicated to the suffering masses. The Mother eats Her lunch at five in the afternoon and even then, only one or two balls of rice or a few pieces of steamed vegetables. She has Her supper at five a.m. and has nothing later in the morning except perhaps one or two sips of tea or coffee. Even when She does take Her lunch or supper at those odd hours, She will be either reading a letter from a devotee or giving instructions to a brahmacharini or devotee concerning their sadhana. Or She may be consoling a devotee while making him or her feel that they are under Her protection, or possibly talking to a resident about the administration of the Ashram. The Mother says, "My wish is that even when I breathe my last, my hands will be resting on someone's shoulder, that I will be consoling and caressing someone."

Today after lunch Mother sat on the roof of the meditation hall along with some of the brahmacharins. Brahmacharini Gayatri was also present.

One brahmacharin: Mother, what is the significance of a vow of silence?

Amma: The shore is there to obstruct the waves of the ocean. What is there to obstruct the waves of the mind? That is the purpose for the observation of a vow of silence. The movements of the mind can be diminished through a vow of silence.

Question: Even though we don't speak while taking a vow of silence, the mind does not keep quiet, does it?

Amma: Haven't you seen the water in a dam? Though there are ripples on the surface, the bottom is calm. Nor does the water flow out. Likewise, while observing a vow of silence, there will be thought waves on the surface of the mind, but no energy will be expended or wasted. It is enough if you do not forget the goal. In the beginning, a vow of silence is indispensable for subjugating and sublimating the mind. Not much of the vital force will be lost. One's life span, health and vitality are decreased through talking. A person who breathes quickly will have only a short life span. This is why pigeons live only for a short time. More vital air is needed when we talk. At that time, the organs within us will undergo more wear and tear.

Another brahmacharin: It is difficult to understand everything that Mother says.

Amma: Faith is enough.

Question: Is everything that we experience the fruit of our past actions?

Amma: Yes. Every action that you do will have a reaction. Good actions will have positive reactions and bad actions will have negative reactions. The actions that we did in the past are known as fate in this lifetime. Fate is very powerful, but fate can be overcome to a certain extent by performing good actions in this life.

Question: Whether one is a householder or a *sannyasin*, food is needed to sustain the body; so what is a *sannyasin* to do?

Amma: A *tapasvi* need not wander in search of food. If his surrender is complete, whatever he needs will come in front of him. The spider, after weaving the web, sits in it. The prey which it needs will reach the web. Above all, a *tapasvi* lives to go beyond the body and to know the Self; a *grahastha* lives to sustain his body. A real meditator can live even without food. Whatever nourishment he wants will be had from within. He is not a slave to food like a worldly person; he is master of it. During Mother's period of *sadhana* She lived for months without even drinking water.

Two kinds of desire

Question: Both the desire to lead a worldly life and the desire to lead a spiritual life are desires. What is the difference between the two?
Amma: In worldly life first there comes the desire to pass the college examination. After that is fulfilled, the next desire is to immediately get a job. After one gets a job, next comes the desire to get married. If that is also fulfilled, then other desires follow one after another. Thus, there is no end to the desires of a person who leads a worldly life. It is like a never-ending circle; it goes on and on. The person toils and struggles to get all his desires fulfilled. In the process he dissipates all his energies and finally collapses. Even then, there still remains a chain of unfulfilled desires. But due to the weakness of his sense organs, he becomes unable to fulfill or enjoy them, and the individual remains dissatisfied forever.

But with a spiritual seeker it is not so. His one and only desire is to realize God. He does everything with that as his goal. He has no worldly desires to fulfill. He withdraws his senses from worldly objects and fixes them on the form of his Beloved Deity. He sees that form in whatever he beholds. He tries to do everything selflessly. Therefore, there is no dissipation of energy. All desires end in his desire for God. His desire is for the highest and if that desire is fulfilled, he can save thousands from the cycle of rebirth. He becomes like a tree giving shade and fruit to all humanity. He gives peace and tranquility to any person who approaches him.

The desire of the person who runs after worldly objects is of a lower nature. He is always selfishly motivated. He can neither save himself, his family nor society. He becomes an abode of chaos and confusion. But it is not only his own mind which becomes agitated; he creates the same agitation in the minds of others as well.

Both a thief and a doctor use knives. The thief, to fulfill his own selfish ends, kills people with his knife. The doctor, on the other hand, saves the lives of thousands of people with his. Likewise, the desires of a person immersed in the world destroy himself and others, but the desire of a spiritual person to realize God saves himself and also others from destruction. Such a person becomes eternally satisfied. That is the difference.

Now, what Mother wants to ask is why you children enter into disputes about a hundred things? Meditation is what is needed. Haven't you seen the gods and goddesses carrying weapons in their hands? These are hints about the sadhak's inner life. Maturity will come only through constant fighting with the lower mind. But in order to successfully carry out that inner fight, japa and meditation are necessary.

Brahmacharin: Mother, please forgive us if you find our doubts meaningless. To whom else can we turn to get our doubts cleared except you?

Amma: Do not worry, son, go ahead and ask.

Question: Was Vamana's pushing Mahabali down into the netherworld correct?[12]

Amma: What is the inner meaning behind it? Mahabali had performed intense *tapas* in order to merge into the Lord. In order to show the world what is true devotion, the Lord tested Bali to see whether

---

[12] Mahabali or Bali as he was called, was a king in ancient times. In order to test his devotion to truth, Lord Vishnu incarnated Himself in a dwarfish form as Vamana, a young *brahmacharin*, and came to a fire sacrifice which Bali was performing. Seeing Him but not understanding who He was, the king got up and offered Vamana a boon. Vamana requested only three strides of land using his stride as the measure. Bali asked Vamana to ask for something more but on refusal from Vamana, agreed upon the former's request. Lord Vamana then assumed His Universal Form and with the first stride, He covered the entire earth. With His second stride He covered the heavens. He then asked Bali where to place the third one as the entire Universe had been covered by the first two. Bali humbly offered his own head as the spot to place the Lord's foot. Doing so, the Lord sent Bali down to the netherworld and made him the king there.

he had any desire for external things. The Lord made Bali merge in Him. Bali first gave all of his wealth to the Lord. Then the attitude of complete surrender came. When even his head, that is, his ego, had been dedicated to the Lord, when he had no other desires to be fulfilled, it was then that *Bhagavan* pushed Bali's ego down into the netherworld. The inner meaning is that the physical body, the product of ignorance, disappeared and his soul was liberated for all eternity. Bali's ignorance was eradicated and his soul merged in the Lord. Whether in the netherworld or in heaven, the Self remains the same; it does not undergo any change or pain.

Question: Mother, what is the meaning of the saying; the world is a projection of the mind?

Amma: Whatever is seen is the projection of the mind. Suppose you have a dream in which you see that you are fighting with another person in the middle of the road. It is daytime, and therefore, many people assemble to see the fight on both sides of the street. Some reproach it while others encourage it, and some try to stop the fighting. As your opponent is stronger than you, you receive a lot of beatings, kicks and blows. Finally, the police come and arrest both of you. You are placed behind bars for three days. When you come out, you are full of shame, hatred and revenge. You cannot contain it. Just at the same time you wake up from the dream. You become very restless. You think, "What a disgrace! Now how can I possibly face my friends and others? I should not have fought with that man. I could hardly return one single blow." Thinking in this way, your mental agitation increases. Somehow you want to get out of the situation. Therefore you sit down and slowly contemplate everything and slowly realize that the fight, the road, the opponent, the policeman, the jail, the people, the shame, the hatred, the revenge, all of it, was nothing but the creation of your own mind. Similarly, all that we see and experience in this world is a long dream. It is nothing but the jugglery of the mind. When we awaken into the state of God-Realization, we will come to know this fact through direct experience.

When there is no mind, there is no world. In deep sleep there is no mind and therefore no "you" or "I," day or night, wife or children, cars or television, yesterday or tomorrow. Immediately upon waking up, the sense of "I" comes and then everything else follows. The goal of spiritual sadhana is to eliminate the mind which consists of thoughts and desires. The Self is beyond all these. To know the Self, the mind should be eradicated.

Question: What should be done if friends come and talk about worldly matters?

Amma: Let them talk. Children, you should go on chanting your mantra within and remember your Beloved Deity. While looking at your friend's face, you can imagine your Beloved Deity's face there as well. If you are sitting, you can draw a triangle or circle on the ground and mentally do archana to your Beloved Deity using stones instead of flowers. Remember the Self, your Real Nature, while doing each action. Before going to bed and immediately after waking up, meditate for some time sitting on your bed. Don't lie down to sleep. Lie down to wake up. Spiritual Realization is not possible without undergoing suffering. We are not perfect by birth. We should progress through action.

Don't row a moored boat

Amma: Children, you should give special attention to cutting the worldly bonds. (Pointing to a *brahmacharin*) That son says that he wants to go home every month. Once Mother sent him home in order to understand his mind. Afterwards, She did not let him go as She found that his attachment to his family remained. Had there been no attachment in his mind, Mother would have allowed him to go. How can a boat that is tied to a post possibly move even if you row it? It will move only if you row it after untying the knot.

Otherwise, what use is there in rowing? Likewise, no progress will be gained if one does *sadhana* while being attached to the family and the world. (Smilingly) One fights with Mother for not getting the intended result, the complaint being that Mother is not showering Her grace. Mother doesn't show any such partiality to anyone. All are equal to Mother. She can give each one only what they deserve.

One brahmacharin: (Hesitantly) Mother, can we see the movie, "Kumara Sambhava?" It is a devotional movie.

Amma: Children, you are watching a film when you sit in the meditation hall, are you not? Could there be a more interesting movie than this world around you? If only Mother could see that the screen of Her children's minds was white! Movies, even if they are devotional, will dissipate energy. Power will be lost even if you look carefully at something. It is better for a *sadhak* not to see devotional movies, especially in the beginning stages. Even devotional movies are not fully devotional. There are also many scenes which are capable of creating mental agitation.

A devotee who was a highschool teacher came and prostrated before the Holy Mother and silently sat near Her.

Amma: Not only that. There is no money here for such things. We can feed the poor if there is that much money. Worldly people simply waste money indulging in pleasures. How much are they wasting for trivial, selfish things like chewing betel leaves, smoking cigarettes and indulging in other bad habits! None of these people will spend any money on a good cause or even think that if the money which is spent on cigarettes and other indulgences is given in charity, a *brahmacharin* could be helped to live with minimum comforts. Many people are starving in our country. How many are without food, shelter, a proper education and without even a single penny to give their daughter in marriage? How much money are the politicians squandering away in the name of propagating their party and doing service to the nation! Everyone talks about service to the poor, but they do little to solve the situation. Spend the money which you unnecessarily waste on silly things to save the poor and needy.

The chain smokers, betel chewers, avid movie-goers and lovers of politics sincerely think that they can do a lot to help the suffering masses. Let them save a part of the amount which they spend on these meaningless things and use it to feed the poor, to build a small hut for the homeless, or to help a poor man perform his daughter's marriage.

At this point the Mother paused for a while and looking at the headmaster's face, smiled meaningfully at him. He had come to see the Mother only for a few minutes and therefore prostrated and took leave of Her. Having come out of the room, the headmaster told one of the brahmacharins, "Mother meant me, I am quite sure about it. I chew betel leaves and smoke a lot." He sighed and then he said to the brahmacharin, "I take this as Mother's command. Instead of telling me directly to stop it, She adopted a much more powerful and pointed method." From now onwards, this devotee began saving all the money which he used to spend on cigarettes and betel leaves and would either bring it to the Ashram in cash or in kind, or he would buy food for the poor and needy. Thus he completely got rid of his bad habits. Such incidents always happened around the Mother. Countless are the people who have completely refrained from all their bad habits by the mere sight of the Mother.

While talking to a group of people, the Mother knows how, when and towards whom to aim Her arrows. Aiming at someone who is sitting nearby, She might be talking to a person who is sitting next to him. Whatever is going on, Her arrow definitely hits the target and the right person will understand it in the right way. Sometimes the Mother will not tell someone to stop doing a particular thing directly, but in his presence, while talking to another person or to a group of people, She will mention whatever is necessary for him to hear. It will penetrate into his mind and transform him.

Question: Some Western psychologists say that spending time in solitude and meditation without being involved in worldly life is a mental disease.

Amma: Their perception is that the refuge for man is woman and vice versa. It would be difficult for them to live abandoning this idea as the guiding factor in their way of life. This is why they say that. It is difficult to change their opinion as long as they remain in this state. They will learn when they develop more spirituality. Westerners are unable to think of a world forsaking material pleasures. Their slogan is to enjoy life to the maximum; body, body, body. Some of them go a little higher, up to the level of the intellect. There they stop and do not move one inch further.

As far as a spiritual person is concerned, neither man nor woman is his place of refuge. Human beings are not a refuge for human beings. All human beings are imperfect and an imperfect person cannot protect another imperfect person. Both will struggle like a small snake swallowing a big frog. The only perfect being is God or a God-Realized Soul. Therefore, the real place of refuge is God or one's own Self.

Actually, those who live an exclusively worldly life are victims of the mental disease of worldliness. They waste most of their energy on trivial matters and have very little mental balance. A small problem is enough to upset them. They may even commit suicide out of desperation and are enslaved by sense objects. They have no real wisdom or peace of mind. A spiritual being conserves his energy and uses it to save thousands of worldly people from going mad by giving them peace and mental comfort.

Question: It is said that celibacy will create diseases like dullness or mental aberrations.

Amma: Maybe it is true concerning worldly people because they do not do any *sadhana*. If the conserved semen is not channeled properly, it may create problems. The spiritual person withdraws it inwards and converts it into purified, vital energy. He will not have any mental disease but will have only bliss.

One brahmacharin: It was I who made today's vegetable dish. Did Mother eat it?

Amma: Mother cannot eat anything that is tasty. Mother does not know why. The mind does not go in for such things at all. Children, how is it that all of you care so much about taste and other external things? It is That Taste which we have to get. Without giving up the taste of the tongue you will not get That Taste, the taste of Self-Realization. The taste of the heart will not be had without giving up the taste of the tongue.

One *brahmacharin* spoke loudly. The Holy Mother commented,

Amma: What noise is this? A spiritual seeker's voice should be very soft. He should talk in such a way that the person who listens will be able to hear it only if he keeps his intellect, mind and sense organs concentrated.

At this, one brahmacharin approached the Holy Mother.

Amma: What is the matter, my son?

Brahmacharin: (Referring to another *brahmacharin*) Somebody is fast asleep in the room. (All laugh.)

Amma: That is all right. Last night he kept awake until very late. Even then, to sleep in the daytime is not good for anyone. A *sadhak* especially should not sleep during the day. At that time the air in the atmosphere is polluted. That is why the yogis utilize the night for doing *sadhana*. Exhaustion will be felt when we get up after sleeping in the daytime. When we wake up after having slept during the night, we feel more vigor.

Brahmacharin: Sometimes it seems to me that Mother looks less vigorous. Is it only a feeling of mine?

Amma: Within, Mother is totally unaffected, always blissful and vigorous. But if those children who have surrendered everything to Mother do something wrong, that would affect Mother's body.

Since you children have dedicated everything to Mother, your wrong-doings will affect Mother's body. Children, your happiness is Mother's health. Mother even removes your fate by taking such *prarabdhas*[13] into Her own body. This also will affect the body. It is the law of Nature that the body must suffer and undergo change. Mother does not care about it. Let this body become like fertilizer for the spiritual growth of my children.

That statement really touched the brahmacharins' hearts. Some of them silently shed tears. Brahmacharini Gayatri could not control her emotions. There was a long pause after which Gayatri said, "You suffer a lot for us. Give part of your suffering to me."

Amma: (Looking at her lovingly and affectionately patting her on the back) Mother knows your pure love and innocent faith. But daughter, your body cannot bear even an infinitesimal part of the suffering that Mother's body takes on, not even for a moment. If I were to give it to you, you would collapse in a moment.

Question: Is it not the goal to go beyond all bondages?

Amma: Yes, to love everyone without getting attached. A spiritual person should become like the wind. The wind blows everywhere; it caresses and embraces everything without difference. It blows over fragrant flowers and foul-smelling excreta equally. It neither blows for a longer time over the flowers, nor for a shorter time over the excreta. It is not bound by anything. It is beyond all attachments.

One brahmacharin: Mother, there is no steadiness in the mind and concentration is not attained.

Amma: That is due to lack of *vairagya* (detachment). A strong and determined will is necessary to progress spiritually. Without this, you should at least have pure love and devotion towards your Guru. Attachment to the Guru will withdraw the mind from all worldly thoughts and objects. It will help to fix the thoughts on the Guru,

---

[13] That part of one's accumulated past actions which are bearing fruit in the present life is called "*prarabdha*."

and then steadfastness will slowly increase. Once the mind gets distracted from the goal or the Guru, it will immediately turn towards the objects of the world. Love is the force which binds the disciple to the Guru, and it is the same love which makes him realize God.

When the mind is constantly engaged in the thought of your Guru, what other thoughts can come? All other thoughts will be restrained; thus concentration will be gained.

Faith in the Guru and his words is another factor. Faith in the Guru will always protect you as a mother does. Faith that your Guru is omniscient, omnipotent and all-pervading is what is needed. This kind of faith will give you mental strength and power to cross over all obstacles that might arise on your spiritual path. Spiritual beings are the ones who have to guide the world. They should not be weak-minded. They should be like lion cubs, not like sheep.

Question: Why is it that good people always have to face opposition?

Amma: Good and virtuous people always fight against evil and vice. Society consists of more evil-minded and selfish people than good and wise people. Therefore, it is quite natural that they have to confront more challenges than others. To let yourself flow with the river's current is easy. But it is quite difficult to swim against the current, is it not? Likewise, the general tendency of human beings is to indulge in more and more evil. When one or two people come who want to propagate the message of *dharma*, it goes against the general tendency, just like swimming against the river current. Naturally, it will be a difficult task.

Protests and opposition which come from the outside are easy to tackle when compared to the protests and opposition which come from within. Because the outer enemy exits in the present only, you know who, what and from where it is. But the inner foes are more powerful because they gather their strength from the past as well. All the habits and latent tendencies come together to fight with you. You do not know who or what they are, or from where they come.

In most people, virtue is less powerful than vice. In other words, at present Maya is more powerful then God.

In the case of a devotee, it is God who creates the sorrows and obstacles in his life. As far as a true devotee is concerned, all the sorrows which he confronts will serve as a bridge to cross the Ocean of Transmigration. He takes them as a blessing sent by God to cut off his attachments to the world. They will serve as fertilizer for his mental flower which will blossom and spread its fragrance all around.

Another brahmacharin: Mother, when I asked in the office for a postcard, they didn't give me one. I want to write a letter.

Amma: Children, in the beginning stages a *sadhak* should not do things such as write letters or read newspapers. If it is absolutely necessary, you can write to your parents. They should get a little bit of consolation, shouldn't they? Don't write to other relatives or worldly friends. The friends will write back about worldly affairs and family members will write to you about family affairs. Then, even though you have left the house, what have you children renounced? Our *vasanas* will awaken when we read letters. If you write to them, then it is your turn to wait for a reply, and all that time will be wasted in waiting. In the olden days, *sadhak*s lived in the forests, in huts made of grass. They had no contact with the outer world. Therefore, you have to live in the midst of all this constant fighting, without becoming prey to it.

Image worship

The Holy Mother uttered Her favorite mantra, "Shiva, Shiva." The *brahmacharins* anxiously looked at each other, thinking that She was about to get up. Such occasions to ask questions and clear their doubts were not always possible.

As they all looked at the Mother, She went into *samadhi*. A few moments later, having travelled all alone in the highest plane of consciousness, the Mother came down, again uttering, "Shiva,

Shiva." The *brahmacharins*, who had been meditating during the short period of time when Mother was in *samadhi*, opened their eyes when they heard the Mother chanting.

Brahmacharin: Mother, Swami Dayananda Saraswati saw a rat stealing the *naivedyam* (the food offering to God) when he visited a temple, and found that the statue remained unmoving. He consequently decided that there was no God in the image and thus he started opposing image worship.

Amma: *Brahman*, the Absolute, is motionless. The statue also is motionless. If the statue is to move, a *Jnani* (a Self-Realized Soul) should make the *sankalpa* (resolve) for it to do so. They are creators. They are the ones who instill power and vital force into the statue. Because they give their power to the statue, the statue will even speak. In reality it is the power of that particular *Mahatma* which is reflected in the image. If they want to, they can even make an inert plank move and do other such things.

How is it that the all-pervading God ceases to exist in the statue only because the rat happens to eat the naivedyam? To say that God is all-pervading and to say, at the same time, that He is not in the image, is contradictory, is it not? If God is not in the image, then He is not all-pervading; and then, He is no God. God is there, even in the rat. Why can't you take it in this way -- that it was God in the form of the rat who ate the naivedyam? If you say that God is not there in the rat, then again it is imposing a limitation on God; whereas, God is limitless. What logic is there if you say that Ganesha does not exist because ants crawled into the molasses which had been kept as naivedyam for Him? (Smilingly) Ants and rats have no food ration card! Can't you imagine that God has allowed them to eat a little because of that? (All laugh)

Question: I have heard that different kinds of experiences will occur during the period of *sadhana* but I am not having any.

Amma: You will get the wages only if you work. You will get experience only if you do *sadhana*. After all, children, why do you bother about such things? Do *sadhana* as best as you can and do not think about the result. If you sit thinking about the result, then you will not be able to do your *sadhana* with all your attention. A *sadhak* is not supposed to care about such experiences. Run straight towards the goal.

Question: Is not *Advaita* superior even to God?

Amma: Children, you don't need *Advaita* now. Cultivate love and when the time is ripe, all other knowledge will come of its own accord. Devotion is the foundation on which you have to build your spiritual life. Non-duality is not something that should come from your lips. It is something which should be experienced.

There was a person who used to come every day to milk the cow in the Ashram. This particular day he did not come and so in the evening nobody had their usual evening drink of milk. Without saying anything to anyone, the Mother Herself milked the cow. Later She said,

Amma: Dependence on others will cause problems and pain. We should try to become self-reliant as far as possible. If we milk the cow ourselves, the hundred rupees that we give the milkman will be saved. What Mother thinks is that the same amount could be used to accommodate one more *brahmacharin* at the Ashram. Children in search of God are coming with intense longing, looking for a place where they can perform *sadhana*. Due to lack of sufficient funds, it is impossible to allow everyone to stay here. The money saved can be utilized for that. We may have to do the work ourselves. Even if we have to put up with a little bit of pain, let us serve and help others with good intentions.

Mother doesn't see anything as mithya (unreal). To consider a thing to be unreal means to waste it, not understanding its real value. Mother milked the cow not to gain money, but because She sees the goal and purpose behind doing so. She does not consider any work as lowly.

Mother noticed one brahmacharin beating his fingers rhythmically. She said,

Amma: Wherever they sit or stand, spiritual people should remain still. Don't move the hands, legs or body unnecessarily. To help you to achieve that, imagine that the body is dead. Thus in the beginning if you imagine that you are dead, it will later become natural. It will become possible to remain still. A spiritual being should strive to make the body as if dead.

On hearing the Mother's words, everyone sat still, without moving any part of their body.

Question: Mother, which is best, devotion or knowledge?

Amma: Devotion fortified with knowledge is what is needed. Look at the tree and the creeper. If the tree is not there, the creeper will not grow upwards. You should approach *jnana* through *bhakti*. *Bhakti* which is not based on essential principles (*tattwas*) will only help to bind one. That is harmful. There are certain creepers that keep the trees completely bound. Likewise, *bhakti* without *jnana* will only help one to get bound more and more. *Jnana* means to grow straight upwards. *Tattwa bhakti* is that which embraces *jnana* tightly. Then it will not come down.

Bhakti and jnana, though seemingly different, are not two. Bhakti is the means and jnana the end. Bhakti without jnana and jnana without bhakti are both harmful. In fact, bhakti is the easiest and least complicated way. Anyone and everyone can follow it. Bhakti culminates in jnana. The Lord of a true devotee and Brahman, the Absolute Reality of the Jnani, are really one and the same. Bhakti is usually prescribed for people who are predominantly emotional, and jnana for intellectuals. Jnana without bhakti is dry, and bhakti without jnana is blind.

On the seashore

Twilight was approaching. The Holy Mother, along with the brahmacharins and Gayatri, went to the seashore. Everyone sat facing the sun as it set over the vast ocean. The reddish rays reflected on the Mother's face, lending a special glow to Her already radiant countenance. As the sun set on the western horizon it looked like a big, red-hot iron ball floating on the surface of the expansive sea. The day slowly took its leave and gave way to the night. The ocean waves sang their never-ending lullaby. The Holy Mother and the brahmacharins were deeply immersed in meditation. It was truly a wonderful sight to see the Mother and Her children sitting together, meditating in this calm and serene atmosphere.

Here and there, a few fishermen stood watching the group. Who knows what they were thinking? The fishermen's children, who had been somersaulting in the white sand, stopped their play and stood still, gazing at the Mother and the brahmacharins. They were hoping to receive their usual share of toffees from the Mother.

After the Holy Mother and the brahmacharins had finished their meditation, the Mother sat, fixing Her eyes on the roaring sea. Without turning Her eyes away from the ocean, the Mother said,

Amma: The ocean is the *Akhanda Satchidananda* (Undivided Pure Being, Awareness and Bliss). The *Mahatmas* are the waves of That and its bubbles are the ordinary human beings.

A short distance away, groups of fishermen pushed their boats out into the water, and with great speed, proceeded to row away from the shore into the ocean. Like worldly people hurrying through the dense darkness of this world towards nowhere, the fishermen rowed their boats away into the ocean in the darkness of the evening. A flock of seagulls flew down and sat on the waves. The seagulls are like yogis full of detachment who are unaffected by the ocean of transmigration. The ocean cannot do anything to the seagulls. They sit only on the surface and can fly away whenever they want.

Pointing to a boat on the ocean, the Mother said,

Amma: Look, haven't you seen that in order to take the boat beyond the waves, the fishermen are rowing hard without paying attention to anything else. The people standing on the shore are encouraging them by waving their hands and making noise, but those in the boat aren't paying any attention to that. They have only one thought in mind and that is to somehow go beyond the waves. Only when they reach that point will they take rest, for beyond the waves there is nothing to fear. Children, you too are among the waves right now. You will be able to reach your goal if you proceed without paying attention to anything else, keeping only the goal before you. If you are not alert, the waves will lift you and toss you over. In the beginning a *sadhak* should not pay attention to anything around him.

The external world is there in the mind itself. The traits of all animals exist within us. Just like chameleons, human beings change their character every moment. The tiger, snake and all other animals are there within man and all these should be sublimated through sadhana.

Having come to the seashore, you should imagine a lotus flower on the horizon at the point where the sea and the sky unite, and visualize your Beloved Deity sitting on that lotus.

A sadhak should not speak unnecessarily. Power will be lost if he talks too much. Nor should he get angry. He should always be rejoicing in God. A sadhak should wear clothes which cover his entire body and should not converse very closely with worldly people. A brahmacharin who has left everything of the world, keeping spiritual life as his goal, should not enter any house without being invited in by the family. He should remain outside until he is given permission. After entering the house, he should sit only in the shrine room if there is one. If people ask him something, he should answer but he should not speak unnecessarily.

Do not be too attached to anyone. Brahmacharins should never sleep in the bedrooms of worldly people. Inhaling the air which is permeated with worldly vibrations will awaken worldly thoughts in us. Do we have the same mental attitude when we enter a temple as we do when we go to a night club? There is a difference, is there not?

Thoughts and subtle germs

The Mother continued,

Mother: Inside decaying objects, tiny worms and other creatures take their birth. When milk gets spoiled, small worms will be born in it. Likewise, subtle germs take birth according to the thoughts of human beings. In response to each and every thought of ours, subtle germs will take birth of their own accord. These germs will remain in the atmosphere and are capable of creating vibrations in the minds of others. Some day modern science will prove all this.

Children, in the beginning, a sadhak should not use a mirror or a comb. It is enough if you comb your hair with your fingers after wiping your head dry. Otherwise, time will be wasted. Not only that; instead of helping to remove body-consciousness, such actions will only increase it. We are trying to go more and more inward, not outward. By lessening external actions, we should make time to do sadhana. Our aim is to develop the inner spiritual beauty, not the outer physical one, is it not?

A sadhak should wear clothes of a single color. If you wear different colors, then the next thing will be to choose the nicest colors. Whatever object you perceive, it should be with the idea that it is your Beloved Deity. While handling books or clothes or while opening a door, mentally bow down, imagining that your Beloved Deity is standing in front of you. There will be no waste of time if you practice in this manner.

It was past six-thirty. The Mother got up saying, "Come on, children, let us go. The sea breeze at this time is not good for one's health." Everyone got up and returned to the Ashram.

After reaching the Ashram, the Holy Mother immediately began the usual evening bhajan. Having told everyone to sing the bhajan while visualizing their Beloved Deity in the heart, the Mother sang,

> *Through my mind, speech and actions*
> *I am remembering Thee incessantly.*
> *Why then art Thou delaying to show*
> *Thy mercy to me, beloved Mother?*
>
> *Years have passed*
> *But still my mind has no peace.*
> *O darling Mother, please grant me*
> *A little relief.*

Again She sang,

> *O Mother, for the satisfaction of my life*
> *Give a drop of Thy love*
> *To my dry, burning heart.*
> *Why, O why dost Thou put burning fire*
> *As fertilizer to this scorched creeper?*
>
> *Bursting out crying, how many hot tears*
> *Have I offered before Thee?*
> *Hear Thou not my heart throbbing*
> *And agony coming out as suppressed sighs?*

The songs were filled with pathos, the inner call of an aspirant to become one with the Supreme. Ecstatically singing the bhajans, the Holy Mother soared to the heights of supreme devotion. As Her feeling was reflected in Balu, he became intoxicated by the devotional fervor which pervaded everywhere and he burst into tears.

Rao also entered into the same mood. The singing reached its peak of devotion and supreme love. The Mother seemed to be sending out a never-ending stream of bliss. The brahmacharins and other devotees swam in it. There are no words with which to express the devotional feeling which pervaded the atmosphere.

The bhajan ended at eight-thirty. After vespers, the Holy Mother went out into the coconut grove and roamed there for about fifteen or twenty minutes, Her hands clasped behind Her back. There was an extraordinary seriousness and glow on Her face. During such occasions, no one dared to go near Her.

Once again the Mother came and sat in the sand in front of the temple. Hoping to hear more of Her nectarous words, some of the brahmacharins gathered around Her.

Brahmacharin: Mother said not to mingle with *grahasthas*. But sometimes you also scold us for not taking proper care of them when they come here. Why is that so, Mother?

Amma: What Mother said was to keep away from *grahasthas*. But you should always serve *grahasthashramis*. However, they must be real *grahasthashramis*. A *grahasthashrami* is one who leads a spiritual life while staying at home with his family. A *grahasthashrami* is one who has made his home (*graha*) into an ashram. Children, although it is true that the purpose of your life is to serve everyone without differentiating, until you acquire a balanced state of mind and strong discrimination between the real and the unreal, it is better for your own spiritual progress that you maintain this sense of difference.

The subject of grahasthas is very interesting. When the sun sets, small children are unhappy, thinking that the sun is lost. But when the dawn comes, again they rejoice, thinking that the sun has come back again. They don't know the eternal nature of the sun, that it neither rises nor sets. Worldly people are like that. With gain and loss, they rejoice and grieve, not knowing that nothing is really theirs. They do not understand the nature of their True Self.

5 January 1984

As it was a Devi Bhava day, the Holy Mother came to give darshan to the devotees in the hut. It was ten past nine in the morning, but before going into the hut, She visited the brahmacharins' quarters. As the Mother came out of each room, the brahmacharins who were inside would come out and follow Her. Suddenly She turned to a brahmacharin who was looking here and there and said,

Amma: A spiritual being should only look ahead. Looking this side and that shows a lack of concentration and alertness. When you walk along a road, look straight ahead, visualizing your Beloved Deity in front of you and proceed. Many things may be happening on either side of the road. Already there are many pictures in your mind. Do not take any more pictures with your mental camera. To remove the ones which have already been taken will take a long time. If you are adding more, be aware that the distance to reach God will increase.

Mother remained in Sreekumar's room for a while. Balu thought that it was the right time to clear his doubt. He asked,

Balu: Mother has said that a *sadhak* will have to suffer a lot if he re-enters worldly life after doing *sadhana* for a long time. Why is that?

Amma: A spiritual person will certainly have to undergo suffering if he re-enters worldly life. The subtle aura which the *sadhak* has developed around him through spiritual practices during his period of *sadhana* will bring calamity to the *sadhak* who re-enters worldly life. When he stops his *sadhana*, the *vasanas* which he was trying to subjugate will double in strength and cause a tremendous outburst of passion in him. When he fails to fulfill these cravings, negative feelings like anger and lust will overcome him and destroy his peace of mind, causing him to be like one gone mad. He will not have mental peace even for a moment. His or her family life will be an utter failure always troubled by obstacles.

Balu: Mother, some people have come from Germany today. I have just seen one of them standing in front of the Ashram smoking marijuana. Shall I ask him to leave?

Amma: Be patient. Politely tell him that Mother has said that he should not smoke marijuana here, that it is the duty of each one to maintain the sanctity of the place. Tell him that he is not free to do as he likes, that there are rules to be followed wherever he may be.

Balu left and returned within a few minutes. From the expression on his face, it seemed that his mission had met with failure.

Balu: Mother, I told him everything that you said but he became very angry and retorted, "I am my own boss. I won't obey anyone!" Then, he immediately left the Ashram.

Hearing this, the Mother smiled and said, "Everything is for the best." Balu could not understand what Mother meant by that statement regarding that egotistic and arrogant visitor. He therefore asked Mother,

Balu: Mother, what do you mean by saying this about such an arrogant person?

Amma: Wait and see.

Having said this much, the Mother went towards the hut to give darshan to the devotees.

6 January 1984

Cast off shyness

Last night the darshan finished at three-thirty in the morning. After that, the Mother met with a family of devotees who had been eagerly waiting to talk with Her privately. Following this, She went around to make sure that all of the devotees had something to lie down on. It was nearly five o'clock when She finally went to Her room.

Almost all the devotees who were staying at the Ashram this day had seen the Mother the previous day, and therefore, the Mother came only for the evening bhajan. After the bhajan the Holy Mother came to the dining hall. The supper was still being served. Today during the evening bhajan, Kunjumol, because of her shyness, did not sing when the Mother asked her to do so. Referring to this the Mother said,

Amma: Shyness is the first thing that a spiritual person has to give up. Shyness is a quality of women. Whether it is a man or a woman, once one comes to spiritual life, one should develop some assertiveness. (Turning to Kunjumol) What can be done if you, who will have to move in front of thousands of men some day, feel shy? Do one thing. Every day sing at least one *bhajan*. Mother will also make you deliver a speech in front of others. In this way you can remove this shyness of yours.

After saying that, the Mother walked out of the dining hall and went into the kitchen. Seeing all the cooking pots and other vessels lying in disorder, the Mother said,

Amma: Orderliness and cleanliness are very important. Every day when the cooking is over, you should wash the vessels and keep them in an orderly way. External orderliness leads to internal orderliness. You should always try to keep the surroundings clean and tidy. External disorder indicates your internal disorder. If things are in disorder, the mind will also be affected.

The Mother Herself started arranging the vessels in order. The brahmacharinis also joined Her saying, "Mother, we will do it," but She would not stop. Only when everything was clean and in order did She leave.

8 January 1984

Today just before the Mother arrived at the hut for *darshan*, Balu spotted the same German man who had arrogantly left the Ashram a few days ago. He was standing by the temple. Remembering the man's rude behavior, Balu felt a bit angry and avoided him. He thought to himself, "What business does he have here?"

At nine-thirty in the morning the Mother came to the hut to receive and give darshan to those who had come for the Devi Bhava. She was cheerful and fresh as ever. The Mother began calling the devotees one by one. On seeing the German man enter the hut, Balu stood near the Mother, expecting the man to create further trouble in Her presence. Much to Balu's amazement, the Mother received the man with love and affection. Smilingly She asked him, "Son, what happened? Which boss caught you?"

On hearing those words of the Mother, a sudden shock passed through his body. With an astounded look on his face, he gazed at the Mother and burst into tears. Mother continued to pat him on the back to console him, all the while having a mischievous smile on Her face. "Come on, son, do not worry, tell Mother what happened," She said.

Balu stood with eyes wide open watching the drama unfold before him. He could not make out the meaning of the man's mysterious behavior.

German man: (Weeping) Mother, it was you who made everything happen. After I left here the other day, I went to another town to the south with my friends. The very same day they left me there to myself. While I was sitting on the seashore smoking marijuana, two policemen suddenly approached me and put me under arrest. I was taken to the police station and put behind bars for twenty-four hours. I spent a sleepless night thinking of the arrogant way that I had behaved when I was here and wept to Mother for forgiveness. O Mother, please forgive me. You have taught me a good lesson.

He sobbed like a small child. Once again consoling him, the Mother said,

Amma: Son, it was out of ignorance that you acted like that. Do not brood over it anymore; you have regretted enough. Now forget it. Son, we should always try to cultivate humility. When the police caught you, you could not tell them that you are your own boss, could you? Similarly, if you do not stop when the traffic police ask you to, you may kill yourself and others. You cannot tell them that you are your own boss. Rules and regulations are needed for our spiritual development. We should lead our life in accordance with spiritual principles. It is the ego which says, "I am my own boss." Unless the hard shell of the ego breaks, Self-Realization is impossible. For that to happen, a *sadhak* should cultivate obedience first and foremost. Child, this repentance of yours has made your mind pure.

Upon saying this, the Mother wiped his tears with Her hand. After a few seconds, Mother looked at Balu who was watching the whole scene.

Amma: Now do you understand why Mother said that everything was for the best? He has regretted his mistake and has been transformed into a devotee. Isn't that good?

Balu silently listened to the Mother's words. He thought, "Mother, what do I know? You know that I do not know anything." He could not reply to the Mother but humbly bowed down before Her.

One young man wanted to dedicate his life to spirituality, but since he came from a poor family, circumstances would not allow it. When the Holy Mother heard about his wish and the impediments in his path, She said,

Amma: Even though one comes to spiritual life, if there is no one to protect one's parents, it is the son's duty to do so. If there are other children to take over the responsibilities, then it is all right. It is not necessary to obey one's parents if they are an obstruction to one's spiritual practices. A spiritual aspirant can serve his parents, but he should do so seeing them as his own Self. If there is intense detachment, then there is no harm in relinquishing the family, whatever the circumstances may be. In such a case, no effort towards renunciation is needed; it happens spontaneously. God will not make a true aspirant's parents suffer. God Himself will take care of them. A real renunciate becomes the benefactor of the whole world. Compared to a small family consisting of a father, mother, wife and children, the world family is much greater. Dedicating one's life to God for the good of the world is far superior than sacrificing it for the few people in one's family. But if detachment is not that intense, one should look after one's family while performing spiritual practices as best as one can until real detachment arises. Try to slowly detach yourself from worldly bonds.

Brahmacharin: Mother, what is true love?

Amma: Devotion imbued with wisdom is real love. That is what is needed. Love is of two kinds. Love towards the world and worldly objects is love of a lower nature. Love towards God is devotion, love of the highest kind; that is pure love. Everyone has love within him but it fully manifests only when it is directed towards God.

Question: Mother, why should one control one's diet?

Amma: It is very important to do so. Chilies, turmeric, salt, oily and fatty foods, mustard seeds, onions, fish, meat and other non-vegetarian foods will create more semen which, in turn, will cause more sexual desires to arise. These are all *rajasic* foods (those foods which increase passions) which will aggravate anger, lust and other negative tendencies. It is also not good to eat yogurt or drink buttermilk at night. Do not fill your stomach fully. Fill it half with food and one quarter with water; the other quarter should be left empty for the passage of air. It is better not to eat at night. If you feel hungry, eat some fruit. Sleeping immediately after eating will create problems.

The food that we consume has a strong influence on our character. Look at the traditional brahmins of India who do not eat any tamasic (that which increases lethargy) or rajasic food. Compare them with those who do eat such food. The former are relatively more sattvic (that which is conducive to clarity), calm, quiet and serene than the latter. Don't you know that food constitutes the body? The nature of the food that we eat will reflect in our physical and mental natures.

Question: Mother, why should one meditate on the aspects of God with form? Why not on the Attributeless *Brahman?*

Amma: Can you think of a quality, for example, love or truth, unrelated to a form? It is not possible to do so because qualities are formless in themselves. To think of a quality, we need an object which has that quality as its attribute. Then what can be said of the Attributeless *Brahman* which is beyond all conception? Our mind is so gross that we cannot possibly think of a God Who is formless, changeless and attributeless. Therefore, we need an object which is endowed with divine attributes. Krishna, Rama, Buddha or Christ are such Beings.

Our mind has the habit of always leaning on something as a support. As children, we are fondled by our parents and want to be loved and looked after by them. Afterwards when we grow a little, our interest is to play and be with friends of our own age. Then in school we have many other friends to talk to. Again in college we have our boyfriends or girlfriends to share our heart with. After getting married, our wife or husband is there to share our problems and worries. Thus till death, somehow or other we always have someone to whom we can open our heart. Such a mind which is dependent on others for its solace cannot conceive of a God who is formless and attributeless. We need a name and form to worship. So we say that *Brahman*, the Attributeless, is embodied in Krishna, Rama or Christ and that we should develop a relationship with Them. It is not Their bodies that we are adoring but rather the great ideals that manifest through Them.

Even to meditate on the Formless requires a sublime conception. Those who from birth itself are endowed with an extremely subtle mind can meditate on the Formless. But how many such people are there? Ninety-nine percent of the people are gross-minded. They have no subtlety at all. Can we ignore the fate of the majority for the sake of the few subtle-minded devotees?

Question: Is there any special benefit in meditating on the forms of gods and goddesses?

Amma: By meditating on the forms of gods, concentration of mind and mental purity can be gained. We will get the qualities of the god upon whom we meditate. The basic thing that one should strive to acquire is concentration and attenuation of *vasanas*. To look at one point with open eyes is also a good practice for gaining concentration.

Study of scriptures

Question: Mother, is the study of scriptures indispensable?

Amma: Children, everything will be attained through meditation. Even then, meditation coupled with the study of scriptures is usually better than meditation without it. The awareness, "I am not the body, I am the Self. Can anyone hate me or get angry with me?" will assert itself in the mind. Mental equipoise will be gained. If a coconut tree is grown by a person who has studied agriculture, the tree will grow without any harm coming to it. He knows when and how to use fertilizer and pesticide and also knows the remedy even if it gets infested with worms. The coconut tree will be ravaged if it is looked after by a person who does not know these things. Likewise, a person who has studied the scriptures will have the ability to control himself when dangerous thoughts come into his mind, by reflecting on what he has learned from the scriptures. If used properly, scriptures can lead us to Perfection without much trouble. However, it is usually seen that the study of scriptures without a Guru and without doing *sadhana* will only help to inflate the ego.

Question: Will God assume a form?

Amma: God is omnipotent and omniscient. He can assume a form if He finds it necessary, but eventually, He will return to His real Formless Nature. Ice cannot remain as such for long but will ultimately revert back to its original state as water. We make salt from sea water. It will not remain as salt but will dissolve and become watery after a while. Similarly, God, the Omniscient, Omnipotent and All-pervading, assumes a form for some time and then returns to His Formless Being when His purpose is fulfilled.

Question: When is the best time to enter into spiritual life?

Amma: Right now is the best time. Son, there is no particular time to enter into spiritual life. Whenever you have the strong urge, that is the best time. One who is determined will start immediately without wasting a moment. But do not wait until all your desires are fulfilled. That will be like waiting for all the waves to subside before going to bathe in the ocean. It is better not to postpone. If you postpone, you may never start. Postponement shows lack of earnestness. Either you should come when you are young, or you should come after a real spirit of renunciation arises.

Love is what is needed

Brahmacharin: I am always feeling miserable.

Amma: Hmmm. That is good. Melancholy! And that too, even after coming here! Go ahead, be miserable. Maybe that is what you need. It is only possible to give what each one needs, is it not? Worldly people also say that they are always miserable. That is good if it is caused by the anguish to see God. That is bliss, not misery. But if your dejection is caused by something other than that, it must be due to unnecessary desires. (Smilingly) Mother knows the cause for each child's sadness after they come to stay here. If Mother talks to one person, another one becomes sorrowful. If Mother praises one person, another one feels miserable. Another one is sad if Mother sits talking with *grahasthas*. Your misery is due to jealousy.

Desire is the cause of sorrow. Mother felt a desire for certain things when She was young. It so happened that such desires would be fulfilled immediately. Once when She saw a beautiful sari, Mother thought, "How heavenly it would be if Devi could wear it!" On that very same day a devotee offered a sari of the same kind to Mother. After that, Mother stopped desiring anything.

Having created desires, what a pity it is for a brahmacharin to be sorrowful. What is the difference between you and worldly people? One who is separated from one's beloved will always be thinking about them. The husband will always be thinking about his loving wife. Similarly, a sadhak should always think of his Beloved Deity. Do not let the mind wander towards other things. If you do not control the mind, misery will follow.

God undoubtedly exists. Even if one does penance for many births, it is impossible to attain Him without a hunger, a yearning to see Him. Love is what is most important.

The brahmacharin who had said that he was in misery sat with his head hung down. Later he told one of the other brahmacharins, "Mother knows everything that is going on within us as well as outside. We cannot hide anything from Her. She knew that my sorrow was due to jealousy, and by making me aware of it She has enabled me to overcome it."

The power of tapas

Question: Many people who come here say that their prayers to Mother always get fulfilled. Does Mother hear whatever things they say wherever She may be?

Hearing the question, the Holy Mother burst into laughter.
Amma: God is hearing all our prayers. In truth, the Lord knows each and every thought; He does not have to hear the prayers of His

devotees. He is all-pervading. People's thoughts exist in God only, but they do not know it.

Children, Mother is crazy; She doesn't have any powers. All powers belong to Him. But whatever a tapasvi says or thinks will certainly happen. That is the power of tapas. Through sadhana one gains power; one becomes a storehouse of inexhaustible energy and vigor. Even in trying situations, one becomes capable of doing proper actions without breaking down. It is at such times that one will have to save the people who are wandering in samsara.

Worms and germs grow in places where water stagnates and this will create trouble. If one goes near this water, one may become sick. The trouble is eliminated if such stagnant waters are directed to the ocean through channels. That is what we have to do; the mind should be made to flow towards God through sadhana.

Question: Once God is realized, there is only happiness, is it not so, Mother?

Amma: God is neither happiness nor unhappiness. Happiness and unhappiness belong to the world. God is Pure Bliss (*ananda*). Happiness is limited but bliss is unconditional. It is the very nature of the Self. It is beyond everything. Supreme Bliss is that in which you will become established forever upon realizing God.

One devotee: Is the costume really needed for *Bhava Darshan*?

Amma: Is that all? What costume is there which Mother has not donned? Children, when we see the uniform of a postman are we not reminded of the mail? Likewise, a lawyer's coat and a policeman's dress remind us of law and order. Therefore, dress also matters. There are many people who care about dress. Intellectuals may say that this is all nonsense, but how can Mother discard the majority, who are ordinary people, for the sake of a few intellectuals? The intellectuals should try to understand the real significance behind the dress.

Devotee: All costumes are Mother's.

The Holy Mother laughed in gay abandon as if intoxicated. It seemed as if She was unaware of Her surroundings.

Siddha and avatar

Question: Mother, is there any difference between an *Avatar* and a *Sadhana Siddha* (one who has attained the state of Perfection through spiritual practices)?

Amma: Yes, there is a difference between *Avatars* and those who have reached the state of *nirvikalpa samadhi* (absorption in the Self) through *sadhana*. It is like the difference between a person who goes to Bombay and returns immediately and a person who has been born and brought up there. If you ask whether they know Bombay, both of them will say yes. But the knowledge of the native is different from that of the casual visitor. *Avatars* come down with full awareness of Reality. They have no limitations except those which they themselves accept. It is not the same in the case of those who have attained that state through spiritual practice. They have certain limitations. We do not look upon them as equal to Sri Krishna, do we? Many such people lived during Sri Krishna's lifetime, yet they were all worshipping Him. The waves are not different from the ocean, yet they cannot be said to be the ocean itself. We can see differences amongst those who have gained the state of *nirvikalpa samadhi*. The conduct of a *karma yogi*, a *jnana yogi* and *bhakta* will all be different from each other. Even though they all experience *samadhi*, one can see different moods in them corresponding to the spiritual practices which they have been following. The moods that were seen in Sri Ramakrishna were not the same as in Ramana Maharshi. The same is true of other Realized Souls as well. Therefore, even though they were all great souls, their Realization manifested differently. This depends on the path through which they attained the goal.

Question: Sometimes we don't understand all that Mother says.

Amma: Those who have learned the scriptures and have the power born of *sadhana* will properly understand what Mother says.

Question: Mother, is it very harmful for a *sadhak* if he loses his semen?

Amma: Cow dung is burnt and mixed in water in order to make sacred ash. The pure ash is obtained by draining away the water. In the same manner, if molasses is kept in a pot with a small hole in the bottom, a fluid will ooze out from there. That is not real molasses. It is the useless water content which is flowing out. What remains will be pure molasses. It will not be so harmful if you lose your seed unknowingly. It is not the real seed that you are losing at that time. Real seed gets lost only when it comes out due to lustful thoughts. Even if the seed does get lost, do not feel upset. You should do meditation and *japa* during the whole day. If lustful thoughts still come, observe silence and do *mantra japa* the next day. Teach a lesson to the mind by observing a fast.

Another devotee: Mother, I have been doing *sadhana* for a long time now but there is no progress at all. Mother, you should bless me.

Amma: Son, when cooking oil is heated sufficiently for frying, you can hear a crackling sound. Until then we might feel that it is not yet ready, despite the fact that we have been heating it for such a long time. A little more time might be enough for the oil to become fully hot. In the same way, at a certain stage, a *sadhak* may feel that he has not gained anything even though *sadhana* has been performed for a long time. But a little more striving may be enough to see the result. Son, proceed courageously. God will take care of the rest.

One thing that you have to remember is not to dissipate the energy which you conserve through spiritual practices. Doing spiritual practices and at the same time indulging in worldly pleasures is like drawing water from a well using a leaky bucket. By the time the bucket reaches the top of the well, there will be no water in it.

Question: There is a saying that only a crying child will get milk.

Amma: So it is said, but it is the same mother who raises both types of children. She knows when they are hungry and will give them milk. The mother's mind will always be on the child who doesn't cry because she knows that he will not cry even if he is hungry. She will be thinking, "Oh, is that son hungry? Where is he? If it is the other one, he will cry when he is hungry. It will be sufficient to feed him then."

Question: Mother, what is the best time to do meditation?

Amma: Night time is the ideal time to do meditation. True seekers meditate at night. Ten hours of meditation in the daytime is equal to five hours of meditation in the night. Even if you sleep the whole day, you will not get the same freshness and happiness which you will get from a few hours of sleep in the night. This is because in the night the atmosphere is calm and quiet. There are fewer worldly vibrations. Pure air is expelled from blossoming flowers and relatively few worldly thoughts make the atmosphere conducive to meditation. In the daytime there are poisonous germs in the air. The atmosphere is completely polluted with the worldly thoughts of people who are running after material pleasures.

Question: Mother, what a pity it is that human beings in this era are so bad.

Amma: The ocean has no color; the color that we see is the reflection of the sky. In a similar manner, the feeling that others are of bad character is only because of the reflection of our own character in them. Son, purify your mind and then you will see everyone as good. Virtuous people see only good everywhere, while evil-minded people see only bad. Therefore, try to see the good in everyone. Then many others will do the same when seeing your example.

Question: Is it possible to lead a spiritual life without a Guru?

Amma: To a certain extent it is possible. But if the attenuation of *vasanas* is to come about, one must live in the company of a *Satguru*. The Guru's grace should be received. The aspirant himself cannot remove his subtle *vasanas*. To overcome adverse circumstances one needs the guidance, instruction and grace of a *Satguru*.

Life after death

Question: What determines the conditions of the next birth?

Amma: The next birth is in accordance with the thought that one has at the time of death. Only intense and unfulfilled desires will come at that time.

Question: Then would one become a house in one's next life if one thinks of a house at the time of death?

Hearing the question, the Mother exploded into laughter. The other devotees also laughed loudly. Finally the laughing subsided.

Amma: If one dies thinking of a house one will not become a house, but one may become a person who builds houses. Otherwise, if the thought is about a half-built house, one will take another birth to fulfill the desire of completing it.

Question: The *Bhagavad Gita* says, "One who leaves his body thinking of Me (the Lord) will merge in Me."

Amma: That is true. But son, do you think that it is so easy to think of the Lord at that time? To think of Him at the time of one's death requires life-long practice. Only one who has directed all thoughts towards Him through constant practice can think of Him at the end. Otherwise, what will come in the mind at that time will be the prominent, unfulfilled desires.

There was a rich merchant who was very cunning and wicked. Having heard the story of Ajamila[14], he thought that it would be

---

[14] Ajamila had led a virtuous life in his childhood but later went along the wrong path and committed numberless sins. At the time of death, he called out to his son in fright on seeing the messengers of Death. His son's name was "Narayana" which is a name of Lord Vishnu. Hearing their Lord's name, the messengers of Lord Vishnu came and released Ajamila

easy to merge in God at the time of death if he gave Divine Names to his children and called them then. Therefore, he named his three sons Rama, Krishna and Govinda respectively. He never thought of God nor did he do any spiritual practice, thinking that it would be enough to call the names of his children at the time of death. His sole intention in life was to somehow make a profit. Through corrupt and evil ways, he made a lot of money. Finally, when he grew old and was completely bed-ridden and about to breathe his last, he called the names of his children loudly, "Rama, Krishna, Govinda!" Upon hearing their names, they all came. The old man looked at their faces and asked, "What? If all of you have stayed home, who is in the shop?" Immediately after saying this, he died! It is the previously acquired tendencies and nature that guide us on the death bed. To think of God at that time is impossible if one's thoughts and actions were not pure while one was active in this world.

15 January 1984

Today was a Bhava Darshan day. People had already started coming before noon. Many inquisitive grahasthas and young men also came since it was a public holiday. The Holy Mother came to the darshan hut a few minutes past nine. The first person to go for Mother's darshan was a gentleman from a village north of Cochin. He prostrated to the Mother but did not get up. He remained in that position like a log of wood for two or three minutes. The Mother did a most unusual thing. She placed Her feet on his head. The man suddenly sprang to his feet and danced in joy. He was laughing and weeping at the same time. He finally calmed down after some time and sat near the Mother. Afterwards, when leaving the hut, he explained to the devotees who questioned him that he had cherished an intense desire that Mother should place Her feet on his head, and had

from the grip of the messengers of Death, declaring that one who repeats the Name of God at the time of death deserves Liberation.

decided that he would not get up after prostrating to Her until She did so. Intuiting his wish, the Mother graciously granted it. Even afterwards, the mere remembrance of this experience would send this devotee into ecstasy, much to the chagrin of his family.

Until noon the Mother received the devotees and sat talking with them. During lunch the Mother Herself fed all the devotees with Her own hand, giving each one a ball of rice. It was really a charming sight to see the Mother feeding the devotees with motherly love and affection. Having gone to Her room at one in the afternoon, the Holy Mother again returned at three. She sat on the temple verandah and as usual, the devotees sat around Her.

Faith

One young man: Isn't it blind faith to say that there is a God?
Amma: Children, everyone lives by faith. Having the faith that there is nothing harmful in front of us, we take each step. We do not place our foot down if we think a poisonous snake may be in front of us. Would you have started from your house to come here if you knew that there was going to be an accident on the way? Of course not. You set out because you had faith that there will not be an accident on the way. Isn't this blind faith? We eat food from restaurants because we believe that there is no danger in doing so. But there are people dying from food poisoning, aren't there? Life itself will become impossible if we do not believe blindly. We believe the bus driver and we believe the doctor. Thus, there are so many people in whom we believe blindly. Disbelieving everything is a kind of mental disease, isn't it? In certain kinds of mental illness, one can see the patient not believing anything. Life is possible only through faith.

Real faith, however, is different from the aforesaid ordinary faith. Faith should be born of meaningful principles. Only then can it be called faith. It was through such faith that our ancestors lived, abiding in God. None of them believed blindly. Those who have seen God directly become witnesses to His existence. Their testimony does not become invalid simply because we have not seen Him. Those who have seen Him prescribed the way for others to see Him. It is not right to reject their testimony without following their advice on a trial basis, is it? Isn't it a kind of blind faith to reject something without experimentation?

The young men remained silent. A few seconds passed.

Question: It is said that diseases can be cured using divine power. Is that possible?

Amma: The methods of treatment were introduced by the Lord Himself when He incarnated as Dhanvanthari (the first physician) in ancient times. Why did He do that? Because most people have the belief that disease will be cured only through doctors and medicines. However, the Lord will directly take care of one who has the attitude, "There is no one else who can save me; You alone are my refuge." The Lord's grace alone will cure the diseases of people who have that kind of faith and devotion. How many experiences are there as proof of this! If you don't believe all this, then gain conviction by sincerely taking refuge in the Lord and experience it for yourself.

Some say that divine power is not necessary, that the doctor can cure the disease. Couldn't it simply be the Lord who made available the help of a good doctor? However good the doctor may be, can he stop the soul from leaving the body? If so, let him hold his own soul back. Let him try not to die himself. In this way, we can see that it is the Lord who saves even when we say that it is the doctor.

Question: Can one force the mind to meditate?

Amma: To make the mind meditate by force is like pushing a hollow log under water. It will shoot up to the surface as soon as you remove your hand. The same is the case with the mind. If you force it to do something, it will revert to its original nature as soon as possible. That is the nature of the mind. Mere suppression or force will not help. You should slowly try to conquer the mind by giving it new ideas, and cultivating good habits in the place of old and bad ones. Control the mind by using discriminative thinking.

Anyhow, in the beginning stages of meditation, you will have to sit and apply a little force. Otherwise it is difficult to teach patience to the body and mind. Once you start getting a taste for meditation, to sit will not be difficult and slowly it will become spontaneous. Until then you must strive hard.

In the olden days the atmosphere was conducive to meditation. There was no impure air. But in those days one had to do more penance to achieve anything. Today the atmosphere has become polluted, but one will progress as a result of doing even a little sadhana if it is done sincerely.

Question: Mother, is *japa* by itself enough?

Amma: Remembrance of the form of God is also necessary. Do not do mere *japa* for a long time without also remembering the form. Otherwise the deity presiding over the mantra will get angry.

At that time, a brahmacharin approached the Mother and prostrated to Her.

Brahmacharin: Mother, news has come from home that a relative has died. May I just go there and come back?

Mother: Children, *sadhak*s should not go to places where there is death or places where marriages are taking place. If they go to a place where there is death, they will see people sorrowing for a non-eternal object. A peculiar smell will arise from the dead body which spreads germs which will harm the *sadhak*. There, the relatives cry over an illusory thing, and lament about the unavoidable and unsolvable.

What if you go to a marriage celebration? Everyone thinks about marriage. The children think about their marriage which will happen in the future. The elderly think about their marriage which occurred in the past. Whom to marry is the thought of young men and women. Thus the whole atmosphere is filled with thought vibrations of marriage. The mind of the brahmacharin who is in that atmosphere will unknowingly go to that world, at least for a moment. That may become cause for his degeneration. Therefore, during the period of sadhana, do not go to such places.

21 January 1984

At eleven o'clock in the morning, the Holy Mother unexpectedly came to the kitchen. She took a bit of the vegetable curry which was made on that day and tasted it. She found that it was a little too tasty.
Amma: (In a very serious tone) You should not add more flavor like this for the *brahmacharins*. What they need is the taste of the Self, and this is an obstacle for attaining that.

The Mother then came out. Hearing the brahmacharin talking angrily to someone, Amma warned him.
Amma: A *sadhak's* words will remain in Nature. Be careful. If you utter improper words, the reaction will come back to you. A *sadhak's* wrong-doings will evoke the wrath of God. The result of his errors will be multiplied by ten. How insignificant are humans before a cyclone. Likewise, nobody can say how great the power of God's wrath will be.

The Holy Mother went out and sat on the front verandah of the meditation hall. Meditation hour was over. Some of the brahmacharins came and sat near Her.
Brahmacharin: Mother, how many years of *sadhana* are needed to attain the Ultimate Goal?
Amma: Even four years are not needed to attain the goal if you do *sadhana* as Mother says. You can reach the destination sooner than others if you travel in a non-stop express bus. One who has the guidance of a Perfect Master and a strong determination to reach the goal will not commit mistakes. Such a person will be like the non-stop express bus. But it cannot be said how much time it will

take to reach the destination by a person who travels in an ordinary bus which stops in several places while picking up and dropping off passengers. In other words, it is difficult to say how long a person who has no Guru and who is of weak determination will take to reach the goal.

Question: Mother, what is the best time for meditation?

Amma: The time from five p.m. to eleven a.m. is good for meditation. If you meditate for one hour, you should sit silently for at least two hours afterwards. It is good to observe silence every morning until eleven o'clock. Energy will be wasted if you speak. Don't waste your energy like a person squandering his hard-earned wealth on mere peanuts.

Some people say that they have been doing sadhana for four or five years but still there is no benefit. Even while they sit in meditation, they are thinking of what they are going to say afterwards. In this way they waste all their acquired energy by indulging in worldliness. Afterwards they complain that they have not gained anything even after long years of spiritual practice. Energy will also be dissipated by spitting too much. Saliva is energy. But you should spit out the phlegm.

Once in a week you should live only on fruits. This will benefit both the body and sadhana. As far as possible, you should say "we" instead of "I." This will be helpful to reduce the ego.

Question: Why should one try to enter the spiritual world which is gained through so much hardship?

Amma: Who told you that it is so difficult? Difficulties arise only after entering into this impure body. *Sadhana* is not a suffering or a hardship for one who has the determination to reach the goal. Even if you feel that it is a hardship, the purpose is to eliminate all of life's other difficulties in order to gain bliss. For that, one has to undergo a little suffering. Why do students study? To get rid of all the hardships of study, and to obtain a permanent job so that they can live happily. Likewise, *sadhana* is done to remove all the difficulties of worldly life so that you can become a true servant of the Lord and the world, and thereafter lead a blissful life of mental equipoise.

Question: Even Nature has become polluted nowadays.

Amma: God's creation has not become polluted. It is human beings who are so. Through their evil thoughts and actions, they trespass Nature's laws and pave the way for their own destruction. Even animals, who live in harmony with Nature, are better than most human beings. At least a spiritual being should lead a pure and straightforward life. A spiritual being should be like a tree which gives shade even to the person who cuts it asunder. A spiritual being should be like the wind that blows equally over both excreta and the flower. Desires are the cause of *vasanas*. Therefore, you should control your desires. During *sadhana* a *sadhak* will become lean like a lizard. Later, if he wants, he can put on weight.

Wherever they go, sadhaks should either repeat their mantra silently or meditate. If it is a noisy place, they should sit in one place reading a spiritual book. Those who observe the disciplines correctly are the ones who really love Mother.

Mother got up and went to Her room at one-thirty. Again, at four-thirty, She came to the meditation hall. From four-thirty to six was meditation time. All the brahmacharins came, sat in their respective places, and started meditating. The Holy Mother closely observed them both internally and externally. By calling their names, Mother made those brahmacharins whose concentration had decreased become alert. To some She said, "See, you are losing your concentration on your form of meditation." To another one She said, "Be alert." It is Mother's habit to keep a few pebbles near Her while observing the meditation of the brahmacharins. She throws them at the brahmacharins to bring back their attention. Throwing one of those pebbles at a brahmacharin, the Mother warned, "You are thinking about something else. Open your eyes and repeat your mantra." Thus She sat there observing and instructing them until their meditation became deep. Bhajans began at six-thirty. The Mother sang,

> *O Beloved of Radha, Lord of my heart,*
> *Destroyer of misery and Support of all,*
> *Is it not Thee only,*
> *The Embodiment of Consciousness,*
> *Who has occupied my mind?*
>
> *Pleasure and peace, the intellect and mind,*
> *All household goods and*
> *A means of livelihood,*
> *Is it not Thee Who has kindly blessed me*
> *With all these?*

The brahmacharins and other devotees responded. The Mother abruptly stopped singing, feeling that some of the brahmacharins were singing without love and devotion.

Amma: (In a serious tone) Other than losing the power that you acquire through meditation, *bhajan* serves no purpose if it is not sung with concentration and love. Do not sing if you cannot sing with concentration. If the *bhajan* is sung with one-pointedness, it is beneficial for the singer, the listeners, and Nature as well. Later when the listeners reflect on the songs, they will try to live in accordance with the lessons enunciated therein. *Bhajans* should be sung with eyes closed. You should hear the song you yourself are singing and grasp its meaning. While singing, you should imagine that your Beloved Deity is listening to the song while sitting in your heart or standing before you. You should be able to shed at least one tear at the Lord's Feet while singing. During Mother's *sadhana*, She could not even utter the names of Krishna or Devi. If She did so, She would immediately become lost to this world. Mother desires to see Her children crying for God. That is how you can make Mother happy.

Having said these words, the Mother sang the rest of the song. The atmosphere became saturated with spiritual vibrations. It seemed that the Mother's instructions went straight into everyone's heart. They all lost themselves in the glory of chanting the Divine Name.

4 February 1984

It was nine-thirty in the morning. The Holy Mother came out of the meditation hall after sitting with the brahmacharins during their meditation. Some householder devotees from the eastern part of Kerala had just arrived. Among them were some new people. It seemed that they were very interested in seeing the Holy Mother. As the Mother came towards them, the devotees became very happy. They all prostrated to the Mother and one elderly devotee who used to visit the Ashram frequently said, "Mother, we brought a few new people with us (pointing to three middle-aged people). Though they are from the same town as we are, these three work abroad. When we told them about Mother, they wanted to see you immediately."

Her countenance lighting up with a benign, unfading smile, the Holy Mother affectionately stroked each of them on the arm. As She patted the third man, the Mother said, "Don't worry, son, you will get another job by the time you get back." In amazement he looked at the other devotees and again turned towards the Mother. He was about to say something to Her, but by that time the Mother had already proceeded towards the darshan hut calling, "Come on, children."

The Mother Herself spread a mat on the floor for the devotees to sit on and then She Herself sat on the cot. But the next moment She got up and sat on the floor with the devotees. Her innate simplicity, humility and innocence were always an attraction and a source of inspiration for the devotees. When everyone was seated, the surprised devotee asked,

Devotee: Mother, for the last twenty years I have been living in America with my wife and children. I hardly had any contact with my native town. For many years I have worked for a big firm, but last year, due to some misunderstandings, I lost my job. Since then, I have been searching for another one. Mother, my question is how did you come to know about the whole thing?

As he finished the last sentence his eyes filled with tears and his voice became choked. The Holy Mother, who was smiling all the while, looked at him calmly and said,
Amma: Son, forget about it. You will get another job which will be awaiting you by the time you get back. It is enough for you to know that.

As the devotee sat amazed and overwhelmed, the elderly man who had brought him said, "Sreedhar, what you have experienced is nothing. You are yet to experience many more wonders." Uttering, "Namah Shivaya," the Holy Mother said,

Amma: Children, Mother doesn't know anything. The only thing She knows is that She doesn't know anything. Everything happens because of the children's innocent devotion and pure intentions.
Devotee: Mother, only you can say that. That is your nature.

Exactly as the Mother had said, the gentleman did, in fact, receive the appointment order for the new job the very next day after his return. He wrote a very touching letter from the States in which he said, "O Mother, O my God, what made you shower so much grace upon this insignificant child of yours? As Mother had said, the very next day after returning here I received an appointment order. Holding that in my hand, I saw Mother's smiling and compassionate face. I could not control the stream of tears that flowed from my eyes. Even now, as I write this letter, I am offering flowers in the form of tears at Mother's lotus feet."

Another devotee: Mother, one of my friends tried to destroy my faith in you even though he has not even seen Mother.

Amma: Do not try to argue with such people. Immediately leave them. If you remain with them, they will create agitation in your mind. Their arguments themselves are born out of faith, the faith that they can corner the believers with their arguments. They believe that there is no God. That belief itself is a faith, but a negative one. Protesting and revolting against anything and everything, such people will destroy their own lives. Anyhow, one day or another, in this birth or in any of the coming births, they must call God. When bitter experiences toss them up and down, when they become totally helpless in life, then they will call God.

Destroying someone's faith is a sin equal to the killing of a pious brahmin. Why should those who cannot save anyone shatter the faith of others? Anyhow, do not trouble yourself by worrying about such people. God will take care of them. Their mental makeup is their own. Let us proceed with our own. Such occasions can be used to test the strength of your own faith, to see whether it will shake or not upon hearing their words. Son, if they have the faith that they can shatter someone else's faith, let it be your faith that nobody can shake yours.

Another devotee: The spiritual path is very difficult. One does not even know how long one should strive.

Amma: Son, everything is in the hands of Time. One should perform one's *sadhana* sincerely and wait patiently. If you work hard, certainly you will get the result. Are you not familiar with the saying, "Bhishma's vow and Bhagirati's efforts." Bhishma of Mahabharata fame stood by his vow of celibacy inspite of all temptations, and finally he attained Liberation. Likewise, Bhagirathi, a king of ancient India, persisted in his *tapas* in order to bring down the celestial river Mandakini to earth so that it would wash the ashes of his ancestors whose souls would then attain peace. He succeeded and legend has it that the present-day Ganges River is that river. Every aspirant should have the firmness, courage, persistence and patience which Bhishma and Bhagirathi had.

It is good if one starts when one is young. If children between the ages of five and twelve come to spiritual life, they can gain spiritual experience before the age of twenty-five. If intense spiritual practices are done, one will start experiencing glimpses of one's real nature.

Question: Mother, why is it said that it is not good to sleep during dusk? And why do people chant the Divine Name at that time?

Amma: During the twilight hours, the atmosphere is filled with polluted air. It is the time when day and night meet. Thieves will think of the thefts that they want to do in the night. It is a time when different kinds of passions arise in pleasure seekers. In order to overcome these negative vibrations and keep one's mind unaffected and serene, it is better to focus one's attention on the Supreme Lord. One should not sleep at this time either. That will create a tendency always to sleep at that hour. One should chant the Divine Name and glorify the Lord. By doing so, the atmosphere will be purified and one will become peaceful and tranquil, keeping the mind concentrated on the single thought of God.

Question: Isn't it due to lack of self-confidence that one places so much faith in the Guru?

Amma: Self-confidence is good but what if it is only egotism? The difficulty in taking refuge in the Guru is due to the fact that the ego does not agree to surrender itself, is it not? Our discrimination has not developed properly. What is real confidence and what is not? We need someone who has real Self-confidence, the confidence born of awareness of the Real Self. Such a person can weigh the validity of our self-confidence and make corrections if necessary.

However long excreta lies in the sun, unless the wind blows on it, its bad smell will not go. However much tapas one does with the attitude of "I am a great tapasvi," the attenuation of vasanas will not take place. For this, the Guru's grace alone is needed. To go to an unknown place, one must put one's faith in a guide. When such is the case for reaching a physical destination, what could be the objection to placing one's faith in a Realized Soul in order to reach the supremely subtle and mysterious Inner Reality?

As instructed by the Mother, a brahmacharini brought a decoction made with pepper, ginger, molasses and basil leaves. The Mother drank a little and put it down.

A householder devotee: Mother, you should tell the neighbors not to soak coconut fibre in the backwaters surrounding the Ashram. It smells terrible.

Amma: Son, there is no bad smell when there is the attitude that it is "mine." Nobody cares about the putrid smell of one's own wound. With how much affection do we remove the excreta of our own child. Sometimes we might even vomit on our own body. Are we not accepting all those without complaint? Once the attitude of "mine" comes, then none of these are a problem at all. Think of the coconut fibre as ours, (Mother laughs) then there will not be any smell. (Laughter)

When we are working in someone's factory, we will always try to skip work. We will have little enthusiasm and feel tired quickly. But if it is our own factory, the attitude changes. Then, even if we can't eat or sleep, we will be enthusiastic. There will be no fatigue because it is our own. If you develop that attitude of "mine" towards everything, then all problems will disappear.

A new devotee: Mother, I have visited many spiritual places but have received nothing.

Amma: Children, reverential devotion should be coupled with the cultivation of a loving relationship towards your Guru. Reverence is helpful for our progress but real benefit will be gained only from that bond with the Guru. Without that, there is no meaning in complaining, "I received nothing." It is difficult for a seedling to grow if you plant it in the midst of densely growing trees. It will have to bend to this side and that in order to get sufficient sunlight. If the trunk is crooked, a boat or any other such thing cannot be made using the wood from that trunk. The tree would have grown straight if there had been no obstacles to its getting light. We can easily and directly reach the goal if we remove the obstacles beforehand. To achieve that, attachment to the *Satguru* is necessary. That will rid us of all other attachments. Those who wander from one Guru to another are not fit for spirituality.

New devotee: Mother, what should I do?

Amma: Crying to God for five minutes is equal to one hour of meditation. If tears are not coming by themselves, try to cry by thinking, "Why am I not able to cry?" Son, try to develop devotion. That is the easiest way.

Question: What is the difference between spiritual bliss and material happiness?

Amma: It is like the difference between the water in the river and the water in the drain. You can no doubt quench your thirst by drinking drain water, but afterwards you will fall ill. If you drink river water, your thirst will be quenched and you will not become sick.

Question: What are the scriptures for?

Amma: Scriptures are like a map. Knowing the path, we can travel in unfamiliar strange places. Otherwise, there will be delay and we will wander about unnecessarily.

Sraddha (attention)

One of the devotees asked the Mother's permission to sing a song in front of Her. Mother said, "Sing, sing. Mother is happy to listen to God's Name." He sang,

> *O man, who craves for the pleasures of this world, do you have peace even for a moment? This precious human birth is not for that, but has a sublime purpose. Just as a moth sees a flame and jumps into it, you get deluded by*

the illusory objects of this world and begin to end your life without reaping any benefit.

That Ultimate Goal can be reached only by relinquishing pride and the desire for wealth and wife. O man, that is the only way to escape from this bondage.

Hearing the song, the Mother went into deep samadhi. Tears of bliss rolled down Her cheeks. The song and the Mother's high spiritual mood created a meditative atmosphere. Some devotees and brahmacharins meditated while others sat gazing at the Mother's blissful face. A few minutes passed and the Mother opened Her eyes uttering "Shiva, Shiva." It seemed that the Mother was struggling to come down to the mundane world again.

Amma: (After a long pause) Mother always maintains the attitude of a child while singing. If that attitude is not there, the mind will completely merge with God and then afterwards it will become very difficult to come out.

Some of the *brahmacharins* were observing silence and fasting on this day. When the Mother saw one of the *brahmacharins* passing by the side of Her hut, She asked him, "Son, are you keeping silent today?" As an answer, he nodded his head in the affirmative and continued walking. As he was coming back, the Mother again enquired, "Son, did you eat anything today?" Without thinking, the *brahmacharin* answered, "No." Immediately he realized his foolishness. Forgetting that he was observing a vow of silence, he had spoken. The Holy Mother and the other devotees burst into laughter.

Amma: Mother was testing to see how much *sraddha* (attention) you have. Children, you may feel that as it is Mother who is asking, why can't I talk? (Looking at the devotees) He is not at fault. (To the *brahmacharin*) Even then, you should be careful; Mother will test you like this. Children, you should always proceed with discrimination.

Question: Mother, what is the benefit of following a controlled diet?

Amma: A controlled diet is good in every way. The body is made up of food. The good and bad qualities of the food will reflect in the body. As the body and mind are interdependent, whatever happens in the body will affect the mind, and vice versa. Do not use too much vegetable curry in your food. Use just enough to mix the rice together. If too many spices like chilies and tamarind are eaten, there will be an increase in semen which, in turn, will create more passion.

Seeing one brahmacharin sitting idle, Mother called him near.

Amma: Son, do not sit idle like this; God will get angry, and bad thoughts will arise in you. It is much better if you dig ditches and fill them again than to sit idle. How much work is there to do if you really look. You should spend your time doing some physical work if you do not have the mind to do meditation and *japa*. Sitting idle means letting the mind brood on unwanted things.

Brahmacharin: (In a sad tone) Mother, now and then there is a break in my *sadhana*.

Amma: Even if honeybees are sitting on the dates, he who desires them will somehow climb up and get the fruit. He who is intent on the goal will move forward and proceed, overcoming all the adversities.

Question: Is the graveyard a fit place to do *sadhana*?

Amma: Yes, it is. Normally a graveyard is very peaceful and calm. That is why it is recommended as a good place for meditation. Usually graveyards will be in a remote corner away from the noisy town or city. Therefore, the tense and chaotic vibrations of the city will not be there. Human beings with all their negative thoughts and vibrations are not there. Therefore, the atmosphere is conducive to meditation. But one needs mental strength and courage to sit there. The graveyard is also beneficial in reminding us about the transitory nature of life. Using ash from the cremation grounds is helpful in protecting one from poisonous germs.

Question: Doesn't a pilgrimage to holy places benefit a *sadhak*?

Amma: In the beginning it is good for *sadhaks* to go on a pilgrimage. Travelling in a spirit of renunciation will be an aid to understanding the nature of the world. But do not do too much travelling. It will become a habit, and then it will become difficult to do *sadhana* sitting in one place. Without wasting time, it is better to stay in one place and do *sadhana*.

In the olden days, however far it was, people used to walk all the way to the pilgrim center. Along the way they would stop here and there to take either food or a little rest. Whatever came to them of its own accord was accepted as God's prasadam and they were content. They bothered little about their bodily needs, comforts and climatic changes. Pilgrimages were undertaken with an attitude of renunciation. It would take months, sometimes even years, for them to reach the pilgrim center. Due to their renunciation and detachment, by the time they reached their destination, they would have gained a lot of mental maturity and spiritual advancement. That is why it is said that one who goes to Kasi will get Liberation -- because of the way the pilgrimage was performed. Now everything is gone. Nowadays pilgrimages are more or less like picnics. If one travels about without having acquired the energy born of spiritual practice, one will just get tired.

Question: Why is it said that *sadhaks* should not eat certain foods?

Amma: It is because some foods are not helpful for developing positive qualities. However, it is difficult to say that a particular food should not be eaten at all. The nature and habits of human beings will differ from place to place as will the climate. *Sadhaks* who live in hot places will not eat certain vegetables that will heat up the body. Those who live in the Himalayas will eat them because it is cold there. Similar is the case with tea and coffee which may be considered as stimulating in a hot climate but as a necessity in a cold one.

Question: Nowadays sudden changes occur in the climate. Why is it so, Mother?

Amma: In the olden days the atmosphere was purified by performing Vedic rituals and sacrifices. But today no such practices exist and the atmosphere is polluted; it is filled with poisonous germs. Everything has become unnatural and artificial. People live out of harmony with the laws of Nature. Though devoid of a discriminative intellect, animals live in harmony with the laws of Nature. But the so-called intelligent human beings continuously break those rules and lead a less than animal life. The human mind has lost its harmony. In the olden days, this harmony was kept up through spiritual practices and righteous living. Now that is gone and Nature also has started reacting.

When trees diminish, rain also becomes less. Even the rain that does come, comes at the wrong time. Similar is the case with sunshine also; either it will be too much or too little. It is all because of the evil doings of human beings; no one else is to blame.

Vows

Question: Mother, what are vows for?

Amma: The atmosphere will be more polluted on certain days such as the eleventh day of the lunar month and the day of the full moon. It is to escape from this pollution that vows are observed on these days. Importance should be given to *sadhana* on these particular days, because on such days our mind can become more concentrated. Just as there are planets outside, there are subtle planets surrounding each organ of our body, whose movements are similar to those of the planets going around the sun. More concentration can be gained when these subtle planets reach a certain state of vibration. Only fruit should be eaten on these particular days since they are less affected by the atmospheric pollution due to their having skin. The polluting effect will be greater on grains and vegetables. In addition, you should remain silent on these days. The more you talk, the

269

more you breathe in the polluted atmosphere's air. Mental control will increase when you lessen food, and concentration will increase.

One devotee: In many ashrams there is no importance given to *sadhana*. Book learning is most important.

Amma: *Sannyasins* and ashramites of the modern age think that Realization is the same as the study of the scriptures. They give more importance to preaching than to meditation and *japa*. The result is that they become egotistical. Mother is not saying that preaching is useless, but without acquiring

any spiritual power through *sadhana*, how can one's preaching be effective or useful? The subtle aspects of the scriptures can be grasped only if *sadhana* is done. If one studies the scriptures in the very beginning, then later one cannot sit and meditate. One's desire will be to teach others. The attitude will be, "Am I not *Brahman*? Then why should I meditate?" Even while meditating, the ego will rise up repeatedly.

5 February 1984

Today was a Devi Bhava day. Though it was a sunny day, the weather was nice and cool and the sea breeze which blew from the west had a soothing effect. The Holy Mother was in the coconut grove at eight-thirty in the morning. It seemed that She wanted to be alone. At first She walked to and fro by the side of the backwaters. Then, after some time, She sat on the bank and became absorbed in Her own world of Pure Consciousness.

At this time a group of devotees consisting of young men, elderly people, women and children entered the Ashram premises. They were very happy when they saw the Mother sitting in the coconut grove. They wanted to go and meet Mother there but Brahmacharin Pai prohibited them, saying, "No, please, don't go to Her now." They were a bit annoyed, but as there was no other choice, they waited.

It was nine o'clock and still the Mother did not move. Pai, with soft steps, walked towards Her and looked at the Mother's face. She was in the same mood as before. The sun's rays filtering through the palm leaves and the blissful smile which danced on the Mother's countenance lent a divine beauty to Her being. Pai remained gazing at Her face for a long time. He turned and sat at a distance watching both the Mother and the devotees in order to prevent them from going near Her.

Finally around nine-thirty the Mother moved slightly. Pai, who had been watching Her closely, went near. The Mother was sitting with eyes opened. He waited for a few more minutes until She turned around and looked at him. The Mother smiled and was about to ask him something when She saw the devotees who were anxiously waiting to come near Her. The Mother waved Her hand and called them. That was enough; in a moment all of them came running.

Everyone prostrated to the Mother after placing before Her the fruit which they had brought as an offering. The Holy Mother asked all of them to sit down. When they were all seated, the Mother lovingly inquired, "Children, have you had your breakfast?" One devotee replied, "No. Today, whatever Mother gives is our breakfast." Uttering "Shiva, Shiva," the Mother gave one banana to each devotee. Everyone was very happy. Another devotee said, "Mother, you should also eat something." Smiling at him, the Mother took a small piece of banana and ate it.

At this point, one devotee said, "Mother, may I ask a question?" Mother gave Her consent through a smile. When satsang began, some brahmacharins also came and sat with Her.

Self-effort and grace

Question: Can everything be gained through human effort alone?
Amma: Nothing will be gained without effort. But we can only put forth the effort. It is God who has to give the fruit. To open the lock

271

we should go to the locksmith's workshop. If we have to open the lock of the ego, which is made of our likes and dislikes, we must get the key which is with God. However much we work, nothing will be gained without God's grace.

During Her childhood, Mother and the children from the nearby houses used to play a game. Everyone would hit one person's palm and then run. The person who comes to catch us cannot do anything if we reach a certain coconut tree. They will stand waiting for us to let go of the coconut tree. Now and then, we will run, leaving the tree to be chased by the person who comes to catch us. But again, if we hold on to the coconut tree, he cannot catch us. In the same manner, nobody can do anything to us if we keep holding on to God. Then there is nothing to fear. But if we let go of God, then the objects of the world will haunt us.

Question: Can one reach the goal through faith in the Guru?

Amma: One can reach Perfection through faith in the Guru, but external love alone is not sufficient. Devotion strengthened by knowledge of spiritual principles is needed. Dedication of the body, mind and intellect is required. If one has faith in and obedience to the Guru coupled with knowledge of spiritual principles, *vasanas* will quickly get destroyed.

There is no point in strutting about making a display of one's devotion to the Guru and prayers to God. Sincerity is needed. One should cry and pray to God thus: "O Lord, don't You see me lying down below? O Lord, shower Your grace upon me through Your Hands of thousands and thousands of stars. O Lord, please give me the strength to remember You always. O Lord, give me sorrow so that I will constantly remember You. You alone are my refuge and consolation. How blissful is Your divine world! How beautiful it is! Lift me to Your world of thousands of twinkling stars. Do You not see the ferocious animals of lust and greed coming to swallow me? Are You not seeing me enveloped by poisonous germs and enduring tortures?" Such prayers will quickly bear fruit.

One brahmacharin: Mother, do you intend to establish new ashrams in different places?

Amma: Children, it is not necessary for you to think about ashrams and money. Don't worry, all will come at the right time. What you have to do is to reach the goal of life through *sadhana*.

One devotee: Mother does not reveal certain things so easily.

Amma: Spiritual matters should not be fully told to everyone. Some curiosity should remain in them. We should not make anyone feel satiated.

Achara - code of conduct

Question: Is it necessary to get entrapped in customs forever? Should one not go beyond them?

Amma: Good customs should be observed at least to set an example to the world. If spiritual people do not respect and practice *acharas*, who else will give importance to them? *Acharas* are necessary for a *sadhak*'s spiritual progress. Just as there is a way to act in front of a policeman, there is also a way to conduct oneself before a Guru, elders or in a temple or holy place. Customs will instill a sense of humility and obedience in a *sadhak* which will be an asset in his or her spiritual life.

Previously Mother made no differentiation between men and women. She was really crazy. Then the brahmacharin children came to stay and the Ashram came into existence. It was at that time that Mother started paying attention to acharas. Only if Mother acts as an example will the brahmacharins and others follow. God will make rules and require discipline but He is never bound by that.

One devotee: Mother, it seems that a devotee or *brahmacharin* who visited here from another ashram didn't like the huts and the minimal facilities.

Amma: Having been attached to another ashram first, wherever else one may go, that attachment will remain. This will incline one to find fault with other places. Only through discrimination can one escape from this.

A sadhak: Mother, what is the way to avoid doing that which is wrong?

Amma: Son, you know in your mind that what you are going to do is wrong. Then why should you still do it? Use your discrimination and try to withdraw your mind. If you are mentally weak and have a tendency to do something wrong, then physically remain away from places where you will be tempted.

God will not reside where there is ego and selfishness. If these are there, God will move a thousand feet away from us. He will come close if we call sincerely. Just one moment is enough to jump into the well. The difficulty lies in climbing out. To lose God is easy, but to regain Him is difficult.

Character is most important

Amma: If you want to gain God, the *vasanas* should be conquered and a good character should be developed. Action is what gives value to a person. Even if one is an I.A.S. officer (Indian Administration Service), others will give him the status of a peon if he commits a crime. Good character is most important. Gradually, you should win over the *vasanas* and the goal should be reached.

As it was Bhava Darshan day, people continued to come. The conversation ended and the Holy Mother then called the devotees one by one and gave a few minutes for each one to tell Her their personal problems.

At twelve-thirty the Mother asked everyone to go and have their lunch. When She was about to get up, a few more people came and saluted Her. The Mother gave them Her personal attention as well and finally went to Her room at one-thirty.

After lunch, the devotees came and sat in front of the Mother's hut and waited. After reaching the Ashram, the devotees would have thoughts of nothing but the Mother. Spending their time in Her presence was their greatest joy.

At three-thirty the Mother called them in. The devotees entered the hut. The room was not very big, and therefore, everyone had to squeeze and sit jammed in. Even then, all were so happy in Her presence that no one felt the discomfort. Those who could not get in the hut sat outside. The Holy Mother got up from the cot and sat down on the mat with the devotees. Someone among the devotees asked, "Didn't Mother have Her lunch?"

The Mother replied, "My children's happiness is Mother's food." The Mother had a pain in Her back. One of the women devotees massaged Her. The devotee was overflowing with joy. The Mother commented, "All the other daughters must be feeling jealous now. (All laugh) Each one of you should imagine that it is you who is sitting and rubbing in her place."

Control of mind

Question: Mother, what is the way to control the mind quickly?
Amma: You can control the mind quickly only through *japa*. Son, there is no short cut on the spiritual path. Whatever the way, a good amount of effort is needed. That is not like going to the market and buying something. Even then, by doing *japa* you can keep the mind from thinking unnecessary thoughts. However, concentration is absolutely necessary.

There is a benefit in following the path of devotion. One will get bliss from the very beginning itself. Thus one will be encouraged to perform sadhana. In other paths like pranayama (control of the breath), bliss will be gained only at the end. Just as one gets fruit even from the base of a jackfruit tree, bhakti is the path from which one gets fruit from the very beginning onwards.

Question: Why is so much importance given to concentration?

Amma: Nothing can be done properly without concentrating the scattered mind. Even ordinary actions can be performed perfectly only if there is concentration. Then what can be said of attaining the knowledge of God, the subtlest of the subtle? It is through the heat born of concentration that sexual energy gets converted into *ojas* (pure vital energy). Concentration is needed if unbroken celibacy is to become fully beneficial. It is said that it is harmful if worldly people practice celibacy. Do you know why? Because if they don't do *sadhana*, the seminal energy will not get converted into *ojas* and will remain stagnant in the body.

One devotee: So many different types of people come to see Mother. They all feel and experience that Mother is their closest relative. Mother dances to everyone's tune.

Amma: (Laughingly) Mother doesn't dance according to anyone's tune. The love that radiates from Mother to the whole universe influences them. Thus they feel that Mother is their own. Many of them do not know anything about spirituality. Some householders come and tell Mother all kinds of mundane things concerning their quarrels with neighbors and other such problems. Mother will sit as if She is listening with great interest. Do you know why? Because without going to their level, Mother cannot catch them and save them. A person who walks, catching hold of the hand of a child, must walk slowly along with the child. Otherwise, the child cannot keep up with him. If he walks making long steps, the child may even fall down.

One devotee: The Mother will pretend that She is acting in accordance with everyone's wish. But finally She will make everyone dance to Her tune.

(All laugh, including the Mother.)

Amma: Those who do not call God even once can be heard calling Him a hundred times when a thorn pierces their foot. But God will protect those who constantly remember Him from all dangers.

Character affects the world

Question: How polluted the world has become! How is it possible to correct this situation?

Amma: The nature of the things in the world will be in accordance with our actions. A king was separated from the rest of his party when he went hunting in the forest. As he was walking, tired and weary due to hunger, he saw some forest dwellers. He asked them, "Which fruit is good to eat?" They replied, "Any fruit in this forest is good to eat. Even naturally bitter fruits are sweet here." The king was astounded and enquired as to how it could be so. They said, "The king who rules this country is a repository of good qualities. Therefore, the subjects are good-natured. Maybe it is because there is no one evil in the country that the trees give sweet fruits only. Nature is pleased with the good acts and qualities of the king and his subjects." The forest dwellers did not know that it was the king himself who was standing in front of them. Even so, they received him in a respectful way.

It was as an egoistic person that the king returned to his city. He was inflated with ego thinking that because of his greatness, even bitter fruits had become sweet. As a result, he started doing unrighteous actions. Later the king once again went to the forest. The forest dwellers saw him as he was about to eat some fruit and said, "Everything is spoiled due to the evil rule of the king of this country. Due to his wicked behavior, the subjects also are acting in an evil way and Nature has become displeased. None of the fruits here are good to eat." The king was shocked and returned home thinking about all his evil actions with repentance.

Our character will be the cause of both good and evil in the world. Knowing that, you should live cautiously. The actions of human beings are the basis of Nature's goodness.

Glossary

ACHARA: Traditional customs and observances.

ADHARA: Substratum.

ADVAITA VEDANTA: Philosophy of Non-duality.

AGNANA: Ignorance.

ANANDAM: Bliss.

ANACHARAS: Contrary to custom.

Arati: Waving burning camphor before the Deity as the conclusion of worship.

ARCHANA: Worship through repetition of Names of God.

ASANA: A seat; a posture in Hatha Yoga

ASANA SIDDHI: Perfection in sitting unmoving in one posture for more than 3 hours.

ASURA: A demon.

ATMA DHYANA: Meditation on the Self.

ATMA GNANA: Self-knowledge.

ATMA VICHARA: Self-inquiry.

ATMACHAITANYA: Spiritual power; the illuminating soul.

ATMAN: The Self.

AVATAR: Incarnation of God.

BHAGAVATI: The Divine Mother.

BHAGAVAN: The Lord.

BHAJAN: Devotional singing.

BHAKTI: Devotion.

BHAKTI MARGA: The path of devotion.

BHARAT: India.

BHAYA BHAKTI: Devotion with fear and reverence.

BHOGA: Enjoyment.

BHAGAVATAM: Scripture about the life and deeds of Lord Vishnu's Incarnations.

BHAVA DARSHAN: The Holy Mother giving an audience in the mood of the Divine Mother or Krishna.

BHAVAS: Moods, feelings or attitudes.

BIJAKSHARAS: Seed letters preceding mantras.

BRAHMACHARIN: A celibate student studying the scriptures and undergoing spiritual guidance and discipline under a Guru.

BRAHMAN: The Absolute.

BRAHMACHARYA: Celibacy and sense control.

DARSHAN: Audience or vision of the Deity or holy person.

DASA BHAVANA: Attitude of being a servant.

DEVATA: A god or deity.

DEVI BHAVA: Divine mood as Devi, the Goddess.

DHARMA: Righteousness.

DHYANA: Meditation.

DHYANA RUPAM: Form on which one is meditating.

DOSHA: Evil or defect.

DVARAKA: City where Sri Krishna lived.

EKAGRATA: One-pointedness.

GAURANGA: Sri Krishna Chaitanya, considered as an Incarnation of Sri Radha-Krishna, who lived in Bengal about 400 years ago.

GRAHASTA: One living in a house, i.e., a married person.

GRAHASTASHRAMI: A spiritual-minded grahasta.

GURU: Spiritual master.

GURU BHAVA: Attitude of a Guru.

HRIM: A seed letter associated with the Goddess.

ISWARA AMSA: A partial manifestation of God.

ISWARA BHAVANA: The attitude that oneself is identical with the Lord.

JAPA: Repetition of a mantra.

JIVA: The individual soul; life force.

JIVANMUKTA: One who has achieved Liberation even while tenanting the body.

JIVATMA: Individual soul.

JNANA: Spiritual wisdom or knowledge.

JNANA MARGA: The path of knowledge.

JNANI: A Knower of Truth.

KALIYUGA: The present Dark Age of materialism.

KARMA: Action.

KARMA PHALA: The fruit of action.

KAURAVAS: The enemies of the Pandavas during the Mahabharata War, representing unrighteousness.

KIRTANA: Devotional singing.

KRISHNA BHAVA: The divine mood of Krishna.

KUMBHAKA: Retention of breath during pranayama.

KUNDALINI DHYANA: Meditation on the kundalini.

KURUKSHETRA: The battlefield on which the Mahabharata War was fought.

KAMA: Lust or desire.

LAKSHANA: Symptoms or signs.

LAKSHARCHANA: Worship by repeating the Divine Names 100,000 times.

LAKSHYA: Aim or goal.

LAKSHYA BODHA: A mind intent on reaching the goal.

LALITASAHASRANAMA: The 1000 Names of the Goddess Sri Lalita.

LAYA: Merger or absorption.

LEELA: Play.

MANONASA: Destruction of the mind; permanent subsidence of the mind.

MITHYA: Unreal.

MOKSHA: Release from the cycle of rebirth.

NIRGUNA: Without qualities.

NIRGUNOPASAKA: One who meditates on the qualityless Absolute.

NISHTA: Established; regularity in practice.

NITYA: Eternal.

NITYANITYA VASTU VIVEKAM: Discrimination between the eternal and the transitory.

NAMA: The Divine Name.

OMKARA: The divine sound OM.

PADMASANA: Lotus posture.

PARAMAHAMSA: A God-realised Soul.

PARA BHAKTI: Supreme devotion.

PUJA: Ritualistic worship.

PRANA: Life force.

PRASAD: Consecrated offering to God or a saint.

PREMA BHAKTI: Loving devotion.

PREMA SWARUPA: Of the nature of love.

PURVA SAMSKARA: Previously acquired tendencies.

PURNAM: Full or perfect.

RAJAS: The principle of activity; one of the three gunas or qualities of Nature.

RASA: Taste; juice; elixir.

RADHA BHAVA: Attitude of being Sri Radha, Beloved of Sri KRISHNA: supreme devotion.

RAJA YOGA: The Royal yoga; the eight-fold yoga of Liberation.

SAGUNA: With attributes.

SAHAJA SAMADHI: The Natural State of being established in the Supreme Reality.

SAMA CHITTATA: Equipoised mind.

SAMATVA BHAVANA: Attitude of equality.

SAMATVA BUDDHI: Mind endowed with the equal vision of beholding all as One.

SAMATVAM YOGA UCHYATE: "Equipoise is yoga."

SAMADHI: The equipoised state of Oneness with God.

SANKALPA SAKTI: Power of resolve or creative imagination.

SANATANA DHARMA: The Eternal Religion of the Vedas.

SARVATRA SAMADA: Equal vision everywhere.

SASTRA: Scripture; science.

SAT KARMA: Good or virtuous action.

SATTVA: Principle of clarity; one of the three qualities of Nature.

SEVA: Service.

SHANTI: Peace.

SHIVOHAM: "I am Shiva."

SIDDHI: Psychic power; perfection.

SISHYA: Disciple.

SVADHARMA: One's own duty.

SAGUNARADHANA: Worship of God as having attributes.

TAMAS: the principle of inertia; one of the three qualities of Nature.

TAMASIC: Pertaining to tamas (see above).

TAPAS SAKTI: The power generated by austerities.

TIRUVATIRA KALI: A village dance.

TRIGUNAS: The three gunas or qualities of Nature, sattva (tranquil), rajas (active), and tamas (inert).

VAIRAGYA: Detachment.

VANAPRASTHA: The third stage of life in which one leaves all worldly activity and devotes oneself to austerities.

VEDAS: The revealed scriptures of Hinduism.

VETTUCHEMBU: A kind of tuber root.

VYAVAHARA: Empirical.

YAMA AND NIYAMA: The do's and don'ts of the path of Raja Yoga.

www.ingramcontent.com/pod-product-compliance
Lightning Source LLC
Chambersburg PA
CBHW071208090426

42736CB00014B/2752